AN OPEN SECRET

An Open Secret

The Family Story of Robert & John Gregg Allerton

NICHOLAS L. SYRETT

The University of Chicago Press   Chicago and London

The University of Chicago Press, Chicago 60637
The University of Chicago Press, Ltd., London
© 2021 by Nicholas L. Syrett
All rights reserved. No part of this book may be used or
reproduced in any manner whatsoever without written
permission, except in the case of brief quotations in critical
articles and reviews. For more information, contact the
University of Chicago Press, 1427 E. 60th St., Chicago, IL 60637.
Published 2021
Printed in the United States of America

30 29 28 27 26 25 24 23 22 21   1 2 3 4 5

ISBN-13: 978-0-226-63874-4 (cloth)
ISBN-13: 978-0-226-76155-8 (paper)
ISBN-13: 978-0-226-75166-5 (e-book)
DOI: https://doi.org/10.7208/chicago/9780226751665.001.0001

Library of Congress Cataloging-in-Publication Data

Names: Syrett, Nicholas L., author.
Title: An open secret : the family story of Robert & John Gregg
    Allerton / Nicholas L. Syrett.
Description: Chicago : The University of Chicago Press, 2021. |
    Includes index.
Identifiers: LCCN 2020036091 | ISBN 9780226638744 (cloth) |
    ISBN 9780226761558 (paperback) | ISBN 9780226751665 (ebook)
Subjects: LCSH: Allerton, Robert, 1873–1964. | Allerton, John
    Gregg, 1899–1986. | Gay men—Illinois—Biography. |
    Philanthropists—Illinois—Biography. | Gay couples—Illinois. |
    Gay adoption—Illinois.
Classification: LCC HQ 76.35.U6 S97 2021 | DDC 306.76/620922
    [B]—dc23
LC record available at https://lccn.loc.gov/2020036091

♾ This paper meets the requirements of ANSI/NISO Z39.48-1992
(Permanence of Paper).

Contents

Illustrations

Introduction

On March 4, 1960, Robert Allerton became a father. He was eighty-six years old at the time and his newly adopted son, John Gregg, was sixty. The pair had already been living together and calling themselves father and son for almost four decades. Thus, the adoption, while legally affirming Allerton and Gregg's filial status, paradoxically had the effect of bringing that very status into question. Allerton was an immensely wealthy benefactor of the arts, both in Illinois—where he and Gregg maintained legal residence and where the adoption took place, the first adoption of an adult child in the state's history—and in Hawai'i, where the two had lived for twenty years. The adoption was newsworthy in both places. The *Champaign-Urbana Courier*, covering the jurisdiction where the adoption was finalized, announced: "Companion Is Adopted by R. Allerton." Other papers used similar sorts of headlines: "Robert Allerton Adopts Friend." "Robert Allerton, Piatt Park Donor, Adopts Companion of Many Years." Even more ambiguously the *Honolulu Star-Bulletin* titled its article "Have Been Friends for 38 Years. Kauai's Allerton, 86, to Adopt 60-Year-Old Son," referring to Gregg as both a friend and a son before the adoption had even occurred. The reporter explained that "Mr. Allerton and Mr. Gregg have lived at Lawai-Kai on Kauai since 1938 and many friends believed that Gregg already was Allerton's adopted son."[1]

Despite the fact that the adoption did make them father and son in the eyes of the law, it also had the public effect of calling into question the very thing it was most designed to assert: that Robert Allerton was John Gregg's father, and not something else. And yet, as the *Star-Bulletin* noted, perhaps despite itself, it is difficult to become something that one claims already to be. In a similar vein, the *Chicago Tribune* reported that Gregg had had "the status of son" for thirty years under the headline "'Son' 30 Years Is Adopted by Allerton," the quotation marks around "son" suggesting doubt about Gregg's real status over those decades. This conundrum—who Robert Allerton and John Gregg were to each other and how they explained themselves to the world—had been, in many respects, the fundamental question of their then thirty-eight years together.[2]

This book tells the story of their lives. Born in the late nineteenth century to one of Chicago's richest entrepreneurs and raised among its elite, Robert Allerton was expected by most around him to assume the responsibilities of his father's business, marry an eligible young Chicago socialite, and produce the next generation of Allertons. In one respect—taking on some of his father's business interests—he did so, but he also engaged in socializing at home and abroad with a cosmopolitan jet set that included artists, musicians, and socialites, gay men among them. He had at least one affair with a man, the British composer Roger Quilter; there were likely others. And in 1922, nearing the age of fifty, he met a college student named John Gregg, twenty-six years his junior. From that day forward, they were rarely apart, splitting their time between an English manor house in downstate Illinois and a tropical paradise on the southern shore of Kaua'i in Hawai'i. They referred to one another as father and son from the 1920s until the death of John Gregg in 1986, securing that status in the law in 1960.

Robert Allerton and John Gregg were a handsome and popular pair. Well-read and worldly, they entertained frequently and traveled the globe with their friends. They also dedicated themselves—both in their own homes and through generous philanthropy—to the arts, focusing in particular on architecture, landscape design, and decoration. Allerton's employees describe a generous man who looked after the needs of those who worked for him. Their letters show a keen sense of humor as well as exacting temperaments; Allerton, in particular, had precise ideas of how he wanted things done, and his wealth meant that he did not often have to compromise. They were both also quite private, Allerton even more so than Gregg. While Allerton's wealth meant that he was often the subject of media coverage, he rarely agreed to be photographed or give interviews. Allerton's choice to live away from Chicago in rural Piatt County, Illinois, also indicates that as much as he liked to socialize, he was not at all opposed to living in solitude with his books and his dogs. In sum, Allerton's wealth, which he came to share with Gregg, allowed him to set the terms on which he engaged with the rest of the world. Deciding when to be private and when to have company were two facets of this privilege; calling John Gregg his son and having the world acquiesce to those terms, even if they were not quite believable, was another.

The years of Robert Allerton's life, 1873–1964, encompass an almost-century-long arc during which homosexuality in American culture was first discovered, diagnosed, pathologized, and persecuted. By the time of his death, those named by the category had begun to assert their own rights. If we include John Gregg's final years—he lived until 1986—this century also encompasses the birth of gay liberation and the beginnings of the AIDS crisis. Because of this, it is possible to see how one man, eventually joined by another, negotiated changing understandings of same-sex sexuality in America (and, at times, in Europe and Asia). In some ways, Allerton typifies what we have come to know about the history of same-sex intimacy in the nineteenth and twentieth centuries. From his earliest days, for instance, he was involved in a romantic friendship with a childhood companion, the painter Frederic Clay Bartlett. The intensity of that friendship ended, however, when Bartlett married. Allerton then met a series of queer men while traveling in Europe and elsewhere. He had an affair with at least one of them, and with others practiced a sort of queer mentoring that had long been popular among gay men in Europe. Finally, looking to settle down more permanently with only one man by the 1920s, he met John Gregg. It was at this moment that Robert Allerton's story becomes unique and anomalous, though revealing about queer history, nevertheless.

Allerton and Gregg met at a moment when persecution of same-sex desire was on the rise. While it would have been possible for the two to see each other clandestinely for sex, as historians have demonstrated many self-identified gay men were doing by the 1920s, they wanted something else. They wanted a partnership, and yet there were few viable models for how to do that at the time, especially when one of the partners was already quite well known. The pair was clearly understood as being a couple by many of their close friends, but they also lived a public life and they needed to come up with some story to account for why two single men might choose to live together, never seeking marriage with women. Even women who had once lived together in "Boston marriages"—long-term partnerships between women that were common in the late nineteenth and early twentieth centuries—were starting to meet with prejudice and suspicions of lesbianism by the 1920s. That Gregg's parents were both deceased certainly lent credibility to the story. And Allerton's immense wealth went a long way toward insulating the pair from most suspicion and prejudice. What, after all, could their detractors do about the relationship? Gossip about them, certainly. But it is unlikely that the police would have responded to anonymous tips and bust down the doors of Allerton's family homes in Chicago or Monticello, Illinois.[3]

So Allerton and Gregg fashioned a cover for their relationship that was something of an open secret, but it was one that let them move about in public together, socializing with Chicago's elite and allowing them to make new friends on their extensive travels abroad, and eventually in their second home on the island of Kaua'i in Hawai'i.[4] How they publicly staged their relationship has much to tell us about how at least two gay men navigated their lives in a world before they were able to be open about their devotions and desires. It is clear that Allerton was not interested in having Gregg be regarded by Allerton's peers as a secretary, companion, or chauffeur, a sort of second-class sidekick. Other wealthy gay men did pursue this option, but it would never have allowed Gregg to enjoy all the perks of Allerton's life. In order to gain that kind of access for Gregg, they needed a different story; claiming him as family solved this problem.

The Allertons are interesting for other reasons, because they were not just a pair of gay men who used filial ties to elude persecution (had there been any); there was no moment, even later in life, when they became publicly gay and admitted to using the legal device of adoption in order to secure their partnership. Until his death in 1986, John Gregg Allerton (he took Robert's last name only following his death in 1964) always publicly referred to Robert as his father. They actually lived like a father and son in other important ways as well. Because they were separated in age by twenty-six years, Gregg ended up caring for Allerton as he entered old age; he lived until he was ninety-one. Gregg, with little in the way of inheritance after the death of his parents, was also poor in comparison to Allerton, with his immense family wealth. Allerton controlled the purse strings throughout their relationship, and Gregg never worked for pay after he moved in with Allerton a few years after their first meeting. Even in the years before that, Allerton used his connections to find Gregg employment, much as a wealthy and connected father might do for his son. In Allerton's later years, he also set up Gregg financially, buying him pieces of land and residences in his own name, so that he might achieve a certain modicum of independence, not just at Allerton's death, but before that as well.

Robert Allerton and John Gregg are significant, then, not just because they provide us with an example of how one pair of gay men navigated a long-term partnership together before it was safe to do so, but also for how they really did structure their lives in a manner that resembled the father and son they were claiming publicly to be. They are instructive for reminding us that, even in today's world, not all couples behave similarly. While gender has tended to structure the inequalities in heterosexual marriage, same-sex couples, too, have navigated structural differences—in this case, age and wealth—in ways that don't look particularly equal, even if they are not always harmful.

In part, this book suggests that we take seriously Allerton and Gregg's claims to being father and son. No matter the sexual and romantic content of their relationship, their choice to live together as two single men was undoubtedly queer, by which I mean non-normative. Technically both men remained bachelors their entire lives, but bachelors who chose to live with one another in cozy domesticity. In an era when the domestic sphere was coded feminine, this pair devoted themselves to designing, furnishing, and decorating two different homes and adjoining gardens that are so well-regarded, they are both now tourist attractions. In recognition of their philanthropy in the realm of the arts, their names appear as donors most prominently at the Art Institute of Chicago, the Honolulu Academy of Arts, and the National Tropical Botanical Garden. Their focus on the decorative arts, and Asian art and statuary in particular, was itself a part of their queer aesthetic. Even if we take their filial claims quite seriously, Robert Allerton and John Gregg were very visibly queer.

One can imagine that even those who believed they were father and son might have found them perplexing. Why would an adult man need a replacement father just because his own had died? If so, why not a replacement mother as well? Was Allerton also a replacement father for Gregg's siblings? Why couldn't an adoptive father and son be devoted to one another and at the same time pursue what the world expected of them: marriage to a woman? If they were actually single, nothing in the filial relationship prevents courtship and marriage. Allerton could have provided Gregg with a stepmother, and Gregg could have made Allerton a father-in-law. At the risk of stating the obvious, filial relationships are not expected to be exclusive. Many parents have more than one child, and those children go on to romantic attachments with people who are not their parents. Thus, even though their filial claims were what allowed the pair to fashion a public life together, there would always be something decidedly queer about the pair, even for those who took their story at face value.

Because of their enormous fortune, Allerton and Gregg also allow us to see how some gay men chose to live transnational lives and strategically use what they perceived as the openness of other locations in order to forge queer connections or to be together, or both. If queer history's roots in the United States owe much to the community study—exploring how a group of people forged queer lives in one specific place—more recent years have seen queer historians not only exploring movement by queer subjects as a central motif, but also demonstrating how the nation-state itself has not contained queer subjects. The Allertons' transnational story is not one for celebration, per se, in that it is replete with colonialism and Orientalism, but it does give us a sense of how queer men who enjoyed this privilege constructed a sort of queer transnational subjectivity for themselves. Their identities were bound up not just in their ability to explore international locations, but also in the queer aesthetic they brought back with them to the United States, fashioning cosmopolitan homes and identities filled with Asian and European art, costumes, and flora.[5]

In addition to the community study, the story of queer Americans as told by contemporary historians has also partially been a history of LGBT activism, particularly for the period after midcentury. It is a story of struggle and defiance and occasionally of triumph. Robert Allerton and John Gregg have little relationship to that story, even though Gregg lived into the 1980s. While they socialized with other gay men, their wealth also allowed them never to have to publicly identify as gay, much less advocate for rights as gay people. They were both lifelong Republicans, even as the Republican Party drifted ever rightward over the course of their lives, effectively exchanging some political ideals with Democrats. While neither political party actively worked on behalf of gay rights in their lifetimes, by the postwar period northern Democrats had thrown their support behind other disenfranchised groups like African Americans and women in ways that Republicans never did.[6] In one respect, this is not surprising: the Republican Party had long worked in the interests of wealthy northerners like the Allerton family. It was economically in Allerton's and Gregg's interests to support the GOP. And yet so much of queer history is written about activists and leftists and organizers that one sometimes forgets that there have also been deeply conservative gay people as well, especially among those who were also wealthy, white, and male. The Allertons made decisions about how to live their lives, and then combine their lives, that appear fully accommodating of anti-gay prejudice. They will never be heroes in the story of gay liberation. And yet it would be very difficult to accuse them of homonormativity—the tendency by some gays to ape heterosexuality and the perks of normative couplehood—precisely because the strategy they chose in order to be together was so profoundly queer. They were truly products of their particular moment in history.[7]

Robert Allerton and John Gregg were anomalous in the choices they made, largely because they were so wealthy that they had options others did not. Robert Allerton's wealth is what had thrust him into the public eye in the first place and what had necessitated he devise some way to explain the young man who shared his life with him. Two men of far lesser means might simply have lived together as roommates far from the prying eyes of their families. Or a couple with more radical inclinations might have thrown off the dictates of society altogether and lived together openly, flouting convention. Allerton and Gregg did not see either of these as viable options. Their wealth prompted the need for an explanation of their relationship at the same time that it made that explanation possible, and their essential conservatism made openness about their lives impossible. They were not, however, without options and resources. Precisely because of Allerton's wealth, it was extremely unlikely that anyone would publicly question what many took to be a fiction. To many their relationship was an open secret. Those in Allerton's employ were not in a position to question how their boss chose to frame his relationship with Gregg, at least not if they wanted to keep their jobs. And Allerton's friends had little to gain by exposing Allerton and Gregg for what they might have believed them to be: homosexual men involved in an intimate relationship.[8]

Allerton and Gregg were also extremely careful in how they portrayed their relationship. I have never found an instance in which they publicly referred to one another as anything other than father and son. They maintained this version of their relationship even in correspondence with family, friends, and employees. While it is likely that they were more forthcoming with close friends, certainly fellow gay men with whom they socialized, any correspondence where they discuss each other as lovers has been lost or destroyed, if it ever existed. Because Allerton and Gregg were so rarely apart, especially so after they moved in together in the mid-1920s, there was little reason for much correspondence between the two to have ever existed in the first place. Whatever they wrote to one another in the years when they were not yet living together they chose not to include in the archival collections of their papers that are stored at the University of Illinois and the National Tropical Botanical Garden.

Thus there are times when the very subject of this book—Allerton and Gregg's relationship with one another—seems almost illusory, just beyond one's grasp. This is because their ability to be together was predicated on never talking openly about what happened when they were alone. This is a problem of evidence best acknowledged at the outset of this book. I have done my best to fill in the gaps when I can and provide as much context as possible for the decisions that they made in the context of queer history more broadly, as well as various other themes that bore on their lives in one manner or another—like the history of domesticity, design, and philanthropy, areas where Allerton and Gregg have had long-lasting significance. But the fact remains that despite their social prominence, they were a very private pair who, by their own design, did their utmost to keep the most intimate aspects of their relationship with one another a secret. In ways that can be frustrating, that secrecy fundamentally structures this book as well.

Ultimately I see the story of the Allertons as helping us to understand how one early twentieth-century queer couple with almost every imaginable advantage fashioned a life where they could be together. As a contribution to the field of queer history, it is best understood as one focused squarely on privilege, primarily that afforded by class, which was partially predicated on their whiteness. While social class, especially the divide between working- and middle-class men, was key to queer historians' understandings of identity formation at the turn of the twentieth century, the analysis of class is less apparent in work that explores mid-century queers, with the notable exception of lesbian bar culture in Elizabeth Lapovsky Kennedy and Madeline Davis's groundbreaking *Boots of Leather, Slippers of Gold*. This book aims to use class as an analytic to understand the choices made by one queer couple and, as we shall see, by others like them as well. Allerton's and Gregg's class privilege was what allowed them to live a public life that those of lesser means have not had the means to achieve nor the need to do so.[9]

At times, as readers will come to see, acknowledging what Allerton's and Gregg's class and race privilege bought for them means also seeing how unappealing they could be. Like some of their friends and relatives, their correspondence indicates they were both racist and anti-Semitic. They wanted to surround themselves with people of their own ilk, which for them meant other white, wealthy Anglo-Saxon Protestants. While there is no evidence to demonstrate that they took religion particularly seriously—no regular church attendance, for instance—culturally they were prejudiced against people who were not Protestant because that is the world into which Allerton was born and those were the biases he shared with this generation of wealthy Chicagoans. While Allerton and Gregg regularly employed nonwhite people in Hawai'i and working-class white people in their homes in Chicago and Monticello, there was a distinct difference for them between those with whom they socialized and those they employed. When traveling, for instance, they sometimes inquired about whether accommodations were restricted to only white Protestants. At the same time, they also regularly traveled abroad to countries populated primarily by nonwhite people and regularly expressed great admiration for the history, art, and culture of these nations. In this dualism—the ability to simultaneously embrace the culture and yet reject its nonwhite producers—they were not atypical of their generation of wealthy Americans.

I was attracted to the story of the Allertons, then, not because I think it is one for celebration—though some certainly believe so; Robert Allerton was posthumously inducted into the Chicago LGBT Hall of Fame in 2016—but rather because learning more about them enriches our narrative of queer history.[10] It helps us better understand how some queer people in the past developed strategies to be together. Some of those people, like Robert Allerton and John Gregg, were not always entirely sympathetic in their actions and their beliefs. Like most people in the past, they were neither heroic nor villainous. I offer them up not for emulation or admiration, but rather to help us understand the queer past and because most accounts of them to date either do not explore their queerness in any depth or do not acknowledge the more regrettable aspects of their history. Robert Allerton and John Gregg were two men who enjoyed almost every possible privilege and one distinct disadvantage: they wanted to be together in a world that did not countenance love between men. This book describes who they were, the world they lived in, and ultimately how they shaped that world as well. *An Open Secret* is the story of Robert Allerton and John Gregg Allerton, expanding the definition of family long before gay men and lesbians would establish what they called families of choice.

Illinois is today home to a number of landmarks that bear the name Allerton. The Allerton Hotel (now the Warwick Allerton) sits in Chicago's Near North Side neighborhood alongside many other hotels on the city's Magnificent Mile. The imposing entrance wing of the Art Institute of Chicago is the Allerton Building, and numerous collections and pieces within the Art Institute honor Allerton as their donor. Much farther south, the tiny town of Allerton, Illinois (population 291), sits amidst the cornfields in Vermilion County, southeast of Champaign and the University of Illinois, which itself hosts Allerton conferences at Allerton Park and awards annual Allerton scholarships.

Most, but not all, are named for Robert Allerton and his immediate relations. The Chicago hotel, which is part of a chain that also had a New York location, was originally begun in the 1920s by a distant cousin and named for their common ancestor, Mary Allerton, the last surviving passenger on the *Mayflower*. Those that are named directly for Robert or his father, Samuel, all attest to the influence of one family and ultimately demonstrate just how Robert Allerton came to be the subject of this book in the first place. Without the wealth of his forebears, there would, quite simply, be no Robert Allerton and John Gregg to write about. The choices that Allerton made to fulfill his same-sex desires were fully enabled and structured by his wealth. A Robert born to an Illinois farming family not only would be unknown to us today, but would have had his affinity for men constrained in any number of ways not experienced by the Robert who was born to the prosperous Samuel and Pamilla Allerton of Chicago's Michigan Avenue. He likely would have married a woman and become a farmer himself or, if he was particularly enterprising, moved to Chicago, where he might have satisfied his same-sex desires in clandestine encounters with other similarly inclined men in the growing queer scene at the turn of the century. He would not have been in a position to take up with a long-term partner he referred to as his son, travel the world in search of queer pleasures, and make a long-lasting impact in the worlds of art and design. While the latter two claims verge on the obvious, it is worth emphasizing that the very possibility for fulfilling Allerton's queer desires was predicated on his family's money. Socioeconomic class structured the form in which Robert Allerton and subsequently John Gregg were able to live out a queer life.

When Robert Henry Allerton was born in 1873, his father, Samuel Waters Allerton, was already one of Chicago's "Cattle Kings" and had begun to amass a good portion of the fortune that would sustain not only Samuel's family but also Robert and John. But Samuel Allerton did not grow up with money. He had been born in obscurity in 1828 in upstate New York. The Allerton family story in America is one of triumph and of hardship, culminating in Samuel's astounding success in an industrializing Chicago of the mid-nineteenth century. A brief trip backward situates Robert Allerton (and subsequently John Gregg) as part of a quintessentially American family story that begins as the *Mayflower* crosses the Atlantic ocean in the early seventeenth century and ends on a tiny Hawaiian island in the middle of the Pacific nearly four hundred years later.

That story commences with the sixteenth-century Puritan revolt against the Church of England. Isaac Allerton was born in England in the 1580s. Allerton was in his mid-twenties when he left England for Holland with his fellow Puritans as a result of the religious persecution they experienced because of their questioning and criticism of the Church of England. He settled in Leiden, where he married Mary Norris in November 1611; she gave birth to a son, Bartholomew, and two daughters, Remember and Mary. Fleeing persecution once again, this time in their adopted home in Holland, the Allertons and their servant, John Hooke, joined their fellow Pilgrims aboard the *Mayflower* in 1620 and set sail for what would become Plymouth Colony, which they hoped would be a permanent home for Puritans in the New World. Isaac appears in records as "Mr. Isaac Allerton," indicating he was a man of wealth and status. Mary Allerton would give birth to a stillborn child while in Plymouth Harbor and would herself die during that first winter in Plymouth Colony. Isaac Allerton was remarried in 1626 to a woman twenty years his junior, Fear Brewster, daughter of preacher and Puritan leader William Brewster. They would have two children: Isaac Jr., born around 1627, from whom Samuel and Robert descend, and Sarah, born in 1633, who died in infancy.[1]

Isaac Allerton Sr. quickly rose to prominence in Plymouth Colony and then just as quickly fell into disrepute. He served as William Bradford's assistant governor during the colony's early years and in 1627 became one of the undertakers of the colony's debt; in that capacity he made several trips back and forth to England to negotiate with the colony's creditors.

At the same time, he used the colony's credit as collateral in starting a number of business ventures of his own, ventures that failed, leaving the colony further saddled with his debt. In addition to being friendly with Roger Williams—forced from Plymouth for his heresy—Allerton brought the social reformer Thomas Morton with him on a trip back to Plymouth in 1629 and allowed him to stay at his home. Morton had been condemned by the Puritans at Plymouth for his liberal Christianity and for what they believed to be his far too intimate relations with Native Americans at his Virginia colony, Merrymount. Allerton's seeming approbation of Morton did not bode well for his own continued acceptance among the colonists at Plymouth, and Allerton was forced to leave. He settled first at Marblehead, Massachusetts, and later, after being forced to leave Massachusetts, in the colonies at New Amsterdam and finally in New Haven, where he died, insolvent, in 1659. His daughter, Mary, was the last survivor of the *Mayflower*, dying in 1699 at the age of eighty-three. The first generation of the Allertons in America had begun with promise but had ended in obscurity. That said, the very fact of the Allerton family's arriving so early in the American colonial project insured that at least some of their descendants would have access to opportunities for amassing wealth that were rarely available to those who arrived in America as indentured servants or slaves or who immigrated later after much of the land once occupied by Native Americans had been claimed by other white settlers.[2]

For an additional four generations, the Allertons lived in Connecticut, New York, and Rhode Island, with occasional forays into Virginia. Their fortunes rose and fell, and while an occasional Allerton distinguished him- or herself (Robert's great-grandfather Reuben Allerton served as a doctor in the Revolutionary War), for the most part the Allertons, like most Americans, toiled away out of the public eye. Robert Allerton's grandfather, Samuel Waters Allerton Sr., was born December 5, 1785, in Amenia, New York. On March 26, 1808, he married Hannah Hurd. Like his father, Reuben, he trained to be a physician but decided to pursue a trade instead and became a tailor, opening a country store. He also invested in a woolens factory in the late 1820s, but when protective tariffs were reduced in the 1830s, he and many others like him were reduced to ruins. Samuel Waters Allerton Jr. came into the world on May 26, 1828, the ninth child of Samuel and Hannah. When a child of seven, he witnessed the ruin of his father: the sheriff had come to sell the Allerton property, which was claimed to settle Samuel Sr.'s debts. As two highly prized horses were being bid upon, Samuel Jr. saw his mother in tears. According to Walter Scott Allerton, chronicler of the Allerton genealogy, Samuel threw his arms about his mother's neck, promising that he would be a man and care for her. This experience would prove foundational for the younger

Samuel. In speaking about his father and mother later in life, Samuel recalled: "He was one of the most honest, straight men in the world. Much too honest to make a good trade for himself; very hard working and industrious man. My mother was one of the best mothers in the world; as true as steel, very genial and pleasant—would have enjoyed life very much if she had not been so poor. Had she been the man, and Father the woman, they would have made better headway in the world." In these recollections of his parents, recorded after he had made his fortune, Samuel was clear about what it took to be successful, attributes he believed his mother possessed more than his father.[3]

The lesson learned from his father's ruin was fundamental for Samuel: "When I arrived at the age of 11 years I saw if I ever had any money or position in life I would have to get it myself, and as we had been poor, and always went with the best people in the country, we felt it more, and I made up my mind to gain money, and I commenced at 11 to save and work; had no taste for school—[my] mind all seemed to be on how to get money." The financial disaster forced his father to rent a farm to make ends meet; the younger Samuel began to work on that farm at the age of twelve. Eventually they had saved enough to buy a farm of their own in Wayne County, New York. Samuel and his elder brother Henry then set aside enough money to buy their own farm, Samuel's first endeavor in agricultural ownership. He also began, intermittently, to trade in livestock. In time he realized that he knew as much about the trade as the dealers with whom he interacted and decided to sell his portion of the farm he owned with his brother and invest the money in making his entrance into the livestock trade. His brother counseled him: "If you continue as you are [in farming], in a few years you will own the best farm in this country; but if you wish to try the live stock trade, all right, we will settle on this basis. This is all the advice I have to give you; you will run across smart and tricky men, but they always die poor—make a name and character for yourself, and you are sure to win."[4]

Throughout his late teens and early twenties, Samuel drifted between the sale of livestock and farming with his brothers. By the 1850s he had moved west, continuing to trade in livestock. While in Illinois, he met Pamilla Thompson, daughter of a farmer and landowner in Fulton County, about two hundred miles southwest of Chicago. As he was making plans to pursue Pamilla, the economic Panic of 1857 gripped the country. As Samuel put it, "We had 400 head of cattle on our hands and cattle dropped $1.00 per hundred and we lost all we made the first year, and I was taken with a very bad fever and was laid up for 6 months." In the wake of his financial failure and his illness, he returned home to upstate New York, where he partnered again with his brother in a dry goods store. Tiring of that after a year, he "got well and courage came back," and he again headed west, this time with his share of the store and some borrowed money, in search of Pamilla Thompson.[5]

Before marrying Pamilla, he began to trade hogs in Chicago; he wanted to have enough money to feel that he could support a wife, for as he said later, "I did not like to marry until I felt I could take good care of her." Samuel Waters Allerton Jr. married Pamilla Wigdon Thompson in July 1860, when he was thirty-two and she was twenty. While he did not have much money, he had "what was better than money—the courage and knowledge of how to trade," which helped him to "get over the diffidence with the girl I loved better than life."[6]

From that point on, Samuel's story is one of a steady rise upward. In the midst of the Civil War, in 1863, as the federal government was encouraging the formation of national banks, Samuel and five associates founded the First National Bank of Chicago. This was both an astute financial move—Samuel and his children would remain principal shareholders for some time—but was also because Samuel had difficulty in securing funds to purchase large numbers of hogs. He was well known for having cornered the Chicago hog market in May 1860—purchasing all the available hogs in Chicago following a sharp decline in prices—but was only able to secure loans to do so after local bankers received three telegrams from New York banks vouching for his good name. The establishment of the First National Bank of Chicago and others like it would thus make large sums of capital available to Chicago businessmen like Allerton intent on developing their fortunes.[7]

Samuel's next great project was the founding of the Union Stock Yards, which he, along with other businessmen, helped to establish in 1865. For many years, livestock in Chicago had either been kept in small yards near taverns and saloons or increasingly, after 1848, in smaller commercial stockyards developed expressly for that purpose. A number of factors increased the need for a large stockyard that was more conveniently located near the railroad. The first of these was the expansion of the railroad westward, which made Chicago a hub for converging trains and their cargo as well as turning Chicago into a commercial center in its own right. A second factor was the closing of the Mississippi River for north–south commerce during the Civil War, which only increased the traffic through Chicago, particularly of grains and livestock coming from the Midwest and heading east. Both of these factors also brought larger numbers of meatpackers and their livestock to Chicago. This was all good news for a man like Samuel Allerton, whose livelihood was in livestock. But in order to accommodate the influx of hogs, sheep, and cattle, Chicagoans had to build a large facility located near the railroads. Joining with other packers and railroad companies, Allerton founded the Union Stock Yard and Transit Company. The railroads had purchased 320 acres south of the city, and the corporation proposed to spend nearly one million dollars to "fence and plank [the yards], construct suitable hotels and other buildings, and connect the yards with all the railroads entering the city, by constructing railroad tracks, *which shall be free to the stock business* of such roads." The guiding principle was to establish a giant central location in which buyers, sellers, livestock, and railroads would all converge for the convenience and financial betterment of all concerned (save the livestock, of course). Construction began in June 1865.[8]

Throughout this period, Samuel and Pamilla Allerton had been growing steadily richer, as had their fellow Chicago Gilded Age industrialists. In 1863, three years after they were married, Pamilla gave birth to a daughter, Kate Reinette Allerton. A decade after that, she gave birth to Robert in their home on Michigan Avenue. By this point the Allertons were part of an established social set that included Marshall Field, of the eponymous department store; Potter Palmer, who worked with Field on the department store and also founded the Palmer House hotel; and Adolphus Clay Bartlett and William Gold Hibbard, founders of Hibbard, Spencer, Bartlett & Company, at the time one of the country's foremost hardware companies (now True Value). These men and their wives made up some of the elite social set in Gilded Age Chicago, the equivalent of New York's Vanderbilts, Astors, Rockefellers, and Carnegies. While the truly old money would likely have looked down their noses at these *nouveaux riches arrivistes* and the New Yorkers no doubt did not consider the midwesterners to be their equals, families like the Fields, the Palmers, and the Bartletts were at the apex of Chicago society. Samuel Allerton's ties to agriculture and the hog market, as well as his less-than-polished table manners, set him slightly apart from some of their neighbors, but not so much that Robert and Kate were unable to enjoy all the privileges of growing up with others in their elite social set.[9]

Robert spent his childhood playing with the children of these elites: Ethel and Marshall Field Jr., Honoré and Potter Palmer Jr., Frederic Clay Bartlett, and Franklin Hibbard. As one of Robert's employees would later recall, "In the backyard of his family house on South Michigan Avenue in Chicago he had a replica of his parents' house as a play house. There on a little stove he cooked pancakes for his little friends made from batter an indulgent cook whipped up for him." It was, by all accounts, an exceptionally privileged childhood for both Kate and Robert. As Samuel's fortune rose, he moved the family to Prairie Avenue, alongside the rest of the city's elite on Millionaires' Row. The Fields lived on the same block in number 1905; the Pullmans, of the Pullman Palace Car Company, were at 1729;

meatpacking magnate Philip Armour and his family were at 2115. When the census taker came to the door of the Allerton home at 1936 Prairie Avenue in 1880, the household also included Pamilla's younger sister Agnes, as well as a coachman, a gardener, a butler, a cook, a seamstress, and a laundress. In 1884 Samuel purchased a summer home among other wealthy families on the shores of Lake Geneva, Wisconsin. They called the lodge "The Folly," supposedly because when Samuel had returned from his trip to Wisconsin after purchasing the twenty-six-acre property, his second wife, Agnes, had exclaimed, "A fishing lodge? Heavens[,] Samuel, that is sheer folly!" The Allertons soon transformed the more rustic lodge into a magnificent redwood structure, moving the original lodge on the property and then constructing the new dwelling around the original core. Samuel had managed to give Robert and Kate a childhood not only free of the economic insecurity of his own youth, but a life of privilege and luxury.[10]

Four events occurred in the early 1880s that would have a profound effect upon Robert's childhood and indeed the rest of his life. In 1880 Robert and Kate, who were then six and seventeen, contracted scarlet fever. Most common among young people between exactly those ages, scarlet fever is epidemiologically related to strep throat and is similarly spread by coughing and sneezing. While now easily treatable, in the late nineteenth century, scarlet fever had no known cure; its symptoms were sore throat, fever, headaches, rash, and swollen lymph nodes, and it could lead to arthritis, rheumatic fever, and inflammation of the kidney. In many cases, the disease felled entire families. In the case of both Robert and Kate, it led to deafness, likely caused by sinus infections or abscesses of the ear. Sparing no expense, their parents sent them to Vienna, Austria, to be treated by the renowned Dr. Adam Politzer, specialist in otology, where both were operated upon in hopes of restoring their hearing. In Kate's case, the surgery was partially successful. Robert did not fare as well, and he was left with permanent hearing loss. He was not completely deaf, and over the course of his life, he partially made up for his hearing loss with an ear trumpet and later with a hearing aid. He also began the process of learning to read lips as a child. These remedies were successful enough that he certainly never learned to sign and was capable of sustained conversations with other people; he was also a regular attendee at the opera, ballet, and symphony. That said, both he and later John claimed that his hearing loss made him particularly shy with women and around crowds, although his later socializing seems to belie this claim.[11]

The same year as the Allerton children's bout with scarlet fever, Pamilla Thompson Allerton died from the illness, just five days before Robert's seventh birthday. She was only thirty-nine. We know little of how Robert experienced the loss of his mother, only because he rarely spoke about it publicly or in records that survive. But he was still quite young, and her sudden absence must have been a terrible shock to him and his seventeen-year-old sister. Memories of Pamilla Allerton may also have been eclipsed by the fact that within two years Samuel had married for a second time, to Pamilla's younger sister, Agnes, who became Robert and Kate's step-mother, and for nine-year-old Robert effectively his mother. Recall that Agnes Thompson was already living with the Allertons in Chicago in 1880, the year her sister died. This may be because she was nursing Pamilla.

Robert and Agnes grew to be very close, much closer than Kate and her stepmother; unlike Robert, Kate was never able to refer to Agnes as "Mother," in part, one surmises, because she had much better memories of their real mother. She remained "Aunt Agnes." Agnes instilled in Robert an appreciation for gardening, music, and literature. As an adult, Robert was an avid reader like Agnes, and they regularly shared books with one another. In later years Robert credited his stepmother as having given him a cultural education and inspiring him to become an artist, as he was for a number of years. When he donated collections in the memory of his mother to the Art Institute of Chicago, he was doing so in honor of Agnes Allerton, not Pamilla, the mother he lost at a young age. Agnes went on to outlive Robert's father by ten years.[12]

It is worth pausing here to note the age difference between Agnes Aller-ton and her husband, Samuel. He was fifty-three when they married, and she was only twenty-four. Even if Robert did not fully comprehend this difference in ages at the time, as he grew older he would come to appre-ciate that his father was of another generation from his adoptive mother (who herself was fifteen years younger than her sister, Pamilla, Robert's biological mother). As Robert learned more about his family, he would also come to understand that Samuel's choice to marry his deceased wife's sister was itself unconventional. While by no means unheard of, some legislatures and religious denominations had sought to bar the practice at earlier moments in history, arguing that this kind of affinal incest— that is, marrying two people from the same lineal family—made the rela-tionships inappropriate. Perhaps the most important lesson that Robert would learn was how much he could value the woman who *became* his mother rather than the one to whom he was born. What Robert would understand—and later apply to his own relationship with John Gregg— was that a person could become a parent to a child years after that child's birth, and that the relationship was no less meaningful for commenc-ing sometime later in life. Robert had learned his first lesson in quasi-incestuous—arguably queer—family formation at the age of nine, and it had a lifelong impact on him, eventually helping to structure his own choices much later in life.[13]

FIGURE 1.1 Samuel, Agnes, Kate, and Robert Allerton at The Folly in Lake Geneva, Wisconsin, about 1895. Courtesy of the University of Illinois Archives.

Finally, in 1885 Robert's sister Kate, ten years her brother's senior, married Dr. Francis Papin, a Chicago physician, at the age of twenty-two. She moved out of the Allerton home on Prairie Avenue, leaving Robert as an only child with his father and stepmother. Unfortunately, the marriage was short-lived. Papin contracted tuberculosis four years after they were wed and died while seeking treatment in Mexico in 1889. They did not have children, and Kate did not remarry for a decade. In a period of seven years, Robert became partially deaf, lost his mother, and gained a stepmother. One of the only constants in his life throughout this upheaval, his sister, Kate, left when he was just twelve. While Robert's upbringing had afforded him every privilege, money could not protect him from tragedy or the disruption that came in its wake.[14]

As a child, Robert first attended the Allen Academy and then the Harvard School, which had been founded by a graduate of Harvard University in 1865 to train young men to be able to attend that institution and similar colleges on the East Coast. The school also enrolled the likes of Edgar Rice Burroughs, later famous for writing *Tarzan,* and other sons of Chicago's elite. He then followed his friend Frederic Clay Bartlett to St. Paul's School in Concord, New Hampshire, in 1889 at the age of sixteen. (Frederic had preceded him by a year.) St. Paul's, founded in 1856, was a boarding school serving a similar sort of clientele as the Harvard School. Like most college preparatory schools of the era, St. Paul's was single-sex and offered instruction in a variety of languages (Latin, Greek, French, German) and courses in English literature, history, physics, and mathematics. In keeping with changing ideals of masculinity for young moneyed men, it also emphasized sports, including football, tennis, cricket, track and field, and crew. There was also free time as well, and Allerton and Bartlett "built a little house in the woods at the edge of the campus where they could hide away from masters," what teachers were called at St. Paul's. The school had been founded as an Episcopal boarding school; men of the faculty were ordained, and boys regularly attended chapel. Indeed, in the years immediately prior to Allerton's and Bartlett's enrollment, the school built a new chapel, which was consecrated the summer before they began. While St. Paul's did offer some scholarships, this was also a school designed to prepare wealthy white young men for college and career. Tuition in the 1880s was $500 per annum (approximately $13,500 today), this in a period when the vast majority of Americans did not attend secondary school, let alone private high schools. On December 17, 1889, partway through Allerton's and Bartlett's time at St. Paul's, *Harper's Magazine* published an account of the arrival of the "Vacation Special of St. Paul's School," in New York's Grand Central Station. This was a chartered train that ran three times a year between Concord, New Hampshire, and New York to transport St. Paul's students home on holidays. As a historian of the school explained:

They have tumbled out at all the way stations between Concord and New York to cheer the school; they have been singing songs in the intervals snatched from poring over movie and detective story magazines, and for the last fifteen minutes before the train pulls into the terminal they have been standing with impatient expectancy in the aisles. When at last they get out on the platform, instead of immediately hurrying into the station, they assemble in a body and give a deafening St. Paul's cheer. The mothers and fathers waiting inside the gate know that the boys have come.

It is possible that Samuel and Agnes Allerton were waiting at Grand Central for Robert to descend that train, or, more likely, the school simply sent along a staff member to make sure that those who were bound for further afield, like Chicago, were situated in their carriages before the next leg of the journey began. Either way, the article is a testament both to the notoriety of St. Paul's and to the wealth of its student body.[15]

After Robert's three years at St. Paul's, both he and Frederic Bartlett left the school without graduating, coming home in 1892. It is possible that Robert's own religious background as a Universalist clashed with the Episcopalian traditions that students learned in their classes in Sacred Studies at St. Paul's, and this caused him to sever his ties with the institution. A more likely explanation, however, especially considering that Frederic left at the same time, is that Robert had simply tired of school and saw no further need for St. Paul's. This was not a particularly unusual choice for men of wealth, especially in an era when a college or university education was unnecessary for entry into the world of business that their fathers hoped for them. Far fewer Americans attended college in the later nineteenth century than do today, and many who did saw it as more of a finishing school and aggregator of connections than for the intrinsic educational value. Robert Allerton and Frederic Bartlett already had both wealth *and* connections, so finishing high school in order to enter college was not necessary for them. While today the notion of a wealthy young person dropping out of high school might seem unusual, it would not have been seen that way at the time.[16]

Robert and Frederic arrived home to a city that was increasingly urbanized and that was about to play host to the World's Columbian Exposition, which would showcase a Chicago that had now recovered from the 1871 fire that nearly destroyed it and was poised to become one of the most dynamic cities in the United States. The exposition itself was an international spectacle that was designed to showcase the very best of what humanity had to offer in celebration of the 400th anniversary of Columbus's arrival in the Americas in 1492. Covering an area of six hundred acres and utilizing two hundred buildings, as well as man-made lakes and lagoons, the exposition featured people and artifacts representing forty-six different countries. During the six months that the fair was open to the public, more than twenty-seven million people visited. Among the attractions was the Palace of Fine Arts, which housed thousands of paintings and sculptures representing the United States and many European nations, including those that had produced masters such as France (with its own dedicated wing), Holland, and Spain. Their visits to the Palace of Fine Arts were transformative for both Robert and Frederic. As the latter would explain many years later, they saw "miles and miles of pictures," and afterward they were "determined to leave the security and luxury of home . . . and forge out into the world to learn the technique, the secrets, and methods of artists." Robert Allerton and Frederic Bartlett had decided to leave Chicago and move to Munich in order to study painting. Frederic initially met with more success convincing his parents to allow him to make this unusual choice than did Robert.[17]

Samuel Allerton's vision for his son's life was more conservative than Robert's own plan. Samuel had amassed a fortune precisely so that his son and daughter would always be secure and never need to work. As he had written to Robert in 1886, when Robert was only thirteen, "Remember that your father worked a life time that he might be able to leave his children the capital that would put them in an independent position in this life and if you do not keep it your father's work was in vain." This exhortation came along with a gift of thousands of dollars of stock that was meant to be the first step toward Robert's own fortune and thus his independence. At the time, Samuel also wrote to Robert: "Many a young man has been ruined by dissipation and leading a thoughtless life with the money his father has worked a lifetime to acquire. Most fathers are afraid to give their sons money until they have grown to manhood for fear they will lead a thoughtless and dissipated life but I have confidence in my son that he will lead a thoughtful life, remembering that the only true course of happiness is to shun evil."[18]

When Robert decided that he wanted to go to Europe, Samuel surely must have worried that his worst fears about what Robert would do with his fortune were soon to be realized. Samuel expected his son to follow in his own footsteps and join him in the family business; indeed, he was probably mystified that Robert did not see the advantages to this proposition himself. It was not so much that pursuing a career as an artist was risky: Samuel was wealthy enough that he could certainly afford to support his son during this period and even afterward if the venture failed. Most artists at the time came from money precisely because there was so little to be made in the field except by the very most talented and recognized, who only became so through years of hard work, during which they were supported by their families. Samuel probably recognized that Robert was unlikely to succeed as an artist, only because it was well known how difficult it was to become a successful artist. Two things were particularly vexing about Robert's desires. First, Samuel likely feared that the life of a moneyed young art student in Europe was de facto a life of dissipation, precisely what Samuel had warned his son about more than a decade earlier. Second, for a family that had only recently become moneyed and were still seen as *arriviste* by some of their peers, a son becoming an artist was decidedly unconventional. Samuel had worked hard and amassed

an immense fortune so that his son and daughter could behave as con-
ventional wealthy people were meant to behave. His daughter could now
be married off to a suitable man, and his son could follow him into the
business of managing hogs and farmland. While Kate was meeting his
expectations, Robert instead proposed to turn his back on this future and
pursue the unlikely dream of becoming a painter, all to be financed by the
very business in which he wanted no part. Samuel was very likely not only
confused, but also disappointed.

Nevertheless, Robert prevailed and was eventually able to persuade his
father to finance his stay in Munich, where both he and Frederic Bartlett
first studied with a private tutor by day. As Bartlett recounted, "Stimu-
lated by a slight element of competition, the work went faster and faster,
but we found time for long walks in our beautiful Munich with its endless
parks adorned with statues and fountains, its palaces and monuments."
They both applied for admission to the Royal Academy, also in Berlin,
which according to Bartlett only admitted one or two foreign students
per year. To their great delight, both earned places in the school. They
returned home for a summer visit in Chicago and then were back to Munich, where they found "a charming small apartment, within our slender
means, and only a five-minute walk from the Academy." Bartlett explained
that he and Allerton "have both arranged many apartments and houses
since, but I doubt if any installation ever gave us such intense excitement."
Bartlett remembered the precision with which they instructed the wallpaper hanger about how to get just the right effect in decorating their new
home: "This we thought made a wonderful background for pewter plates
and porcelain jugs, on a shelf draped and held at the corners by carved and
painted wooden angels, encircled with gilded wings."[19]

They lived in companionable happiness, taking strolls in the evenings
and dedicating themselves to their artistic practice during the days. The
course at the Royal Academy lasted through the spring of 1896, during
which Bartlett met the woman who changed his own life and that of Allerton. Dora Tripp was touring Europe with her mother, then a customary
trip for a young woman as she was introduced to society. Tripp was only
seventeen years old, and both felt that marriage was impossible at that
stage; besides, Bartlett still had more training he wished to undertake,
this time in Paris. Tripp returned to the United States with her mother
while Bartlett and Allerton made a plan to meet in Paris in the autumn
of 1896, where they would both enroll in the École Collin to study drawing in the mornings and the École Aman-Jean for painting classes in the
afternoon.[20]

Allerton and Bartlett's friendship had changed in a decisive way as a
result of Bartlett's engagement to Dora Tripp. We have no record of how

Allerton felt about his childhood best friend, but clearly the two were devoted to each other, choosing to accompany one another on a series of moves across two continents in pursuit of schooling and art. As Bartlett described his friendship with Allerton toward the end of his long life:

Friendship, ah: what a wonderful English word so seldom carried to the end of its meaning—perfect understanding, perfect loyalty—never needing to say, "Now not a word of this to a soul"—utter confidence that in all things the beloved friend would be trusted, defended, protected, fought for, and forgiven. The friend of a perfect friendship can do no wrong. How such articles could form the code of two lads of nineteen, I do not know, but I do know that after sixty years of life I would not change a syllable.

The union between Bartlett and Allerton has all the trappings of what scholars have dubbed a romantic friendship. As historian Carroll Smith-Rosenberg first described them, romantic friendships emerged out of the relatively gender-segregated worlds of Victorian households and schools. Girls and boys developed passionate and long-lasting attachments to one another in their youth, relying upon romantic friends for affection, camaraderie, and counsel. Documented in letters and diaries, nineteenth-century Americans, who lived in a world without an understanding of homosexuality as a discrete identity, felt free to express their affection with one another without the stigma that would taint such relationships by the early twentieth century. Some romantic friendships were quite chaste, if emotionally devoted, whereas others involved certain degrees of physical intimacy. Importantly, most people did not view romantic friendships as being incompatible with marriage to someone of the other sex. They were, if anything, a prelude or a complement to marriage. Indeed, many women who had conducted years-long intimate friendships with other women continued them well past the moment when they married.[21]

Men, however, were another story. Most evidence indicates that men maintained the intimacy of their dearest friendships until they married, at which point the relationships were fundamentally altered, many men transferring intimacy to their wives, reliance upon a man thereafter cast as emotionally immature and characteristic of a dependence now seen as incompatible with manhood. The break for Bartlett and Allerton was not nearly so stark, in part because Bartlett's engagement lasted two years and he was largely apart from his fiancée during this time, continuing his studies in Paris with Allerton. But Allerton and Bartlett seem no longer to have shared a residence once they relocated to Paris, and they traveled separately during the summers between their years in Paris, even if they occasionally met up in various locales, for example, when they arranged to meet in Florence, Italy (likely in the summer of 1898).[22]

The scholarship on romantic friendships stresses that in a world without the category of homosexuality, romantic same-sex friends were free never to have to consider defining the nature of their relationships with one another. But in reading the letters sent by some, it becomes clear that an announcement of marriage by one party could sometimes be particularly disturbing to her or his friend. In other words, the fluidity of nineteenth-century conceptions of sexuality might have worked best for those women and men who found themselves attracted in equal parts to women and men and who desired marriage to a spouse of the other sex. For those who found their desires to friends of the same sex to be all-consuming, the societal expectation of marriage and the concomitant pressure to break intimate ties with same-sex friends (at least for men) may have been particularly wrenching. This was doubly so when two parties in an intimate friendship felt different degrees of attachment to one another—that is, when one friend opted for marriage and the other did not, as in the case of Bartlett and Allerton.[23]

There is no way to know if this was how Robert Allerton experienced the lessening of his friendship with Frederic Bartlett. Certainly that friendship, even sixty-five years later, was of immense importance to Bartlett, a man who does not seem otherwise to have pursued romantic or sexual relationships with men (he was married to two women after Dora Tripp, both Tripp and his second wife predeceasing him). While he and Allerton remained friends throughout their lives, the break that came with Bartlett's marriage may have been particularly jarring to Allerton. The two remained in Paris for two years, until late in 1898, when Bartlett married Tripp near her parents' home in Westchester County, New York. Allerton was his best man. Frederic and Dora Bartlett returned to Europe, first to Paris, and eventually back to Munich, before coming back to the United States where their son, Frederic Clay Bartlett Jr., was born in 1907. Robert Allerton stayed in the United States, giving up painting altogether and settling on his father's land in Piatt County, Illinois.[24]

While Allerton's choice has largely been written about as a realization that he did not possess the talent to pursue a career as an artist—a career in which Bartlett did go on to achieve some notable success—it is also worth considering Allerton's decision to sequester himself away from the world, at least temporarily, as a reaction to Bartlett's marriage and the end of their friendship as he knew it. After nearly twenty-five years of inseparable camaraderie, Dora Tripp had taken Robert Allerton's place as Frederic Bartlett's companion. Never mind that this was always the desired outcome, at least with some woman, for Bartlett; for Allerton, this might well have been devastating. Romantic friendships existed in a world that allowed for participation by a wide swath of Americans who were under no obligation to define the intimacy that they shared with people of the same sex. In one way, then, nineteenth-century Americans embraced a more fluid sexual system than would emerge in the twentieth century. But this system probably was least painful for those who did not find themselves primarily attracted to those of the same sex—even before there was a name for such an orientation—those for whom a romantic friend of the same sex was more easily given up for a wife or husband, or at least existed alongside that spouse. Frederic Bartlett was clearly such a man; Robert Allerton was not. While Bartlett seamlessly incorporated his new wife, Dora, and his subsequent wives into his life as an artist, Allerton gave up the artistic life when Bartlett married, and he moved to rural Illinois, a location not just geographically far from Paris, but also culturally distant from large cities like Chicago, Munich, and Paris that had heretofore been his home. He had made a decisive break with at least part of his past.

Robert Allerton had been given opportunities about which most could only dream. The Allerton roots, stretching back to the earliest settlement of New England in the seventeenth century, had positioned his father to make a fortune in midcentury Chicago, which at the time was still developing into a midwestern commercial hub. Allerton's earliest friendships were with the children of other members of Chicago's social elite, including Frederic Bartlett, with whom he would share his formative years both at St. Paul's and abroad, immersed in the world of art. By his early twenties, in his quest to become a painter, Allerton had already broken with both social norms of his class and the expectations of his father, even as he relied on his father's vast fortune in order to do so. The choices he would make in his next decade would be, as we shall see, entirely financed by his father as well.

Chapter Two
Robert Allerton's Queer Aesthetic

On February 18, 1906, the *Chicago Daily Tribune* ran a full-page story on Robert Henry Allerton under the headline "Richest Bachelor in Chicago." The piece featured a picture of Allerton surrounded by drawings of pointing and swooning women as well as photos of his home, "The Farms," near Monticello, Illinois. The story, emphasizing Allerton's fortune and his status as a single man, spent considerable time describing him physically: "His features are cleanly cut, and his head is set firmly above muscular shoulders. He is a man of medium height, active, robust, well proportioned." The reporter also made sure to describe those aspects of his temperament that presumably would make him a good husband: "The qualities that combine in the makeup of his personality are qualities that go to make a man lovable—a strong character, personal fearlessness, the gentleness of strength, optimism, and just enough ideality to guide impulse, a strong sense of justice, humanity, generosity almost to a fault. He is democratic and reserved."[1]

This story was not particularly unusual for its era; the next year the *Tribune* ran another piece called "Matrimonial Chances for Chicago Girls," which listed "Bachelors with Incomes from $1,500 to $100,000 a year." Allerton was included in that feature as well, alongside about eighty other wealthy single men, all listed by annual income and occupation. Allerton's annual stipend was estimated at $100,000 per year, about $3 million today. The 1906 piece also described Allerton's Monticello home at length. "The house is low and broad. A massive colonnade joins the two great wings and inside a gallery runs from end to end of the spacious house. . . . The gallery, which is 25 feet wide, is lined on either side by expensive marbles and bronzes which were purchased by Mr. Allerton in the art centers of Europe." Elaborating on Allerton's annual travel—he was actually in Calcutta at that moment—the article explained: "There is not a corner of Europe he has not visited, and scarcely a corner of the earth. In nearly every foreign city from London to Yokohama he has purchased works of art

Robert H Allerton

FIGURE 2.1 "Richest Bachelor in Chicago," *Chicago Daily Tribune*, February 18, 1906, D1.

with which to adorn the walls and niches of his farmhouse." All that said, the *Tribune* assured its more taste-conscious readers that the house was "a modest, severely plain structure." "During the season at the farm Mr. Allerton entertains extensively in spite of his busy, strenuous life. From the beginning of the season to the end, one house party after another is sheltered and entertained in the magnificent 'farm house.'"[2]

The *Tribune* piece neatly summarized the importance of art, decoration, and collection for the persona that Robert Allerton developed in the early twentieth century. If he could not make his mark as an artist, then he would do so as a collector of the art of others, as well as the creation of a home and gardens in which to showcase that art. Upon returning from Europe in 1898, he had commenced the building of Allerton House, the manor home that was the centerpiece of The Farms. While occasionally staying in Chicago for the opera or to visit his parents, who continued to reside there, he lived at The Farms, where he managed, but did not actually farm himself, the thousands of acres of land surrounding the estate, and designed ever more elaborate gardens in the woodland park. He also entertained his friends from Chicago, throwing festive weekend parties, complete with costumes for his guests and picnics on the grounds. Every winter he traveled, primarily in Europe and Asia, bringing back treasures not just for the home and gardens but also for donation to the Art Institute of Chicago, where he was becoming increasingly involved as a trustee and benefactor. Even living in downstate Illinois, Allerton was at the center of a Chicago social whirl that had been established by his parents' generation.

Allerton exemplifies so many of the trends of his elite social set: vast wealth, an elaborate country home, annual travel abroad, art collection, and philanthropy. His initial pursuit of a career as a painter was clearly a departure from the future his father had planned for him and that others would have expected of a young man of his position. He gave up that dream before returning to Illinois, where he acquiesced to his father's desire that he manage the farmland in Piatt and Vermilion Counties. What he would not do, however—perhaps could not do, despite the expectations of all those around him, including the *Chicago Daily Tribune*—was marry a woman. Instead he cultivated the arts of architecture, decorating, landscape gardening, and collecting, combining an English manor home with an Orientalist sensibility. None of these, in and of itself, was inherently queer, and he was in good company among both men and women in these interests. However, one can situate Allerton's pursuits alongside growing understandings of men's interest in the arts, historic preservation, and the decorative arts, as marked by a queer aesthetic. Allerton joined a cadre of moneyed queer men and women who cultivated these interests using the wealth they had inherited.

To name Allerton's interests in the arts as queer is either banal or controversial, depending on the audience. For more than a century, gay men have made note of the traits, aside from the obvious same-sex desire, that they believed made them distinctive from their straight counterparts. Among these were, at least for some, a tendency toward effeminacy, a love of camp, and a predilection for the arts.[3] Historians and cultural critics have been better at documenting these connections than they have been at explaining why they exist, in part because that explanation can irk those gay men who do *not* share these traits and also because it smacks of essentialism, the belief that these characteristics are inherently, essentially linked to some "cause" of homosexuality itself. Whatever the origin, the connections nevertheless do exist. Some scholars have documented particular affiliations between gay men and artistic genres like opera or musical theater, while others have demonstrated that gay men have been overrepresented in specific types of occupations, like fine art, theater, flight attending, or historic preservation, which themselves have sometimes been coded feminine as well.[4]

The sociologist Herbert Gans's notion of a "taste culture" is instructive here. In Gans's definition, taste cultures encompass the class and educational backgrounds of particular sectors of the population and link them to their aesthetic and cultural values and the culture they regularly consume. While Allerton clearly fits within Gans's definition of "high culture," in that he was wealthy, well educated, and moved in the circles of creators of culture, we can expand the definition outward to think about queerness as a taste culture as well. Many queer American and European men at the turn of the century were drawn to particular forms of culture—including the decorative arts, opera, musical theater, ballet, Chinoiserie, and Japonisme—and queer men themselves recognized that this was so. This kind of self-consciousness around taste was what likely led Allerton and those around him to read his interests through a queer lens.[5]

My point here is not to draw a direct causal line between Allerton's same-sex desires and his involvement in the arts, nor is it to mark any of these pursuits as inherently queer. Rather, what I hope to demonstrate is that it is likely that both Allerton and those around him understood the queer connotations of much of what he was doing. By the early twentieth century in at least some circles, "artistic" and "aesthetic" had become not-so-subtle code words for gay-identified men because of these linkages. In some cases, gay men were just called "artists." Gay men's involvement with the theater, for instance, had long been well known in major cities. In some places, like Boston, by contrast, observers noted gay men's predilection for historic preservation and decoration. One conservative resident of Boston's Beacon Hill who objected to the gentrification of her neighborhood by gay men wrote to the *Herald* in 1923: "Beacon Hill is not and never can be temperamental." For those who might be unclear exactly what "temperamental" meant in this context, she continued to lambast those "seeking to find or create there a second Greenwich Village." During his 1882 tour of the United States and Canada, Oscar Wilde lectured a good deal on how to make one's home beautiful, emphasizing the aesthetics of the decorative arts as they could be applied to a home. Many Americans would have drawn links between Wilde, art, interior design, and his 1895 trial for gross indecency. Wilde was queer not just because of his sexual proclivities, but also because he was a man focused on aesthetics. As Christopher Reed argues in *Art and Homosexuality*, coverage of the Wilde trials "made the artist-genius the paradigm of homosexual identity." Indeed, Reed demonstrates that the category of homosexuality emerged at the same time as the avant-garde artist, and the two were often linked, not just in the art world, but also in medical texts and in the public imagination. In demonstrable historical ways, "art and homosexuality have been significantly intertwined."[6]

Men particularly interested in the domestic sphere were similarly understood as queer. The art historian John Potvin has argued that because the domestic sphere was coded female during the nineteenth and early twentieth centuries—itself a product of the rise of industrial capitalism and the construction of ideological "separate spheres" that placed men outside the home in the marketplace—there was something decidedly queer about a bachelor who was devoted to the interior of his home, as was Allerton. As Potvin explains, "Deemed feminine, the care for the home stood foursquare at odds with the goal of getting on with the business of the nation." This was particularly so during the moment when Allerton first devoted himself to the construction of The Farms: the late nineteenth century. In terms of architecture and design, innovations that we would now call modernist were also coded as masculine. Allerton's predilection for the past, both in the seventeenth-century design for his house and for its furnishings, was anything but modern. This was a moment during which middle-class white men, trapped in their offices and fearing a decline in their masculinity vis-à-vis their working-class counterparts, who were more likely to work with their bodies, devoted themselves to what Theodore Roosevelt called "the strenuous life." Designed to take boys and men out of the cities in which they were supposedly becoming feminized, this masculine movement gave rise to the Boy Scouts, muscular Christianity, college football, and other sports. While not all men pursued these activities, it is worth noting that just as masculine rigor was being touted as the solution to problems of male ennui and effeminacy, Allerton was turning inward, attempting to design and furnish the perfect domestic space.[7]

While no artistic pursuit of Allerton's alone justifies the label queer, I argue here that it is applicable to an unmarried man who built an English manor house in the Illinois prairie, furnished it to historically accurate standards, and lavishly landscaped the gardens with Asian statuary; who collected and donated generously in the realm of decorative arts, including an entire collection of "prints and chintzes" named in his honor; and who founded a group called "The Orientals" in order to cultivate the love and appreciation of Asian art. There was more to Allerton's queerness than his four-decades-long partnership with another man; he was culturally queer as much as romantically or sexually. While many heterosexually married men and women, contemporaries and friends of Allerton, also participated in many of the same activities, Allerton's bachelor status combined with these activities marked him as queer.

And it was his fortune that allowed him to be so. While men of lesser means might also have indulged in a penchant for the decorative arts in their private residences, Allerton was able to expend an enormous fortune in pursuit of his queer aesthetic. Like other wealthy queer men, Allerton helped to shape the very idea of a queer aesthetic precisely because it was so dependent on the ability to consume.

When Robert Allerton gave up his brushes, destroyed his canvases, and returned to Illinois, he must have been disappointed. He had given up a dream. He also left behind his dear friend Frederic Bartlett, who would stay in Europe and continue to hone his skills as a painter, eventually to much professional acclaim. But Allerton had also clearly made a decision, which John Gregg later said was based on Allerton's realization that he simply did not have the natural talent to sustain a career as an artist.[8] It is likely that Robert's father would have continued to support him had he chosen to stay abroad, and yet he believed that his talent was simply insufficient to warrant a continued commitment to painting. As it would turn out, Allerton's life in the arts was only just beginning. Though it would take a very different form, his accomplishments at The Farms and his devotion to the Art Institute would have more of an impact upon his life—and the lives of many thousands of others as well—than his continued painting probably ever could have.

When Allerton returned from abroad, it would have made the most sense to live in Chicago alongside his parents. With assistance from his father, he could have also moved to New York, where his sister had relocated following the death of her first husband, and where she continued to live with her second husband, Hugo Johnstone, whom she married in 1898. Instead, he moved into a small cottage on a 280-acre farm his father had given him in 1881, when he was just a child. It was located in Piatt County, 250 miles south of Chicago. He had the cottage moved so that it was close to the Sangamon River, which also ran through the property. He bathed in a nearby spring and had an outdoor privy that he papered with Toulouse-Lautrec posters he'd brought home with him from Paris. He lived with his dogs amidst nature. He also decided that year to dam up the spring to create a pond on the farm's property. The farm itself was surrounded by 12,000 acres of his father's farmland that Samuel would ask Robert to manage for him the next year.[9]

Allerton had returned from five years living in Munich and Paris, years in which he painted and developed his skill, years in which his friendship with Frederic Bartlett had grown. He was now living in a secluded farmer's cottage in rural Illinois, a far cry from noisy apartments on crowded German and French streets with trips to Florence and other destinations in southern Europe. It may be that Allerton desired a respite from the hectic life he had lived in Europe as well as time to adjust to a life that did not have painting at its center. It also seems likely that, having decided to give up his canvases, he felt the need to immerse himself completely in the land and in his rural surroundings. His father had advised a path similar to his own: "Get an education and then get in touch with a farm somewhere; while you work it, your returns will not only be coming in, but you will be laying up health, vitality and character, which are always welcomed by metropolitan enterprises." While Samuel had worked as an actual farmer in his early days, there is no evidence to indicate that Robert ever worked the land with his own hands, instead relying on actual farmers to do that work for him.[10]

The quiet rural existence was not to last for long, though Robert would also never fully return to the metropolitan life that his father had predicted. In 1898 Samuel asked his son, then twenty-five, to formally take over the management of the acreage in Piatt and Vermilion Counties that surrounded his own farm; Robert acquiesced, but on the condition that he be given the funds to build a home there. His father agreed, and Robert set about planning what would eventually be called Allerton House. Unlike his father, he professed not to believe in being an absentee landlord; taking up residence in Piatt County made sure that would not be an issue, at least for part of every year. He hired his friend John Borie, a Philadelphia-born architect, to design Allerton House. Borie and Allerton had first met in Paris in the 1890s at the École des Beaux-Arts, or perhaps earlier in Chicago while Borie was visiting his sister Emily Borie Ryerson, whose husband's family was part of the Allerton family's social set. Borie had attended the University of Pennsylvania before studying in Paris and then worked for the Philadelphia firm of Cope and Stewardson, where he helped to design gargoyles for the University of Pennsylvania. Borie was an occasional student of the American painter Thomas Eakins, who painted a portrait of him in the late 1890s, *The Architect*. Borie agreed to the commission, and the two left for England in October 1898, looking for inspiration for the home and gardens they would design and build along the Sangamon River. By the early twentieth century, some wealthy Americans—particularly those who might be trying to distance themselves from their nouveau riche origins in the hog markets of Chicago— were finding inspiration in traditional English architecture. It was meant to demonstrate the owner's sophistication as well as speak to a sense of permanence and solidity, evoking the impression that the home had been on its land for quite some time. The English country house was the ideal, and it was this that Allerton and Borie sought on their trip.[11]

Allerton and Borie returned to the United States in early 1899 with ideas for the home. They had visited many different estates over the course of their months abroad, and the plan for the home was based loosely on the seventeenth-century Ham House at Richmond, in Surrey: a brick-and-stone exterior, modified H floor plan, and long gallery running down its front. While Allerton House is usually classified as Georgian Revival in design, the influences are actually more eclectic. One scholar has noted the similarities to Jacobean Revival–style architecture of Cope and Stewardson, Borie's former employer; another has seen an Edwardian influence and has compared the grand staircase to those of some colonial American homes. The inspirations, then, were varied, though to the untrained eye, the house gives the appearance of tradition and solidity. Because of his love of nature, Allerton had also specifically requested that he be able to see earth, sky, and water from every room. Borie worked to make sure this was accomplished.[12]

At the end of the trip, Borie returned to his New York firm and completed the plans for Allerton House, its outbuildings, and the gardens immediately surrounding them. Because Borie was not licensed in Illinois, Chicago architect James Gamble Rogers, a former coworker of Borie's at Cope and Stewardson, worked with Borie to prepare and finalize the drawings. Construction began on June 13, 1899. A local contractor, William Lodge, oversaw the excavation and the construction of the foundation. Chicago contractor William Mavor, who had previously worked on buildings for the World's Fair, was in charge of building the home and stable. The total cost was estimated at $50,000 (or about $1.5 million today). Allerton continued to live in his cottage, located across the pond that he had created by damming the spring—the pond that would ultimately serve as a mirror, reflecting the front of the house back to itself. By the spring of 1900, though the house was not fully completed, Allerton had moved in. From New York, and later London, where he lived with the singer Victor Beigel, Borie continued to send drawings for the completion of outbuildings and further gardens. The accompanying stable and gatehouse were completed in 1901 and 1903, respectively.[13]

The house itself is approximately 30,000 square feet in size and, while certainly imposing, is not nearly so large as other country homes constructed at the time or indeed the home on which it was modeled. The main floor of the home is dominated by a long gallery that runs the length of the house and divides the back from the front. To the rear of the gallery are a music room and an office. On either side of the front of the house are a library and dining room; between them is a glassed conservatory that looks out on a terrace with an ornamental pool. The terrace is raised above the pond. Also attached on the main floor are a kitchen, pantry, and servants' quarters. Four bedrooms (later consolidated to three) on the second floor also look out on the reflecting pond, while the fifth back bedroom overlooks what Allerton called the Music Room Terrace at the rear of the home. Smaller rooms on the third floor served as additional guest rooms, and bedrooms over the kitchen and pantry served as servants' quarters.[14]

FIGURE 2.2 Allerton House at The Farms. Courtesy of the University of Illinois Archives.

Across the driveway behind the house and directly opposite the kitchen and servants' quarters are a gatehouse, stables, and other outbuildings. Abutting a meadow beyond the pond are a series of formal gardens connected by paths. Two of these, now called the Brick Wall Garden and the Maze Garden, were also designed by Borie, as was the Gatehouse (designed to be a residence for a head gardener). The creation of the rest of the gardens was a decades-long process, some of them built and then redesigned multiple times. A bridge over the Sangamon River was completed in 1914, and the House in the Woods, located some distance down the road past Allerton House, by Chicago architect Joseph Llewellyn was completed in 1917. The first incarnation of the Sunken Garden, an oval-shaped garden that was the culmination of the formal gardens extending outward from the Gatehouse, was completed in 1915. The overall design process was augmented by Allerton's travel and the purchase of sculpture while abroad, much of which found a home in the gardens. Allerton also invited artists and sculptors to The Farms, and their contributions are still in evidence throughout the gardens.[15]

All of this, of course, was decidedly exotic for Piatt County, Illinois. As Irene Priebe, a local resident and later wife of the farm manager at The Farms, put it, "When he first came to this quiet prairie he caused quite a stir. When in 1899 he buil[t] what the local farmers called 'The Mansion' on a piece of unused land on his father's farm, they, unused to 'city folks,' especially a young artist fresh from Europe, allowed their imagination to invent tales which are the legends of today." This observation summarizes well the relationship between Robert Allerton and the residents of Piatt County. He was different: both a young and unmarried man from Chicago who was an artist, just returned from studying abroad, but also the son of the man who owned a good part of the county's land and had long been a benefactor in that county. He was also only one generation removed from the land himself. His father had, after all, been a farmer and took an active interest in agriculture, publishing *On Systematic Farming* in 1907, and making a good portion of his fortune not just through livestock packaging but also through the ownership of thousands of acres of midwestern farmlands, those in Piatt County making up only a small percentage of the total. While his father had come from upstate New York to Illinois in the mid-nineteenth century, his mother and stepmother were both from Fulton County, Illinois, not that far removed from The Farms. Indeed, he had relatives nearby in Monticello on his mother's side. Robert Allerton was thus *from* rural Illinois in important ways but not quite *of* it. While his wealth and what were seen as his eccentricities set him apart from his neighbors, his connections to the land and the people of the county also made him one of them. In the end, no matter how strange they might have found him, Allerton was always insulated from their criticism by the fact that he and his family owned most everything in sight.[16]

In those first years on The Farms, Robert generally had a live-in staff of at least five. The 1910 census lists the occupants of the home, in addition to Allerton himself, as a butler and housekeeper couple, Ranholt and Sachi Reynolds, as well as a cook, houseman, and laundress. In addition, James Shield, a gardener who had moved from Scotland, lived on the premises with his wife and sons, as did three additional laborers, charged with assisting the gardener in landscaping and maintenance of the home and grounds. Most of his staff would be replaced by 1920 when Allerton hired the Cackett family—Arthur and Edith—who came from England and worked as houseman and housekeeper for Allerton. They were recruited through Edith's brother, Stanley Gollop, who was serving as Allerton's butler by the mid-1910s. Arthur and Edith Cackett would remain with Allerton for twenty-five years, Arthur replacing his brother-in-law as butler. Arthur's sister, Emily, was laundress, and Edith's relatives, Edward and Violet Page, were hired as houseboy and chambermaid; a friend of Emily's, Florence Fry, served as cook. Elmer Priebe—who first worked for Allerton as a houseboy in 1913, later as chauffeur, and finally as farm manager—remembered the yard and house staff in his early years as being just like a family. By the 1920s, they were literally so.[17]

But at a time when household service was generally in decline with all but the very wealthy, Allerton stood out. While his contemporaries in Chicago continued to keep household staffs, it would have been decidedly unusual in Monticello, Illinois, especially a staff of this size.[18] Thus hiring couples (and their relatives) who lived in was wise because they could be expected to stay longer. As Cyril Cackett, Arthur and Edith's son, remembered of some of his parents' more temporary coworkers, "The fact that there were quite a few changes in personnel had no bearing on the relationship they had with Mr. Allerton but a majority of them wanted to better their employment with other occupations." While they remained at Allerton House, however, most reports tend to emphasize a happy working environment, not just among the staff but also in their relationships with Allerton and later with John Gregg. As Cackett recalled of his childhood in the 1920s, "I had [a] wonderful relationship with Mr. Allerton; in fact when I became about 6 he had me in with him just about every evening and he would play different games that he would purchase and he called it 'Little' Cyril's hour between 6–7 PM." Irene Priebe, Elmer's wife, had nothing but kind things to say about Allerton after his death, indeed speaking of him like an old friend, though he had actually been her husband's employer for five decades. Allerton and Gregg corresponded with Irene and Elmer after leaving Illinois for Hawai'i and regularly sent updates and postcards from their travels. There is no reason to doubt that Allerton and Gregg were kind employers, but it is also worth emphasizing that the very forum in which their employees were asked about Allerton and Gregg—interviews for celebrations of their lives—would not have been conducive to honesty had they not been so kind.[19]

Allerton's primary task in those days was the management of the 12,000 acres of his father's farmland. Working with a hired farm manager, Allerton's job was to make sure that the land was cultivated so that the harvests were profitable and made a sizable contribution to the Allerton family coffers. Principal crops at the time were corn, oats, wheat, and clover hay. In addition, large numbers of cattle and hogs were raised and marketed from the farms closest to Monticello. Elmer Priebe explained that when he first started working on the farms in 1913, thirty-six men were required to work the land. The farms were divided up, and each was supervised by what Priebe called a "strawboss," a more junior supervisor reporting to the farm manager (John Phalen until the early 1920s), who would in turn report to Allerton. Each farm had its own farmhouse, dormitory, barn, and set of equipment. Each strawboss had a crew of six working for him, and each morning at sunup the strawboss received the day's orders from the farm manager. Using the time-honored practices elaborated by his father in his 1907 publication, On Systematic Farming, as well as newer methods, Robert developed a number of model farms on the property, experimenting with the latest techniques in farm production. Like his role as supervisor of household help, and despite the fact that laborers worked from sunup to sundown six days a week, Allerton was remembered as a kind and generous boss. The farms at The Farms continued to be run this way until 1932, when they began to be managed by tenant farmers, the profits divided between the farmer and Allerton. Until that time, when Allerton delegated increasing responsibility to his farm manager, Allerton took an active interest in the management of the lands, which, of course, provided for his own livelihood as well.[20]

When Allerton was not busy traveling beyond Monticello or managing his farmland, he could often be found walking his estate twice a day with his dogs. Allerton was particularly fond of strolling the grounds partially dressed or occasionally without clothes altogether. He also liked sunbathing in the nude, but only when guests were not present. In his free time, Allerton was a voracious reader with eclectic tastes. The library at Allerton House at one point housed at least two thousand volumes, many of which were inscribed with a date and location by Allerton, his stepmother Agnes, or occasionally John Gregg or another relative. These inscriptions suggest that the books were actually acquired and read by those who signed them instead of being purchased in bulk simply to furnish the library. The fact that they were published and acquired over at least a fifty-year period, from the 1880s through the 1930s, also suggests that they were purchased for the purpose of reading, not mere ornamentation. Not surprisingly, Allerton read many volumes on architecture, design, and gardening. He read widely in history, both ancient and modern. Fiction also clearly appealed to him. He read Kate Chopin's feminist classic, *The Awakening*, the year it was published, in 1899, as well as Edgar Rice Burroughs's *The Return of Tarzan* in its year of publication, 1915. In 1924 he read queer writer and Harlem Renaissance patron Carl Van Vechten's *The Tattooed Countess*, the story of a European aristocrat, née Iowa farm girl, who returns to her rural roots and scandalizes her neighbors, not unlike the story of Allerton himself. He regularly read works by friends and acquaintances, including Maurice Hewlett and Henry James. He also liked mysteries, especially those by Mary Roberts Rinehart, and had a particular fondness for the works of Hugh Walpole, a queer British novelist who wrote many works of fiction in the first half of the twentieth century. Others appearing in his library include Mary Cholmondeley, who was known for satirizing country life; feminist novelists Rebecca West and May Sinclair; and freethinking journalist and novelist Hutchins Hapgood. Considering Allerton's reading habits alongside his own life is illuminating. On the one hand, Allerton clearly learned about worlds beyond his own through fiction and nonfiction, including those of women and other gay men, as well as those living in distant lands. This exposure may have led him to be open to the unconventional life that he eventually chose for himself, and may have complemented his lifelong friendships with women. But learning about people different from himself does not seem to have extended to any particular sympathy for those who were not white or Protestant or those who were disadvantaged by virtue of socioeconomic class. In that respect, Allerton remained a conservative product of his social class, kind toward most of his employees, but more in the role of a benevolent overseer and protector than an equal. Reading opened Allerton's mind, but only so far.[21]

Living in Monticello, it was perhaps inevitable that he would also be an object of curiosity: the wealthy bachelor artist who built a mansion in the middle of the prairies, what local papers sometimes referred to as a "castle" or "palace." Rumors abounded. One claimed that he had released rattlesnakes onto his land to scare off trespassers. Some believed that he disliked women because he remained a bachelor. Others found it peculiar that he walked bareheaded at a time when men customarily wore hats. Still others simply thought it bizarre how much he walked, spending hours each day traversing his acres, from garden to garden, statue to statue. In 1917 the estate was subject to much local curiosity—as well as some national attention—when a lioness was reportedly seen roaming the grounds. In June of that year, Allerton's butler, Stanley Gollop, was reputed to have been injured in a scuffle with the lioness, and this prompted an armed hunt by approximately six hundred local residents, who walked the grounds searching for the wild animal. Newspapers, including the *Los Angeles Times*, reported that Allerton considered bringing in a lion from the Lincoln Park Zoo in Chicago to lure the lioness from wherever she may have hidden. In the end, no lioness was ever found, and Allerton seems to have concluded that it had all been an elaborate plot cooked up by outsiders (presumably in concert with the butler) intent on getting a better view of the estate, which they were afforded during the hunt. Whether or not the lioness ever existed, the incident is telling. That an escaped lioness—from where? No one seems to have known—roamed the grounds of Robert Allerton's estate lent it an air of exoticism. It was plausible to people precisely because they already believed that goings-on at The Farms were strange; it was just the type of place where an escaped lioness *would* go had she escaped from somewhere. If the story was invented, as Irene Priebe says Allerton believed, then it stands as testament to the curiosity that others had about Allerton, his home, and the way he lived; the purpose of the invented lioness was to allow entrée on to an otherwise closed estate. Indeed, the local paper reported that during the hunt so many clamored to get through the gates, Allerton had to make sure that only those men who were armed, and clearly participating in the search, could enter. If Allerton believed the story was invented to satisfy this curiosity, it demonstrates the degree to which he was cognizant of his place in Piatt County, of the manner in which he was regarded. Robert Allerton was a curiosity. And he knew it.[22]

In one other respect did Allerton further provoke his neighbors' inquisitiveness. He entertained regularly, guests usually arriving by train at Monticello, where his chauffeur, Elmer Priebe, would pick them up and transport them to The Farms. As a 1906 *Tribune* story explained, "His friends take as much pleasure in going down to Monticello to 'be with Allerton' as in being the recipients of his generous hospitality. He is well liked as a man likes another man." At The Farms, these guests picnicked in the gardens, took tours of the actual farms, and dined in Allerton House, often in costumes supplied by Allerton. Not only did local residents see the guests arriving at the train station, they sometimes read accounts of their visits—like the one in the *Chicago Tribune* with which this chapter opened—and presumably they heard reports from some of the household staff as well, who would have told stories to their friends and relatives in the village. The guests at The Farms were often notable themselves. In June 1903, for instance, Joseph Medill McCormick, future US senator, and his new bride, Ruth Hanna McCormick, daughter of Ohio senator Marcus Alonzo Hanna, arrived at The Farms for their honeymoon. While Allerton was not himself present for their stay, he had been an usher at the Cleveland wedding and was a close friend of McCormick's. The bridal couple arrived via a special railroad car and was met at the station by the coachman and carriage from The Farms. As the newspaper explained, "No special preparations were made for receiving them either at the station or at the house. It is stated that almost no change in the everyday life of the inmates and caretakers of the big house will be made by the arrival of Mr. McCormick and his bride. They have come to spend two or three weeks quietly and the estate is kept up on such an elaborate scale that they can be taken in and entertained without any preparation." Though the article claimed that Allerton's neighbors had long accustomed themselves to his eccentricities and his famous guests, that rumors abounded about Allerton suggests otherwise.[23]

Most visitors were actually there to see Allerton, the man himself, and not just to enjoy his home. Typical of announcements that regularly ran in newspapers about Allerton and all of his social set was this one from the *Chicago Tribune* in 1927:

There are no more cherished weekend invitations in these parts than those issued by Robert Allerton. He not only owns one of the finest country places hereabouts, down at Monticello, but he knows that the best embellishment of a beautiful house is a collection of congenial guests.

The Alfred Hamills, the Tiffany Blakes, Mrs. Hugh J. McBirney and Ambrose Cramer were invited this week for a Friday-to-Monday visit, and because there are many indoor and outdoor distractions to keep the house party occupied from the moment they arrive until their final adieux, every one is looking forward to a delightful time.

Many of them were good friends of long standing, including Potter Palmer Jr. and his wife, Pauline, son and daughter-in-law of Potter and Bertha Honoré Palmer, the real estate developer and his wife who had transformed Chicago's Gold Coast into the most desirable neighborhood with the construction of their "castle" on Lake Shore Drive. Allerton was also friends with the Winterbotham family: sisters Genevieve and Luritia "Rue," the latter a founder and second president of the Arts Club of Chicago; their brother John and his family; and Rue's husband, John Alden Carpenter, the composer and pianist. Other guests included Margaret and Tiffany Blake, Chicago art patrons, and William Jennings Bryan and Mississippi senator Pat Harrison. John McCutcheon, political cartoonist for the *Tribune*, also visited at least once.[24]

Chauffeur Elmer Priebe remembered most coming down from Chicago on Friday afternoon and staying till Sunday, sometimes Monday. He and Allerton would pick them up in the car—first a Stevens-Duryea and later a Packard—around 2:30 or 3:00. The party would usually change clothes upon their arrival for a walk around the gardens. The next day guests toured the farms themselves, and on the Saturday evening they had dinner in costume. Guests visited the costume room to select an outfit—most of them brought back from travels through Asia—that they would then wear to Saturday's dinner. Because people went to the costume room individually, the actual gathering was a surprise when it was revealed what everyone had chosen. John Gregg explained that part of the reason for the costumes was that during that period—the 1910s and 1920s—dinner normally required that women wear formal attire and men wear tuxedos, which could be uncomfortable. "So [Allerton] thought the best thing to do was to throw everybody into costume; the men wore loose draperies and I don't know how they ever gave them up, but stretched themselves into tight pants; that was the law of evolution, I guess. So the men wore Roman togas and their Japanese kimonos and it made it a little bit harder for the women because they had to put on more clothes then [sic] they would ordinarily have anyway, but that was the origin of the costume room." He also explained, "Robert also taught native dances that went with the costumes," so clearly there was more to it than just an accommodation of comfort. Sunday or Monday they were taken back to the train for the return trip to Chicago. Priebe even remembers one weekend where Allerton's guests included a Spanish dancer, Estrellita, "who was quite good at her profession. After dinner when the servants had their work finished, I was invited along with them to see her perform." While the guest books from this early period have been lost, Priebe recalled: "He had a different group practically every weekend. Most of them were out of Chicago." Newspaper articles from the same period seem to bear out this conclusion, noting that guests prized invitations to The Farms. And while this was in part because of the estate itself and the efforts Allerton undertook to ensure that his guests enjoyed their visit there, it also demonstrated the degree to which Robert Allerton was very much of this society already. He had been born into it and continued his friendships with Chicago's social elite throughout his long life.[25]

By the time that Allerton had made the decision to build Allerton House and the park surrounding it, there were already ample examples of queer men and women who had built, restored, and maintained estates similar to what Allerton planned. Such estates were also quite common among the wealthiest Americans and Europeans in the nineteenth century (and indeed far earlier in Europe). It was generally the case, however, that houses of this size and expense were constructed for a family: a husband and wife and their lineal descendants. Such estates (like Ham House, upon which Allerton modeled his own home), usually passed through families via inheritance—in England regulated by primogeniture, while in the United States simply by will and estate law. Allerton thus was something of an anomaly in building such an estate for himself alone as a bachelor. As we know, about twenty-five years after it was built, he came to share it with John Gregg, but initially it was a large home for one man, even with the staff included.

When Allerton toured England prior to building the home, he may have been influenced by other queer landowners and the estates they had left behind. The Ladies of Llangollen, for instance, was the name given to Lady Eleanor Butler and the Honorable Sarah Ponsonby, two elite Irishwomen who left their homes in Ireland in 1778 and moved to northern Wales. They settled outside the village of Llangollen and moved into a cottage they called Plas Newydd, which they proceeded to update and restore. Over the years that they lived there (they died in 1829 and 1831, respectively), they entertained frequently and welcomed some of the leading literary figures of their day to Plas Newydd, including Byron, Shelley, Wordsworth, and more. Because of their literary and political connections and their unusual living arrangements, the Ladies were famous in their time and are remembered today as queer. But they were often understood that way in their own day as well. Their families had initially wanted them to marry men; they escaped to Wales to avoid this fate. While historians are unclear about whether they had an erotic relationship with one another, they were two women who set up housekeeping together, signed their letters together, and were eventually buried together (with their maid) when they died. As scholar Fiona Brideoake has demonstrated, whatever the actual facts of their relationship, many queer people (including Anne Lister and Lady Troubridge, partner of Radclyffe Hall) embraced the story of the Ladies of Llangollen because they offered a model for how two people of the same sex might share their lives together. And their house, Plas Newydd, was central to the story. Located far from their birthplaces and natal families, and from any city, Plas Newydd became known as a haven for the two women who had escaped the plans their families had made for them; they were accepted by the townspeople of Llangollen despite their eccentric ways. Similar to what Allerton would create at The Farms, it was also a location where visiting dignitaries and those in the arts stopped to pay their respects to "the Ladies."[26]

Horace Walpole (1717–1797) is another example. Walpole, the fourth Earl of Orford, was a politician, novelist, and youngest son of Great Britain's de facto first prime minister, Robert Walpole. Horace Walpole never married and was rumored in his day—and long since—to have been queer, though some biographers suspect he was asexual. Either way, "he drew about him a collection of highly cultured 'dear friends'—men of sensitive taste but lesser background, who shared his obsessions," two of which were art and architecture. Beginning in 1749, Walpole built Strawberry Hill House, an enormous Gothic-inspired mansion in Twickenham, on the Thames. He constructed the home in stages, adding on roughly every decade until 1770. He worked with two friends, calling themselves a Committee of Taste. The mansion sits on approximately fifty-six acres, and Walpole also designed extensive gardens surrounding it, about five acres altogether. Strawberry Hill is generally credited as being a precursor to the revival in Gothic architecture that came later in the Victorian era. In order to create his ideal house, Walpole resurrected a bygone architectural style, just as Allerton did when creating his home in Monticello. He was among the first to do so, even as he was by no means fully faithful to the Gothic tradition.[27]

It is almost certain that Allerton and John Borie would have visited Strawberry Hill on their architectural tour; it is only a mile and a half from Ham House, just across the Thames, and by far the more impressive and storied home. Ham House, which predates Strawberry Hill, was actually the residence of Walpole's niece. One chronicler of Walpole's life has described his home as a "fantastic, incongruous, and yet oddly engaging toy-castle," noting also, "It was inevitable that Walpole should buy a little house somewhere, and make a plaything of it, and cram it with *bric-à-brac.*" This is not dissimilar to how one perceives the presence of Allerton House amidst the corn fields of southern Illinois: an incongruous and oddly engaging toy castle crammed with bric-à-brac, albeit bric-à-brac with a provenance. Architectural historian Marion Harney argues that Walpole created Strawberry Hill to be a sequence of theatrical spaces playing with scale, colour and atmosphere, specifically designed to create surprise and wonder in order to stimulate the imagination. A series of sensory effects and moods, based on contemporary landscape theory, create a background to Walpole's collection of cultural and historical artefacts—each "singular," "unique," or "rare"—artfully displayed to produce their own narrative.

While Allerton may have found architectural inspiration in Ham House as a structure on which to model Allerton House—Walpole himself found Ham House dreary—Walpole's Strawberry Hill was the intellectual and artistic inspiration for how to imagine Allerton House. Unlike Ham House, which stands back from the Thames, Allerton House sits directly behind its small man-made pond and nearby the Sangamon River, which can be seen from its windows. And like Strawberry Hill, the grounds around Allerton House are laid out in a series of garden rooms, each designed to highlight some statuary or plantings. The rooms themselves transport visitors to a myriad of other places, not just to the seventeenth-century England of Ham House, but also to a variety of eclectically imagined couplings of art imported from Asia and Europe with the traditional trappings of an English garden. Like Strawberry Hill, the gardens at The Farms are designed to provoke one's imagination and to amuse with their sense of whimsy.[28]

The Ladies of Llangollen and Horace Walpole's Strawberry Hill are but two examples of queer historical subjects who created eclectic homes based on a combination of architectural revival, restoration, and the inclusion of contemporaneous art and design. They were sites where their eccentric owners held court, entertaining literary and political luminaries. Are these homes exemplary of a queer aesthetic? Maybe so. What matters most is that Allerton would have been well aware of their existence—both were quite famous in the nineteenth and early twentieth centuries—and known about their owners' reputed queerness. It makes sense that Allerton would have then conceived of his own project in design in the context of other confirmed bachelors and maidens who transformed the landscape around them, creating something wholly unexpected in its place.[29]

Throughout the first few decades of the twentieth century, Allerton was also becoming increasingly involved with the arts, this time as a patron and philanthropist. In 1907 he joined a number of other Chicagoans in what they called the Cliff Dwellers Club, which the *Tribune* described as "artists, litterateurs, architects, and others with a penchant for the esthetic" and so named for what was to be their home: a bungalow and roof garden perched atop the Harvester skyscraper at Michigan and Harrison Streets. All design of the building, gardens, and interior of the bungalow was to be completed by the ninety-five men who were members of the organization. The Cliff Dwellers, as envisioned by its founder, Hamlin Garland, was meant to unite artists and writers of various stripes with wealthy men who appreciated the arts and had the fortunes to act as patrons. As one historian has written of the club, "the Cliff Dwellers attempted to offer to its members the solid comfort and good food of a men's club as a base for conversation and as a snare for visiting artists." While its founders were interested in creating a congenial club both for artists and those who appreciated them, establishing clubs like the Cliff Dwellers also served as a way to promote the arts in Chicago, developing it as a city known for its creative endeavors. At meetings of the Cliff Dwellers, Allerton could socialize with other art patrons like Charles Hutchinson and Martin Ryerson, both dedicated supporters of the Art Institute of Chicago (AIC), as well as artists like Lorado Taft and Charles Francis Browne.[30]

Also during this period, Allerton developed what became a lifelong devotion to the Art Institute of Chicago. He had joined the AIC in 1894 at the age of nineteen, and in 1901 he was made a Governing Life Member, largely in recognition of his fortune and the donations he had begun to make to the AIC. By 1918 he had become a trustee, a post he held for many years. He was named a Distinguished Benefactor in 1923, the year he set up a permanent fund for the decorative arts. The year before, he had made his first major gift to the Art Institute: 1,300 shares of capital stock in the Union Stockyards in Omaha, Nebraska. Allerton's generosity to the AIC would continue throughout his lifetime. In 1929 he gave funds to establish the Agnes Allerton Gallery, dedicated to textiles, in memory of his stepmother, who had died five years earlier. Ten years later he paid for a new wing to house decorative arts already owned by the museum, some of which he had donated. The AIC named him an Honorary President in 1956, and following his death in 1964 they named the imposing entrance building on Michigan Avenue in honor of Allerton, the single most generous donor in the AIC's history at that time.[31]

Allerton was obviously in a position to be generous, especially after the deaths of his parents, in 1914 and 1924, respectively, when he inherited most of their sizable fortune outright. And he was hardly alone in this kind of generosity. His friends, Chicago's robber barons and their children and grandchildren, joined him in offering donations to various cultural institutions and serving on their boards of directors. The Art Institute itself had been founded by Allerton friend and neighbor Marshall Field, art collectors James Dole, Samuel Nickerson, and Nathaniel Fairbank, and banker Charles Hutchinson, who also gave generously of his fortune and his time to the AIC. Positions on the boards of trustees of organizations like the AIC were largely earned through generosity that came with varied amounts of responsibility, but they were also status symbols in and of themselves, recognition of one's influence and wealth in a community. Allerton continued this kind of philanthropy even after his later-in-life move to Hawai'i, donating to the Honolulu Academy of Arts and helping to found the Pacific (now National) Tropical Botanical Garden with other wealthy connoisseurs of horticulture. There was nothing particularly queer about any of these endeavors; if anything, he was a conformist alongside his friends and relatives.[32]

What did make Allerton distinctive was that he focused a good deal of the collecting for his own home and his donations in the areas of Asian art and the decorative arts. In somewhat different ways, both fields were feminized and were likely perceived as somewhat queer by Allerton and his peers. As a result of his travels throughout Asia, Allerton was in a position to see and acquire a good deal of Asian art. He not only kept much for himself and the gardens at The Farms, but he also donated a good deal to the AIC. In 1924, for instance, he donated three Chinese Ming family portraits. The next year he gave an architectural tile to what was then called the Oriental Department. In 1937 the Art Institute put on a special exhibition of Javanese batiks that had been loaned to them by Allerton. As late as 1958, Allerton continued his donations, this time an eighteenth-century Japanese landscape screen and four sculptures dating from the fourth through the tenth centuries. These are just a few of the many donations Allerton made to the AIC.[33]

While the original gardens that surround Allerton House are typically English, Allerton also added and augmented many of the original designs once he and John Gregg had moved in together. Robert designed the Chinese Maze Garden, copying a design on one of the many Asian silk costumes he owned. John redesigned a garden to showcase the Fu Dogs that Robert had earlier imported from China. It was adjacent to the Temple of the Golden Buddhas, themselves brought back from Thailand and Cambodia. They also created a walkway to showcase a series of sculptures of Chinese musicians, which were actually carvings crafted in England but made to resemble perceptions of Chinese facial features. In all of this they created a setting both lush, decadent, and, for early twentieth-century downstate Illinois, decidedly exotic. It is clear, then, that Robert's (and later John's) interests in collecting, while not exclusively Asian, certainly included a good deal of material from East and Southeast Asia.[34]

In 1925 Allerton joined together with other Chicago art patrons to found a group that called itself "The Orientals"; they were devoted to the "stimulation of interest in Chinese art," and lest it not be obvious, the members of "The Orientals" were not themselves East Asian, but they had

FIGURE 2.3 Chinese Maze Garden at The Farms. Courtesy of the University of Illinois Archives.

FIGURE 2.4 Fu Dog at The Farms. Originally part of the Chinese Maze Garden, John Gregg later designed a different garden that features twenty-two of these dogs. Courtesy of the University of Illinois Archives.

no difficulty assuming that moniker for the purposes of their socializing and collecting. Allerton was elected a director in the year of its founding. The Orientals thought of themselves that way because they had a fascination and appreciation for the Orient and were able to consume its arts and culture. Other founding members included Allerton's friends Russell Tyson, Potter Palmer Jr., David Adler, and George Porter. In 1920 Allerton was also among the leaders of the "Persian Group," which had assembled in order to put on a "Pageant of the East." And in 1921 he gave a "Chinese Party" for three young women home for the Christmas holidays; it was preceded by a dinner at the King Yen Lo Restaurant in Chicago. While his friend Pauline Palmer and her mother-in-law, Bertha Honoré Palmer, may well have set the standard for Chinese art collection in Chicago, at the time there was also a particular fascination with all things East Asian among queer men. Robert Allerton and eventually John Gregg also are brilliant exemplars of this trend.[35]

Orientalism was hardly new in this era. Since the eighteenth century, Americans (as well as Anglo-Europeans) had used Asian art, ceramics, and other objects in order to demonstrate wealth and sophistication. But the late nineteenth century marked a veritable explosion in these practices, especially as the United States embarked on imperialist expansion. The fascination with Asian art, textiles, and porcelain (among other things) by white collectors was a mixture of both genuine artistic appreciation and exoticization. Collectors like Allerton could truly understand the history and beauty of Asian art at the same time that they could use this appreciation as a way to exoticize Asian people and reduce them to stereotypes. Further, collectors—not just those like Allerton who donated to museums and built gardens around series of sculptures, but everyday ones who simply bought a Chinese bowl or a Japanese kimono for their homes—projected a certain version of themselves to the world by virtue of their possession of Asian art: they were cosmopolitan and worldly and sophisticated. Consuming Asian art was as much about identity as it was about the art itself. It was not just the wealthy who embraced this version of Orientalism. Literary and artistic bohemians, especially those on the West Coast, also used China and Japan, especially, to "enliven their experience and bring more meaning to their lives," as historian Amy Sueyoshi explains. This could take the form of using racially and culturally laden words and metaphors to express emotions, or it could encompass the giving of Asian gifts—a Japanese fan, for instance—or the hosting of a Chinese-themed party or ball. San Francisco's Bohemian Club, for instance, regularly put on plays about Asian countries and read poetry from other cultures. In these plays, white men often dressed in Asian drag to play the parts. And, as critic Mari Yoshihara has pointed out, the fetish for

Asian art, literature, and décor was distinctly feminized, even as it worked to feminize all Asian people as well. That is, white women made up a large portion of those who most became fascinated with "the Orient" during the late nineteenth and early twentieth centuries.[36] Partially for this reason, to be a man and share similar tastes was also to be feminized. The feminized Asian American man was also a stereotype — and a useful one for racist Anglos who sought to discriminate against Asian people and bar them from entering the United States. But for this reason, Anglo men with a particular fascination for Asian cultures themselves became feminized in the eyes of others.[37]

In *Bachelor Japanists*, cultural critic Christopher Reed notes that beginning in the late nineteenth century, Japan, in particular, attracted the attention of sexual dissidents, some of whom were queer. While noting that "nonconformists of all kinds have looked to cultures distant in time and place to forge identities that resist the pejorative terms of their own culture by imagining allegiance elsewhere," he also explains the fascination with Japan in particular during the late nineteenth and early twentieth centuries:

Occidentals alienated — to various degrees and for various reasons — from the sexual conventions of their home cultures turned to the look of Japan, collecting Japanese art, photographing Japan, and making their own art in the Japanese style. In Europe and America, there emerged communities of Japanists, often comprising respected authorities, that rehearsed and elaborated subversive knowledges of Japan.

Because most Westerners could not read or speak Japanese, this fascination primarily focused on the visual, and sometimes included Japanese representations of sexual and gender nonconformity in textiles and porcelain.[38]

Some gay men went so far as to use Asianness and Japanism, especially, as a code for their homosexuality. Sueyoshi has documented a group of San Francisco men who rented a home on Baker Street for the purposes of parties, camaraderie, and same-sex encounters and "also used Chinese and Japanese art, stores, and lodging houses to facilitate their forbidden intimacies." One of these men described how he would approach (or be approached by) other men who were lingering in front of the windows of Asian stores looking at gowns and textiles in the windows. As Sueyoshi explains, "Admiring the storefront window of a Japanese or Chinese store signaled availability for other cruising men." When the Baker Street story broke in 1918 and word of these "temperamental" men's involvement in same-sex affairs as well as interests in Asian art and culture were published in newspapers, the connection between those men who were thought to be "aesthetic" or "temperamental" was more firmly linked with Asia in the minds of a reading public.[39]

It was not just that men like Allerton might be feminized in their fascination with Asian art; Allerton was also particularly drawn to forms of Asian art that were already coded as feminine: textiles and the decorative arts. In 1926, for instance, Allerton gave the Art Institute an East Indian palampore, a large piece of fabric that was "originally intended for covers or hangings and [was] much sought after in the eighteenth century by the English." This one was added to the Robert Allerton Collection of Old Prints and Chintzes. His interests in the decorative arts also extended well beyond those from Asia. In 1920, under the heading "Men 'Set Tables,'" a number of men (and women) displayed place settings at the Art Institute of Chicago; the *Tribune* asserted that "'setting table' is an art." To prove this, Allerton "shows an attractive table with a black and white cloth and plates in which red predominates. The candlesticks are of silver and the candles are black." The headline alone indicates that it was simply unusual in Chicago society for men to take an interest in something so decidedly domestic as setting a table. The decorative arts were understood this way in part because they were ornamental and nonfunctional, two unfortunate and apt descriptors for what people also expected women to be. As Wendy Steiner has argued:

Women and ornament have functioned as analogues. Women wear ornaments (more consistently than men), and have been considered, for better or for worse, ornaments to society and the home. Ornaments epitomize the aesthetic; their primary function is to be beautiful in themselves and so to add beauty to the larger wholes in which they figure. Thus, the aesthetic symbolism of ornament involves a gesture of "pleasing," an openness of appeal that is conventionally gendered feminine.

The condemnation of the ornamental and decorative arts was especially pronounced during the late nineteenth and early twentieth centuries, when proponents and practitioners of modernist art particularly "associated decorative practices with foreign, primitive, criminal, decadent and feminine influences," in the words of art historians Bridget Elliott and Janice Helland. Those who produced decorative art (often women) could be dismissed by this logic as mere amateurs and craftspeople, rather than artists, and those who curated and collected the decorative arts could be feminized if they were men and similarly dismissed if they were women. This kind of feminized coding never stopped Allerton, however.[40]

The decorative arts were a major focus of his work at the AIC. Allerton sat on the Committee on Decorative Arts in the early 1920s, working with architect David Adler (later employer of John Gregg) and Pauline

Palmer to purchase an early Georgian room from the Geffrye Museum in London. Many of his donations were under the auspices of the Committee on Decorative Arts, on which also sat at various times Frederic Bartlett and Alfred E. Hamill. In 1925 Allerton donated a Sheffield teapot and two armchairs as well as a Washington figurine (Staffordshire) and a nineteenth-century compote and Staffordshire dish. In April 1925 he gave a Queen Anne mirror, two pieces of American silver, and thirty-four additions to the Allerton Collection of Old Prints and Chintzes. Also in 1925 he donated twenty-two fragments of French wallpaper and four wallpaper panels as well as eleven additions to the same collection. Listed alongside this particular donation was one large acquisition that the AIC had made with its own funds and then gifts of a pair of brocade curtains, two Italian samplers, two pieces of needlework, 101 pieces of lace and embroidery, two pieces of glass, a Dutch print, toile de Jouy, and four pieces of delft china. These had been given by Mrs. Henry C. Dangler, Mrs. Potter Palmer, Mrs. E. Crane Chadbourne, Elisabeth McCormick, Caroline D. Wade, Mrs. Charles B. Pike, and Mrs. C. H. Chappell, respectively. Robert Allerton was certainly not the lone man interested in the decorative arts; also in the same listing, for instance, the *Bulletin of the Art Institute of Chicago* reported that William McCallin McKee had donated a fragment of American wallpaper, and two other men had joined with Allerton in his donation of prints and chintzes.[41] But it was the case that the decorative arts, both in and outside the rarefied world of the museum, were coded feminine. While everyone understood that the great masters and the great curators were (almost) all men, women were certainly involved in the work of museums, and their involvement was particularly encouraged in realms that were already understood as female, the decorative arts among them. This is, in many ways, the story of the entry of women into many professions already coded as being feminized: those involving helping, nurturing, or decorating. None of these tasks is inherently feminine, but men allowed and encouraged women's participation in these realms because the labor already resembled the work that women did within homes, and their involvement posed no threat to men's hegemony in labor markets that continued to bring greater prestige, management, and pay. So, too, with the decorative arts.[42]

Over the first few decades of the twentieth century, Robert Allerton had cultivated a queer relationship to the worlds of art, collection, and design, that relationship wholly facilitated by his immense fortune. Focusing on the antique, the decorative, and the "Oriental," Allerton had built a large home and gardens, which he had furnished with Victorian pieces and with art and statuary that he had assembled on numerous travels abroad.

The home was all the more unusual because it was located not alongside the mansions of his Chicago friends and relatives, but instead in rural downstate Illinois, where his closest neighbors were all farmers. He had also become an exceedingly valued member of the Art Institute's board of trustees, regularly supplementing the AIC's growing collection in the realms of European painting and statuary, as well as Oriental art, and the decorative arts, textiles in particular. That travel, however, did more than help augment the collections of Allerton and the AIC; it also provided the primary means for Allerton to meet men who were also queer. In order to find the best evidence for Allerton's queer sexuality, we must look to his travels abroad, to which we now turn.

Chapter Three

Travel and Itinerant Homosexuality

Robert Allerton's fortune allowed him to travel extensively, which he did almost every winter. That travel was also a way for him to meet other same-sex-attracted men and to experience cultures that had a reputation for being more accepting of homosexuality. He often visited Europe, but also took trips to North Africa, the Caribbean, and the South Pacific. In Europe—especially Paris and London—he was able to meet other wealthy queer men and women, some similarly interested in the arts, others American expatriates living abroad. Allerton occasionally invited them back to his estate in Illinois for extended visits. These sojourns in developed countries where he socialized with those he perceived as his equals were quite different from trips to destinations that many considered less "civilized." In both places he was always on the lookout for pieces to add to either his collection or that of the Art Institute of Chicago. But in the more exotic locations, sex with local men and boys may also have been one of the attractions. A number of places in southern Europe, North Africa, and the South Pacific that Allerton visited had long held reputations as being particularly hospitable to same-sex affairs or, at the very least, as cultures that celebrated same-sex eroticism.

At the same time that Allerton was crisscrossing the globe in search of queer camaraderie, he also carried on what seems to be a chaste flirtation (and possible engagement) with a woman in the United States, the painter Ellen Emmet, who lived in New York but also visited Chicago and Monticello during the course of their friendship. And much closer at hand was the city of Chicago, which was developing a thriving queer nightlife, as well as a burgeoning literary and intellectual world to which Allerton certainly had access. As a man intent on keeping his sexual desires private, however, Allerton left no record of any interactions he had with queer Chicago. But we know much more about his dalliances abroad. This was partially because many of the men and women with whom he interacted there were notable themselves. It is possible to piece together a sense of Allerton's queer social circles in London and Paris in a way that is impossible for Chicago. This also suggests, however, that Allerton lived an itinerant homosexual existence, taking advantage of queer pleasures while abroad and remaining more circumspect while at home. Given what we know to be his future filial solution to long-term same-sex partnership—the adoption of a son—this should not be surprising; he likely felt he could not be open in his pursuit of same-sex companionship, at least not in Chicago.

Historians have demonstrated that itinerancy has been key to the pursuit of queer pleasures and sometimes to the formation of sexual identities. In part, this was because same-sex-desiring men were able to meet strangers in unfamiliar places, men they would not have encountered at home. Not only did some achieve an anonymity far from home that enabled them to pursue same-sex sexual encounters with less fear of reprisal, the very act of being away led many to feel free in a manner that was not possible closer to home. It bears noting, however, that the itinerant pursuit of queer sex and companionship has varied by class. Working-class men sometimes hitchhiked or rode the rails and met one another in various workplaces—logging camps, farms, and factories—as itinerant laborers, or they congregated in Skid Rows, boardinghouses, and occasionally prisons in big cities and across the great expanse of the American Midwest and West. Middle-class men also used travel and displacement to forge queer connections, eventually also relying upon business travel to facilitate the same ends. Wealthy men like Allerton found queer community by traveling in different circles, including to major metropoles around the globe. The strategies for queer socializing were abetted by travel and itinerancy in all of these cases, though the travel itself varied significantly by class.[1]

Given his penchant for sequestering his queer socializing in other locales, however, Allerton experienced little worry about inviting queer visitors for long-term stays at The Farms, perhaps in part because it was so removed from the world around it, and because he controlled access to it so thoroughly. All that said, the queer world of Chicago was readily accessible to Allerton, and it seems likely that he availed himself of some of its pleasures from time to time when he was staying at the University Club or at his parents' home, especially when they were away at their summer house on Lake Geneva, Wisconsin, or at their winter residence in Pasadena, California. For this reason, it is to queer turn-of-the-century Chicago that we now turn, moving further away from Chicago over the course of this chapter, which explores the travels and the romances of Robert Allerton in the first two decades of the twentieth century.

By the late 1880s, when Robert was still a child, Chicago was already home to notorious houses of vice—brothels—some of which employed, in addition to women, a handful of young male sex workers who catered to other men. Those that employed *only* young men and boys for the pleasure of older men were often called "peg houses." The city's bathhouses were also known for their same-sex activities. This was a period in US history before the solidification of the homosexual-heterosexual binary and when men who engaged in sex with other men, so long as they assumed the dominant position, did not question their own masculinity as a result. Some otherwise "normal" men preferred sex with boys or younger men, and in most cases this would not have raised suspicion about a man's true nature. Only those men who dressed as women or acted in ways perceived as effeminate were censured by their peers. From the 1860s onward, men were also occasionally arrested for violating Illinois's anti-sodomy laws; their names were printed in the papers, serving as a cautionary tale as well as an alert to others who might have same-sex desires. In 1894 homosexuality in Chicago made headlines across the nation when a young man named Guy Olmstead shot his lover and fellow postman William Clifford in the back, so distraught was he that Clifford had ended their relationship. While many papers (rightly) focused on Olmstead's precarious mental health, at least one paper did report that Olmstead tried to end Clifford's life "because he loved him." Publicity surrounding same-sex love and desire—even when it ended horribly—alerted queer people that there were others out there like them. And in a city like Chicago, where men regularly congregated in certain neighborhoods, bars, and, notoriously, under the Randolph Street Bridge, it was not hard to find them.[2]

From 1896 to 1908, two Chicago politicians familiar with the vice trade, John Coughlin and Michael Kenna, organized the First Ward Ball, also known as the Derby, an annual affair that was meant to raise funds for their spring political campaigns by extracting money from those who operated brothels, bars, and gambling establishments. All such owners were encouraged to buy a block of tickets to the ball, and the profits funded the campaigns of Coughlin and Kenna. Few refused to participate because they well understood that to do so risked their businesses. The balls also attracted the city's premier citizens, who had the chance to interact with female impersonators, prostitutes, madams, and other figures from Chicago's underworld. The ball was an annual political fundraiser based in corruption, to be sure, but it also became an opportunity for the wealthy to mingle with the disreputable and to publicly affirm the place of Chicago's queer residents as citizens. It was finally canceled in 1909 when concerned Chicagoans, fearing for the reputation of their city, publicly began to advocate that it be forever banned. Their campaign was successful, and Mayor Fred A. Busse limited the ball's liquor license, which would have cut down on the fun significantly. Police also threatened to arrest any man dressed in women's clothing. As police geared up for the ball in the weeks leading up to it, the organizers realized they had met their match and canceled it. The First Ward Ball's significance lies in demonstrating not only the key role played by queer men in its success, but also the degree of acceptance the balls enjoyed for more than a decade when they were in existence. These were not quiet, clandestine affairs; rather, they were highly publicized events that Chicagoans of all social classes attended. While in one way this affirmed the place of queer people in Chicago, it was also a very particular version of queerness: disorderly, cross-dressing, working class. The First Ward Ball was a spectacle where the wealthy slummed among the freaks, prostitutes, and queers, in essence affirming that they themselves were not any of these things. The balls thus made a space for queerness in Chicago, but not in a way that would have encouraged Allerton to embrace his own identity as a queer man.[3]

In 1911 when Chicago's Vice Commission published *The Social Evil in Chicago*, investigators documented a widespread world of gay men who used certain phrases, glances, and clothing to indicate to one another that they were gay. They spoke in coded language, eschewed the company of women, and worked in particular occupations, many behind the counters at various department stores, including Marshall Field's, which was owned by Allerton family friends. One investigator donned a red necktie and walked down the east side of State Street between four and five in the afternoon; to his surprise he was approached by between fifteen and twenty men who "wanted to go with him to usually one of the prominent hotel lobbies to make assignments." The report estimated that there were as many as twenty thousand homosexuals living in the city and that they formed a distinct subculture with their own bars and other gathering places. Despite the fact that Illinois had anti-sodomy laws on the books, Chicago's new mayor chose not to pursue its growing homosexual underground.[4]

The investigators primarily focused on middle-class and some working-class gay male subcultures, unable to obtain entrée to the more rarefied worlds of the upper-class queer, though they noted that this world certainly existed. They did hear rumors about upscale locales, among them Gerard's, a State Street restaurant, that by 1920 served as a gathering place for wealthy gay men, including, it was said, members of the exiled German royal family. There were some exclusive clubs for Chicago's elite where same-sex male pleasures were also on offer. These clubs, which were only open to members, were often identified with some sort of purpose like athletics, chess, or another activity. One of them, the Chicago Athletic Club, rented rooms to its members, as well as teenage boys, who were available for sex for a price. In 1916 one such teenager, fourteen-year-old

Galen Moon, briefly made a living having sex with the residents at the Athletic Club. One of his clients, a doctor, suggested that he could make $100 per night having sex with another boy for an audience of men at a different "private lounge" called the Officers' Club. Moon accepted the deal, performing one night a week for five weeks for forty to fifty men. The doctor told him it was a club for military officers. The Chicago Athletic Club was reputed to have in its membership "a doctor, a university professor, and a major stockholder in the Chicago Stock Yards," who could well have been Robert Allerton, given that his father was one of the founders of the yards. Two other prominent Chicagoans, George Ade and Orson Collins Wells, were caricatured by cartoonist William Schmedtgen as being effeminate fops for their membership in the Athletic Club in a 1912 cartoon. Like Allerton, Ade was also a member of the Cliff Dwellers Club.[5]

By the 1910s, lovers Harriet Dean and Margaret Anderson were publishing the *Little Review* in Chicago. The magazine regularly included gay and bisexual authors, and because of its coverage of the contemporary fine art scene, it is likely to have been known to Allerton. When the magazine was evicted from its offices for the editorial team's "queerness," the events were covered in the *Chicago Tribune*. The *Little Review* was relocated into new offices in time to cover the lecture of Edith Mary Oldham Lees Ellis, the lesbian wife of Havelock Ellis, who delivered among the first public defenses of homosexuality in the United States. There was a good deal of publicity associated with the 1915 lecture that demanded tolerance for homosexuality, including in the *Tribune*. By the 1920s, Chicago also had its own bohemian neighborhood, Towertown, where queers and other artistic types congregated at establishments like the Wind Blew Inn and the Dill Pickle Club. Patronized by college students, radicals, and homosexuals, among others, these clubs were famous in their day. The first (albeit short-lived) gay rights organization in the United States, the Society for Human Rights, was founded by Henry Gerber in 1924, also in Chicago. The organization published two editions of *Friendship and Freedom* before Gerber and other officers were arrested in the summer of 1925.[6]

Chicago was clearly home to a bustling queer scene. While Allerton actually lived most of the time in Monticello, he regularly came to Chicago for events and to see his friends and family. When they were not at their summer home in Wisconsin or their winter home in California, his father and mother continued to live in Chicago until their deaths in 1914 and 1924, respectively. When Allerton was in the city, he usually stayed at the University Club or at the apartment at 1315 Astor Street that he had inherited from his mother after her death. We do not know, however, if Allerton ever took advantage of any of Chicago's gay nightlife, though he would have known it existed, so frequently did major news outlets like the

Tribune cover it. In addition, Allerton's connections in the art world would have meant he was likely to know about queer publications like the *Little Review*. Allerton may well have visited the Chicago Athletic Club with others of his ilk, well-heeled queer men who sought discreet sexual pleasures behind closed doors. He also might have visited the First Ward Ball, taking in the spectacle alongside other society friends.[7]

For a number of reasons, however, Allerton may have been unlikely to have taken advantage of other parts of queer Chicago, especially those peopled by radicals and the working class. First, he was well-known enough that he may have risked being recognized in bars and clubs. Second, he was decidedly conservative, so the bohemian ambiance of Towertown, with its radical politics, would not have appealed. Third, and perhaps most importantly, for all that Allerton was queer, he was also very much wedded to his role as a staple of Chicago society. He preferred socializing with others of his own kind at events like the opera that were covered by the *Chicago Tribune* or inviting his friends down to Monticello to visit him there.

In 1907 the *Washington Post* reported on the comings and goings of Allerton, including the fact that he had just been in Paris for two months, but was sailing home to be with his parents in Pasadena, California, at their winter home. The *Post* also informed its Washington, DC, readers about the parties that Allerton had at his home in rural Illinois. More curiously, it explained that Allerton had been in love with one of the guests at these parties, a woman named Ellen Emmet, "a beautiful young artist." Just as quickly, however, the *Post* explained that those rumors must have been unfounded and that the families of the "two young people" had been friends for years. Just one year after the *Tribune* had named Allerton the richest bachelor in Chicago and the same year he was included on a list of wealthy prospective husbands, this coverage demonstrates just how public his bachelorhood was and the speculation that arose from his marital eligibility.[8]

Ellen Gertrude Emmet, who went by the nickname "Bay," was born in 1875 in San Francisco but moved to New York as a child. Her cousins included the writers Henry and William James. Like Allerton, she had trained to be a painter in Europe as well as in the United States. By 1900, about seven years before this story was published, she was living in New York City and pursuing a career primarily as a portrait artist. By 1906 she had been given a one-woman show of ninety of her paintings at Boston's Copley Hall. She would go on to paint the portraits of President Theodore Roosevelt, artist Augustus Saint-Gaudens, three different secretaries of state, multiple other artists and performers, as well as her cousins, the

James brothers. She was, in many ways, similar to Robert Allerton. They were both from moneyed families with social connections to one another. They had both decided, uncharacteristically for families such as theirs, to study in Europe in pursuit of careers as artists. While Emmet had a number of relatives who were also artists, which made this choice somewhat less unconventional among her relations than it was for Allerton, that she was a woman in a world dominated by men certainly marked her as an outsider.[9]

The two met in New York City in 1900, where Emmet was living after returning from Paris, and where Allerton had taken an apartment near Washington Square for part of that year. John Borie, Allerton's architect, likely introduced them. He was living in New York and was friends with Emmet's cousin Henry James. It is also possible that Allerton met Emmet even earlier, when he first became friends with Borie in Paris in the 1890s; he had certainly met Emmet's cousin Jane Emmet von Glehn then. By 1901 Ellen Emmet was writing to her sister about Allerton, explaining that she had attended an opera with him and that she would be painting his father's portrait in Lake Geneva, Wisconsin. Allerton and Emmet had themselves begun corresponding by May 1901, as the two were arranging this visit. Over the course of 1901, Allerton's letters to Emmet demonstrate a growing fondness for her and certainly read like the letters of one-half of a courting couple. One of the first letters, for instance, begins "Dear Miss Emmet," but by September he is addressing her by her first name and sending "worlds of love" as he signs off. In these letters Allerton regularly bemoaned the fact that Emmet was busy working, both in New York City and upstate. Her schedule and his own responsibilities in Illinois meant they could not spend time together. He also expressed some jealousy and resentment of her being in New York, which kept her from responding to him, and of the time she was spending with John Borie, their mutual friend.[10]

In July 1901 he wrote to her: "How I wish you were here or I where you are. I miss you so dreadfully." The next month he poured out his heart:

Do you know since I have known you life has become so much easier[?] Before to follow out what I thought I should do was a hard[,] difficult task[,] to bear charity[,] be just and wish people well was always an inward struggle[.] [N]ow knowing you and seeing you has made it all seem so simple and natural. To know and be intimate with two people like you and my mother, well it's the greatest of joys.

Phrases like these, which clearly indicate that Allerton felt transformed by his relationship with Emmet, might indicate that he was pursuing her as a wife. Certainly the increasing affection in the 1901 correspondence would bear out that reading. Between 1901 and 1903, Allerton also repeatedly invited Emmet to visit him in Monticello, and she obliged a number of times; in 1901 she painted his portrait while visiting. His correspondence during this time is marked by his desire to please her with the food she wanted, his plans to buy a new dog for her, and so forth. Those around them certainly thought that marriage was a possibility. Emmet's cousin Jane von Glehn wrote to her mother, "Cousin Henry [James] likes Robert Allerton very much and thinks Bay is going to marry him some day." The correspondence makes it seem as if Allerton is pursuing Emmet more than she him, though it is difficult to know because Emmet's letters to Allerton did not survive. It was also the case, however, that custom dictated that men pursue women, not the other way around. Women's only real power in courtship was the power to say yes or no. Certainly Emmet could flirt, but to openly pursue a man would not have been socially acceptable in their circles. Emmet's livelihood and her success largely depended on her being in New York. Not only was she clearly ambitious, but she was helping to support her family: her father had died during her childhood and her stepfather was increasingly unwilling to do so. Thus she could not simply come to Illinois whenever Allerton wanted her to be there. Marriage to Allerton would have been attractive financially, but it also would likely have involved a move to downstate Illinois—and there is no evidence that Allerton actually ever asked her to marry him in the first place.[11]

What is also striking about the letter excerpted above is that Allerton compares the intimacy he has with Emmet with that he shared with his mother, by which he meant his stepmother, Agnes Allerton. While we know that Allerton and Agnes were incredibly close, the comparison of one's potential spouse with one's mother does not indicate that Allerton necessarily felt a romantic or sexual attraction to Ellen Emmet. Indeed, Allerton primarily reflects upon how he has been changed by his interactions with Emmet, saying little in these letters about Emmet's own unique virtues. There are many ways to interpret their relationship, and I do not want to foreclose the possibility that Allerton was romantically and sexually interested in Ellen Emmet, but I think it is also possible that he pursued her because he felt like this was what he was supposed to be doing, what befitted his position in life. It is also possible that Emmet herself understood that Allerton was unable to give her the kind of marriage that she was interested in, not just because it would likely have to be located in Illinois, but also because she did not believe Allerton's protestations, in which he compared the intimacy they shared with that he also enjoyed with his mother. Through John Borie and Henry James, it is also possible that Emmet knew about relationships that Allerton had had with other men.[12]

The friendship between Emmet and Allerton continued through the first decade of the century and on into the second, with Allerton spending time with Emmet in New York as well as with her relatives in London when he was there. In January 1911, however, Ellen Emmet announced that she was engaged to marry William Blanchard Rand. They wed in early May 1911 in Connecticut. As John Gregg put it many years later:

> The truth of this story is that Robert was very much in love and engaged to this portrait painter Miss Ellen Emmett [sic], who was called Bey [sic][;] I don't know what her real name was. She use[d] to come and stay long times. . . . They were engaged to be married. It's true that morning he read the Chicago Tribure [sic] and read that she had married some one else and he hadn't been warned of it. They were formally engaged and she married somebody else.

Gregg goes on to explain that Allerton had previously withdrawn from his friendship with Emmet because he was deaf and didn't want to burden her with the responsibility of his deafness and also that he found it embarrassing to be in public because people had to speak so loudly when conversing with him. A number of claims here ring patently false, sounding more like a strategy to invent a heterosexual love interest for Allerton in order to distract from the actual way that he decided to live his life. First, while a number of sources close to Allerton retrospectively described him as having been disappointed or upset by the announcement, it seems likely that he would have known about it in advance, given how many friends and relatives they had in common: John Borie, Henry James, Jane Emmet von Glehn. Second, the notion that his deafness would only be a stumbling block for marriage with a woman—but not for any of the travel and socializing he did with men or at his own home or in any number of other very public places—makes little sense. Third, Emmet and Allerton first met in 1900 and she married in 1911. While long courtships and engagements were not unheard of during this period, usually they occurred because the prospective husband was attempting to secure an income for himself before he could settle down; clearly that was not an issue for Allerton. Finally, as we will learn later in this chapter, during the very months that Allerton was supposedly so disappointed to learn that Emmet was engaged and then married, he was writing passionate letters to a composer named Roger Quilter, letters in which he claims that no one could possibly love Quilter as much as he does. There are certainly no comparisons to Allerton's mother in the surviving letters he wrote to Quilter. What is most telling about Gregg's recounting of the Allerton-Emmet engagement is that he insists upon it so decisively, creating a heterosexual past for Allerton in order to inoculate himself and their relationship from suspicions of homosexuality.[13]

The relationship with Ellen Emmet can be read plausibly as Robert Allerton testing the waters with a woman. The two certainly had much in common. What they did not share, however, was residence in the same state. There were ample women close by in Chicago with whom Allerton, the "richest bachelor in Chicago," easily could have found himself engaged. Perhaps it was easier for him to experiment with love when Emmet was many miles away, usually busy with her profession. In some ways, Allerton's relationship with Emmet was not dissimilar to the relationships he was also beginning to have with various men during his thirties and forties: distant, transient, and, because of this, impermanent. What we know is that ultimately Allerton decided not to pursue marriage with Emmet—or any woman—in favor of traveling with a wide variety of queer men in Europe, Asia, and elsewhere. We also know that even after his death in the 1960s, Allerton's adopted son continued to rely upon the mythical figure of Ellen Emmet in order to establish his father's heterosexuality.

Allerton also regularly visited and lived temporarily in New York, where his sister, Kate, had relocated after the death of her first husband, Francis Papin. Following her second marriage in 1898, to Hugo Johnstone, Kate gave birth to two sons, Allerton Johnstone in 1900 and Vanderburgh Johnstone in 1903. Visiting New York allowed Allerton to spend time with his nephews and his sister and brother-in-law.[14]

During this period, New York arguably had the United States' most developed gay scene. Gay men assembled at bars and restaurants, and they cruised for sex in bathrooms and public parks. Washington Square Park, where Allerton resided when he was living in the city, was part of New York's bohemian Greenwich Village. Historian George Chauncey reports that by the early 1900s, men were regularly arrested in the park for engaging in sex with other men. Allerton left no record of his involvement in any sort of queer life when he was in New York. He was only twenty-seven during his first sojourn there, and while he may not have been interested in the working-class venues where "fairies" mingled with and performed in drag for more masculine men, it had always been the perquisite of the middle and upper class to be able to socialize in the privacy of their own homes. New York was no exception to this rule. He certainly knew John Borie and likely knew other queer men through connections with him. Indeed, in 1902 Borie had taken an office in the St. James Building at 1133 Broadway near Madison Square Park, and by 1904 he and his partner Victor Beigel lived only a block from Washington Square Park on Eighth Street between Fifth Avenue and MacDougal. Because Allerton's interests were already so geared toward the artistic, it is probable he was able to meet other like-minded men as he toured galleries, museums, and artists' studios.[15]

Allerton's travels also took him around the East Coast throughout the first two decades of the century. In 1918 he was in Miami with Frederic Bartlett staying at the Royal Palm. Miami was at the time billing itself as a "fairyland" for white and wealthy tourists, especially those interested in the arts and in unconventional sexuality. James Deering, whose father had founded an agricultural equipment company in Chicago, had moved there in 1916 and built an elaborate mansion with thirty-nine guest rooms called Villa Vizcaya. There he entertained many bachelor guests who had come to admire his vast collection of art. Deering had chosen interior decorator Paul Chalfin to design the home. Chalfin lived with his lover and "secretary," Louis Koons. Like Allerton and John Borie, Deering and Chalfin had traveled the world together in search of inspiration, furnishings, and art for Villa Vizcaya, which had been fashioned in the manner of an Italian palazzo. Like Allerton and Gregg, Chalfin and Koons also favored entertaining guests in Chinese costumes. Given Allerton's, Bartlett's, and Deering's shared status as sons of the Chicago robber barons, it seems likely that Allerton and Bartlett would have visited Villa Vizcaya on their trip to Miami. The population of Miami was still fewer than thirty thousand people in 1920, and of those, only a small number could possibly have been among Deering's elite peers. As a testament to the noteworthiness of Allerton and Borie's visit, the *Miami Herald* announced the arrival of the pair. While Allerton already had plenty of experience in developing large homes and gardens in Illinois, Villa Vizcaya and its tropical location may well have served as inspiration for Lawai-Kai, the home that he and Gregg would eventually develop in Kaua'i.[16]

During the 1910s, Allerton also went on driving trips three times along more northern shores of the East Coast to see artwork. With Elmer Priebe acting as chauffeur, they would map out where to stay in advance. These vacations included one in New England, where they traveled to Maine, Vermont, and numerous stops in Massachusetts, including Provincetown, which was establishing itself by the 1910s as one of the largest artists' colonies in the United States, if not the world. In 1899 the Cape Cod School of Art had been founded there; fifteen years later, the Provincetown Art Association opened its doors. By the 1910s, Provincetown had also acquired a reputation as being particularly open and accepting of those artists who led unconventional domestic lives. Journalists also recounted the artists' unusual summertime costume balls, where people dressed in drag and flouted other social conventions. These automobile ventures also included stops in cities like Detroit, Atlantic City, Boston, and Philadelphia. As chauffeur Elmer Priebe recalled many years later, "Mr. Allerton

was very considerate—he always wanted me to have as good accommodations as he had and I always ate at the same table with him and the rest
of the party. We also went to shows together and in Baltimore we shared
the same bathroom."[17]

It is possible that in including Priebe in his socializing and dining out,
Allerton was exploring how he might manage to conduct a long-term relationship with a man in public. I do not mean to imply that Allerton and
Priebe were lovers, but rather to suggest that if Allerton wanted to be able
to travel publicly with a male companion, he would need to have some way
to explain his presence. No doubt some of Allerton's social set would have
found it odd that Priebe was included at dinner if they were sharing the
meal with Allerton's peers. It may be that these early trips with Priebe suggested to Allerton that a different sort of explanation would be necessary
if he were to have a male companion. (As we shall see in the next chapter, some wealthy men styled their partners as chauffeurs or other hired
companions.) In addition to being pleasurable, these trips were produc-
tive for Allerton in seeing new artwork that was being created by artists
in the United States, and for scouting out purchases for himself and the
Art Institute. In order to find what would be most valuable for the AIC,
however—and to make the most of his queer itinerary—he would have
to go abroad, which he did almost every year.

Allerton's travels in Europe were typical for someone of his class. Papers
like the *Chicago Tribune* and the *New York Times* regularly announced those
who were going abroad, who departed on which ship, and who returned
on another. In an era before air travel was commercially available, voyag-
ing to Europe, the Caribbean, or farther abroad was of necessity travel by
ship. In January 1912, for instance, the *New York Times* announced those
sailing from New York to Southampton on the *Olympic*. On board were Allerton, Col. and Mrs. John Jacob Astor, the Prince and Princess del Drago,
and Mr. and Mrs. Reginald Brooks. While the time it took to cross the Atlantic or Pacific had been greatly reduced from the nineteenth century, it
was still long enough (generally four or five days for the Atlantic, longer
for the Pacific depending on the destination) that many travelers chose to
stay abroad for months rather than weeks. Many English and Americans
would take what was called "the grand tour" in the nineteenth century,
visiting numerous countries and seeing a wide selection of highlights of
European culture. Others chose to take up residence in one city—some for
what was called "the season," during which debutantes were introduced
to society and at which they might hope to make matrimonial matches.[18]

Allerton had been engaging in travel like this since he and Frederic
Bartlett first set off for Munich and then Paris to study painting. Over

the course of those years abroad, Allerton and Bartlett had also been to a number of other European cities and towns, visiting museums and galleries, as well as seeing the sights. In the course of his first years in Europe, Allerton had met John Borie in Paris, whom he would commission to design his home in Monticello. It was common enough for wealthy Americans to be abroad that it was also not surprising when they met each other there as well. As a result of this meeting, a number of years later the pair had traveled to England in search of the perfect inspiration for Allerton House. The pair also socialized with other queer men while they were abroad.[19]

The travel writer Ian Littlewood argues that for many people (especially men, though he does not say it), travel and tourism have always been inflected by sex. In part this was because travel throws people closely together—on trains, coaches, and ships—with available sexual partners. It is also because many achieved a degree of anonymity when traveling that they could never have at home. While many think that "sex tourism" is a relatively recent invention, many men who went abroad over the course of the eighteenth and nineteenth centuries paid for sex, often with young people. Others found partners for whom remuneration was not necessary. The queer traveler, especially, was able to meet sexual partners abroad in ways that might not have been possible at home. It was not just that some locations abroad might have had more developed cultures and systems for such meetings—though that was often the case—it was also that people often act and feel differently when they are traveling. Whether or not they actually are more liberated is unclear; that they feel so, or use travel as an excuse to feel so, is demonstrable. In the case of Allerton, the majority of his documentable queer interactions, even those that were likely no more than platonic, took place abroad.[20]

In the decade after finishing his home in Monticello, Allerton made trips to London and Paris. In 1900 and 1901, he also traveled further afield, to China, with a friend, Russell Hewlett, another single man interested in the arts. Hewlett was only one year Allerton's senior and had been born in New York. He had also studied at the École des Beaux-Arts in Paris, which is likely how he and Allerton met. On this particular trip, they toured through Europe, including Italy, where Allerton purchased furniture for Allerton House, and in China he sent back more furniture and scroll paintings for his newly completed home. Four years later, Hewlett and Allerton sailed around the world, including a stop in China at the Peking "thieves market," where they perused ancient Chinese scrolls. As John Gregg explained years later, "They just had a whole pile of these things that had been stolen and they just took them off the ground. . . . Well, some of them turned out to be very valuable." A number of these scrolls made their way to the Art Institute of Chicago, while others stayed at Allerton House. Hewlett and Allerton remained friends after their travels together. Hewlett went on to be a professor of decoration at what was then called the Carnegie Technical Schools and later the Dean of the School of Applied Design at the renamed Carnegie Institute of Technology (what would later become Carnegie Mellon University). He never married and died in 1913 of pneumonia. Allerton went to Brooklyn to attend the service. We do not know whether Hewlett and Allerton were ever involved romantically, or indeed whether Hewlett was queer. Regardless of whether they were involved with one another as something more than simply friends, they also shared a status as single men with atypical interests in feminized fields.[21]

Allerton's travel to Europe, and abroad more generally, picked up significantly in the second decade of the twentieth century. As a result of this travel, his ability to meet queer men also expanded. Allerton met the painter Glyn Philpot in 1913 at the opera at Covent Garden in London. Philpot was twenty-nine at the time, about a decade younger than Allerton. Philpot was primarily known for his portraits and had painted a number of semi-nude studies of both white and black men. He was also queer. It is likely that Allerton was already familiar with Philpot's work because a painting of his, *Tragedienne*, had been loaned to the Art Institute of Chicago in support of a benefit for a local hospital. He had also exhibited at the Carnegie Institute in Pittsburgh, where Allerton's friend Hewlett worked. In the wake of their meeting, Allerton promptly invited him to come visit in Illinois, and Philpot took him up on the offer. When Philpot arrived in New York in the late summer of 1913, Allerton was not waiting for him. Instead, their mutual friends John and Rue Carpenter informed Philpot that Allerton already had another guest, Allerton House architect John Borie. Philpot was not fond of Borie, referring to him as "that beast," so he accepted an invitation from the Carpenters to join them in visiting Vermont. Philpot was clearly upset with the situation, writing to his sister that it "was too much for me just at the moment, and the heat and disappointment finished it." He had already explained to her how excited he was at being able to see Robert; now Allerton was unavailable at the moment of his arrival and was occupied with another gay man, one Philpot himself rather disliked. The trip was not beginning well.[22]

By early September, Allerton and Philpot had smoothed things over, and Philpot was in Monticello, where Allerton set him up in a studio and began trying to get him commissions with his friends. Madame X, a *Chicago Tribune* columnist, devoted almost an entire article to his stay in Illinois, calling him one of the four foremost painters in England at the time:

Glyn Philpot is young, being barely 30 years of age. His English father and Spanish mother are each clearly to be traced in his appearance, which is both attractive and remarkable, a not usual combination. He is rather above medium height, well set up, with a finely modeled head, much after the type of the early portraits of Shelley and Byron. His Spanish blood speaks in his rich coloring and striking dark eyes, large, heavy lidded, with very long thick lashes.

Madame X described his appearance and dress for a further two paragraphs, and then moved on to the purpose of his visit, noting that he has a "great admiration for the negro from the painter's point of view." She expected him to be entranced by the "sky bound expanses of rustling corn" in Monticello.[23]

Philpot stayed at The Farms for three months. When he began to worry that he was overstaying and wearing out his welcome, Allerton apparently asked him, "'We're very happy, aren't we?'" as a means to get him to stay, which proved effective. There is plentiful evidence of Philpot's great attraction to Allerton—he once described him as "everything that is beautiful and true"; less clear is what Allerton felt about Philpot. Philpot explained to his sister, Daisy, while still residing at Allerton House:

I've certainly never had a friend who was so interested in my welfare. He has no opinion whatever of his own importance & says the most childlike things about himself—and yet through it all there comes out the most *beautiful* wise mature character. I wanted to tell you about all this . . . to show you that it is not just a silly infatuation I have for him. Another thing is—he never flatters me at all.

Philpot's biographer, J. G. P. Delaney, credits this as being the most self-revealing surviving letter Philpot would ever write, and it is hardly explicit. It also does not tell us whether or not Allerton reciprocated the feelings or rather saw Philpot as more of a mentee and less of a lover.[24]

During Philpot's stay at Allerton House, he painted a portrait of Allerton, *The Man in Black*. As John Gregg explained years later, Philpot "wanted to paint a figure that was all in black. He wanted to know how you get the tonality of shading it in black, so he asked my father if he would pose for him." In the painting, Allerton stands sideways wearing a black hat and cloak, a white collar visible beneath the outerwear. He faces toward the artist, but his eyes veer slightly to his right, as if he were distracted or looking over the artist's shoulder. It is an arresting and somber portrait that now belongs to the Tate in London. He also painted the commissioned portrait of a society daughter for which he was paid 600 pounds. Allerton and Philpot stayed in touch with one other through the 1910s when Philpot was also serving in the war effort. Philpot again visited Monticello in 1921, this time with the painter Vivian Forbes, who had become his protégé

FIGURE 3.1 *The Man in Black*, 1913, by Glyn Warren Philpot (1884–1937). Courtesy of the Tate, London. Photo credit © Tate, London 2019.

and on-again/off-again lover. On this visit, Allerton connected him with a number of prominent friends whom Philpot painted: Mrs. Potter Palmer and Mrs. Walter Brewster. Whether or not the relationship between Allerton and Philpot had ever been romantic, Allerton clearly took an interest in Philpot's welfare and was doing his best to assist his career. During this trip, Philpot also completed some pieces for Allerton House and its gardens. The first was an overmantel of a faun and satyr. The second was a small plaster sculpture of "primitive man," which was based on nude modeling sessions with Allerton's butler, Edward "Ted" Page; using this as a model, Allerton commissioned two massive figures that stood on two sides of an avenue in a garden at The Farms.[25]

What occurred between Allerton and Philpot could have been entirely devoid of eroticism and simply a one-sided crush on the part of Philpot. His biographer, Delaney, leans in that direction, demonstrating that it was only later in life that Philpot became freer with his sexual desires and predilections. Earlier on he was timid and prone to infatuation with little follow-through. But regardless of whether Allerton and Philpot had a sexual relationship with one another, it seems clear that the fellow feeling established between the two and the interest that Allerton took in mentoring and aiding Philpot had queerness at its foundation. If Allerton could not be an artist, he was interested in aiding those with more talent than he himself possessed. If some of these were young men with similar sensibilities, all the better. Allerton also did his best to aid Vivian Forbes in securing commissions for children's portraits in the course of Philpot and Forbes's visit. Queer aesthetics served as the basis for the friendship with Philpot, whether or not the relationship had a sexual dynamic for Allerton. For Philpot, in its earliest incarnation clearly it did, even if unrequited.[26]

Allerton is said to have met Glyn Philpot at the opera at Covent Garden in 1913, but he could easily have met him earlier than this. Given the other people that Allerton knew in London—all members of a queer London crowd of writers, musicians, and artists, some of whom enjoyed access to considerable inherited wealth—they could have met through friends. During the first two decades of the twentieth century when Allerton was back and forth across the Atlantic annually, he met many other men this way. One of these was likely Charles Shannon, the painter. In 1924 Allerton donated a drawing by Shannon, called *Three Bathers*, to the Art Institute of Chicago. The charcoal sketch features three nude men, one balanced on top of the other as a third dives from above into water below. It is a relatively rudimentary sketch, highlighting the men's musculature. Shannon and his partner Charles Ricketts were notorious aesthetes, artists, and collectors. They were also friends with a number of the men that Allerton himself knew in London. Both born in the 1860s, Shannon became best known for his portraits, some of which hang in London's National Portrait Gallery, while Ricketts, by contrast, was primarily an illustrator, printer, and typographer. The pair met at the South London Technical School of Art in London, where they both studied. Both friends of Oscar Wilde, they also founded a press named after their home, The Vale, in Chelsea. While it is of course possible that Allerton acquired *Three Bathers* at a gallery, the unfinished nature of the work and the fact that Allerton and Shannon were in such overlapping social circles makes it seem more likely that Allerton acquired it directly from Shannon himself. Literary critic Michael Anesko has also demonstrated that the twin sphinx sculptures at The

Farms designed by John Borie also draw on imagery from Oscar Wilde's book *The Sphinx*, which was itself designed by Ricketts. Overlapping circles of queer aesthetes accounted for the generation of numerous artistic projects.[27]

In 1910 or 1911, Allerton also met a man named Roger Quilter via Jane Emmet von Glehn (cousin of both Ellen Emmet and Henry James). Von Glehn regularly hosted salons of artists and musicians in her London home; guests included John Singer Sargent and his sister Emily, Gervase Elwes, Léon Delafosse, and Gabriel Fauré. Quilter was a British composer and the eldest son of William Quilter, 1st Baronet and member of British Parliament. Born in 1877, making him just four years younger than Allerton, Quilter also attended some of the same parties that Glyn Philpot did, like those hosted by wealthy bachelor Frank Schuster at his large country house in Berkshire, whom Philpot knew through their mutual friend Siegfried Sassoon.[28]

The social worlds of wealthy Americans and Europeans overlapped, in part because they married one another and friends became relatives. But these connections aided someone like Allerton when first visiting a city like London or Paris. A subset of this coterie of wealthy sophisticates was also queer, and many of them were artists. Tracing who met whom when thus becomes trickier because they all socialized together, and Allerton was very much welcome in their set. Roger Quilter was like Allerton in many ways aside from their similar ages. He was born into a family where art was not the expected career path and yet he became a musician. Soon after their meeting, Quilter was off on a trip to Egypt with his mother in February 1911, and Allerton was bound for Munich. From there Allerton sent Quilter a letter that is worth quoting at length:

Dearest Roger when I came in to [?] last night and found your first letter and all life has been different since. I never dreamt I could so madly long to hear from any one before. How I wish you were here to hear all the good music and go to the funny balls. We went to a long one last night and feel quite jaded this morning from so much dancing—Susan Metcalf has a concert here tomorrow night we are going of course—It is the most beautiful weather warm and sunny like spring. Do write me what your one act opera is going to be about. I love your music dear Roger all I have heard. It's too heavenly.

In this letter, it seems that Allerton has just met Quilter, whose own first correspondence to Allerton confirms the significance of their meeting and the bond that they had established with one another. The following sentences then elaborate on interests that they share, primarily music, but also their mutual friends, with whom they could attend "funny balls." The letter continues, Allerton referencing an invitation he must already have extended to Quilter to visit him in Monticello:

To think of all the nice things you are going to compose next summer at the Farms[.] [W]hat a divine time we will have together there by ourselves riding over the farm and taking long walks with the dogs. You will like it I haven't a doubt. There won't be any of these beastly seperations [sic] what hell they are. Think what a beautiful time we might be having together now but I must not complain. It's so wonderful to have found you and we have a long life ahead. Life is so much nicer now we are friends and so much more besides[,] even though we are apart you blessed old darling. I do so love you Roger every body that knows you must but no one can as much as I. Your devoted Robert.[29]

This letter, dated from when Allerton was reported to be devastated by the marriage of Ellen Emmet, clearly shows otherwise. Instead he explains that he had not thought it possible to want to hear so badly from another person as from Quilter. He speaks of the songs that Quilter will compose at The Farms and the long life that they will share together as friends, "and so much more besides." The visit, alas, was never to be. As his biographer Valerie Langfield explains, at the time of the proposed visit, Quilter and his father were both sick. Quilter had been seriously ill in the past with both influenza and an ulcer and was repeatedly hospitalized, afterward convalescing in nursing homes. He also suffered from what appears to be depression and anxiety. In sum, Quilter was terrified about whether he could receive adequate care far from home among people he did not know particularly well, even though he clearly wanted to be with Allerton. As Langfield explains, "He was trapped by his fear of the unknown and the unpredictable."[30]

Despite the fact that Quilter did not make it to Monticello, it is likely that he and Allerton saw each other again. Allerton was in England in the winter of 1912 and again in 1913. Nothing else can really explain Allerton's letter to Quilter in February 1914, immediately after learning that his father, Samuel, had died:

Dearest Rog[,] I feel so depressed and sad I had no business to write but your lovely letters—I simply must tell you what a comfort and help they have been. No one could be more lucky than I am to have such a good true dear friend as you are dearest Rog and how I do appreciate it. Words could never explain how much it means to me. I gess [sic] you know don't you dearest Rog. It's the most terrible dissapointment [sic] not to see you. I have been all [?] so looking forward to it. If you could only manage to come over to the Farms this summer—I can't yet believe I will never see my dear Father again he must have been ill only a very short time as all along have been most cheerful happy [?] and weakly [?]. I feel I shall have a violent reaction when I reach my destination (Chicago or California as yet I don't know which) after this incessant driving on from train to train and boats etc, ever since the 10th of Feb when we left Pekin[g]. Thomas could not have been nicer and was the greatest comfort. Eddy was so lovely and I think it was so wonderful of Billy to come over to Paris although I really much preferred not to see anyone but of course he could not have known that. This is a beastly ship. Years ago I crossed on her and swore I never would again—and here I am so grateful to have caught her! She is crowded with dressmakers etc etc She vibrates so one can't read only a few minutes at a time and the old Atlantic is so horribly rough fogs and rains. How glad I will be to see New York alas we are already a day late. I will write you directly I know what my plans are. I want to be with my mother but if she does not come on to stay in Chicago I suppose I [won't] be as of course I will have to be there. All the love in the world darling Rog I do love you so

Your ever devoted Robert

Not only does Allerton thank Quilter for his letters, he also says that it's the "most terrible disappointment not to see" Quilter, as if that were either part of a set plan (Allerton was en route home from Tahiti) or part of a routine. He also mentions a number of mutual friends—Thomas, Billy, and Eddy—who clearly must have been known to Quilter as well, because he does not feel the need to use their surnames. He once again alludes to a possible trip that Quilter might make to The Farms that summer, though that, too, would never occur.[31]

Quilter and Allerton enjoyed an affair that persisted over several years, even if they only saw each other during the periods in which Allerton visited England. Quilter's biographer writes that the relationship with Allerton was the only same-sex affair to which Quilter ever admitted; he later wrote a piece of music for piano and voice dedicated to Allerton: "I Arise from Dreams of Thee," based on the poem by Percy Bysshe Shelley. While Allerton was keen to have Quilter visit him in Monticello, where they could enjoy the privacy of The Farms, he was never able to leave England, and the affair seems to have ended after the death of Allerton's father. The affair with Quilter was just one relationship among the many that he enjoyed with a moneyed set of artists and aesthetes when he traveled to England and France, and because Quilter saved the letters, the only one to which we have access. From it we learn that, despite his ongoing connection with Ellen Emmet, it was with a man that he learned he "never dreamt [he] could so madly long to hear from any one before." The difficulty, of course, was that Allerton lived in Illinois and felt the need to return there for a good portion of every year, and Quilter was unable to travel there at all. If Allerton was going to have a long-term relationship with another man, it would have to be someone willing to live in Monticello, at least part of the year. Men, or women for that matter, with established careers were unlikely candidates for such an arrangement, no matter the other benefits that would inhere in being taken under Allerton's wing.

Allerton's second letter to Quilter was partially occasioned by the death of his father, which occurred on February 22, 1914, in Pasadena, when Allerton was in Tahiti. A funeral service was held two days later in Pasadena. It took Allerton some time to make it home, traveling via Beijing (then called Peking), Bremen, Germany, and then Paris, where he was visited by his friend Billy. He took the SS *Kaiser Wilhelm II* across the Atlantic to Hoboken, New Jersey, where he was met by Frederic and Dora Bartlett and their mutual friend George Porter, another patron of the Art Institute of Chicago. From there, the Bartletts and Allerton headed west by train to Chicago. Once Agnes Allerton and Kate Johnstone had arrived with Samuel's body from Pasadena, Samuel Waters Allerton was buried in Graceland Cemetery on March 14, 1914. More than 150 friends and family members attended.[32]

When Samuel Allerton's will was admitted to probate the next month, the *Tribune* estimated his estate was valued at $4 million, approximately $100 million in today's dollars. Robert received most of the remaining land in Piatt County and environs as well as the house on Prairie Avenue, which he sold soon thereafter, buying an apartment at 1315 Astor Street where his mother lived when not in Pasadena and where Allerton had the option of staying when he was in Chicago. Agnes inherited the homes in Pasadena and in Lake Geneva, Wisconsin. Agnes, Kate, and Robert received shares in various interests, including the First National Bank of Chicago, the Pittsburgh Union Stock Yards, and the Omaha Union Stock Yards. Robert could do what he wanted with his now immense wealth, no longer needing to consult with his father about various expenditures. As it turned out, his priorities remained essentially unchanged; he continued to be generous, both in Chicago and in Piatt County, just as his father had been. He also continued to travel annually during the winter season.[33]

In between trips to England and various other European countries in search of queer camaraderie and objets d'art, Allerton also visited a number of more far-flung destinations. He had been on his way back from Tahiti when he found out about his father's death. The following year he renewed his passport, explaining that he would be going to Australia, New Zealand, and the "South Sea Islands." In January 1919, he ventured to Cuba and two years later to a variety of locations in the Caribbean: Cuba again,

Jamaica, Venezuela, Trinidad, Panama, Martinique, St. Thomas, and Bar-
bados. The next year he included stops in Tunisia and Algeria, as well as
Italy and Spain, into his annual European adventures.[34]

By comparison to Europeans, tourism beyond the bounds of their own
country was relatively rare for most Americans. The very wealthiest Americans, however, had been traveling for most of the nineteenth century, often venturing around Europe or taking a home where they could socialize
with wealthy expatriates and Europeans. But travel of the sort undertaken
by Allerton was slightly more unusual, though certainly not unheard of.
A number of the destinations on his list—including southern Italy, Spain,
North Africa, and the islands of the Pacific—had reputations as being particularly welcoming of sexual encounters between men. Allerton left behind no record of what he did on these vacations, but a brief exploration
of how these locales had become marked as queer should help to contex-
tualize Allerton's travels.

These regions' reputations for tolerance of same-sex relations is somewhat misleading. These were not places, by and large, that had large numbers of gay men as we might think of them: men who were exclusively
attracted to other men. Rather, people in most locations outside of the
United States and western Europe at the turn of the century did not yet
embrace a hetero/homo binary to understand their sexual desires. This
actually remained true for the United States as well. In many cities and
rural areas of the United States in the first decades of the twentieth century, men regularly had sex with other men without believing that doing so constituted a particular identity. Depending on the scenario, so
long as these men acted in masculine ways, or assumed the penetrative
position, or were otherwise married to women, or were the older in the
sexual pairing—the circumstances varied by location and likely by sexual encounter—those involved did not see the older or more masculine
partner as being fundamentally different from those men who exclusively
had sex with women. While historians have demonstrated that this was
particularly so in locations and among populations where women were
few and far between—men riding the rails across the country, in lumber
camps in the Pacific Northwest, among Italian immigrants in New York
City—there were also plentiful opportunities for sex between men when
sex ratios were perfectly even. Queer men knew about these opportunities, just as some knew about those that could be had abroad as well.[35]

In some cases the circumstances that led to the acceptance of same-
sex activity among men were similar abroad. So long as one man maintained some version of masculinity, he was not tainted by the femininity
that was presumed to accompany submission or penetration. But in other
cases, more complex cultural systems account either for the acceptance

of same-sex affairs or Americans' belief that a particular location was accepting. In the case of Italy, for instance, Catholic prohibitions on sex before marriage sometimes made Italian men more likely to have sex with one another if they were unable to do so with similarly unmarried Italian women. Not only did this mean one avoided paying for the services of a prostitute, but Catholic doctrine so emphasized the sin of premarital sex that same-sex sexual encounters simply seemed less problematic by comparison. In the case of Greece, many American and European men believed that traditions of same-sex love and affection passed down from the ancients still characterized Greek culture. These beliefs, made famous by John Addington Symonds and others, sometimes had the effect of making it seem as if contemporaneous Greek culture was also especially accepting of love between men.[36]

Many cultures also had ritualized meanings attached to same-sex sex that Westerners did not fully understand, but publicized if they found these rituals erotic. For instance, Native Hawaiians had long engaged in same-sex practices whereby older men engaged in sex with younger men, a practice called *aikāne*. These relationships were not at all secretive and could continue for a lifetime. The earliest European explorers of Hawai'i and other islands in the Pacific commented upon these relationships. Another common role in Native Hawaiian culture was the *māhū*, a liminal third-gender category (similar to the berdache in some continental US native tribes), a person who assumed a role in between that of male and female and who could engage in sexual relations with those of the same anatomical sex. European explorers from Captain Cook onward were often equal parts intrigued and disgusted by these practices, which they publicized after their journeys, lending various Pacific islands the reputation as being accepting of men who desired sex with other men. This was a misinterpretation of what was happening in Hawai'i and elsewhere. But it stuck, making some locations seem particularly desirable to men in search of sex with other men, or the acceptance of such practices by inhabitants.[37]

Finally, the sheer imbalance in power between rich, white tourists and native peoples led to a variety of forms of prostitution. As the historian Robert Aldrich has explained, this could be outright quid pro quo prostitution where sex was exchanged for money, but in many locations, the negotiations were far more subtle. Travelers paid for expenses with sexual partners—dinner, travel, hotels—and sometimes gave them gifts. No explicit conversations needed to occur in order to make the paying customer feel like he was just that. And in some places, the locals were so well aware of their reputation for queer sex, they did all in their power to facilitate these interactions if remuneration was implied.[38]

It is worth examining a handful of locations Robert Allerton visited in order to see what might have appealed to him, aside from sights that continue to draw tourists to all of these locations. On a number of occasions, Allerton visited Italy, parts of which had long had a reputation for being particularly accepting of same-sex affairs, especially the island of Capri and Taormina on the island of Sicily, both in southern Italy. Indeed, the southern Mediterranean is probably the region, from at least the eighteenth century onward, to most enjoy a reputation as being particularly accepting of homosexuality. This was, in large part, because a series of writers and artists who found refuge in the Mediterranean ended up perpetuating the myth of the homoerotic Mediterranean, and the poor socioeconomic conditions in the region, particularly in southern Italy, encouraged locals to cater to these beliefs and desires for their own livelihood.[39]

This began with latter-day reinterpretations of the ancients and their celebration of pederasty. As Aldrich explains, "The 'homosexual' heritage of Greece (and, to a lesser extent, of Rome) in poetry and philosophy, art and history was the most powerful and most positive image of sexual and emotional relationships between men (or men and boys) available to succeeding generations." Generations of same-sex-desiring men celebrated what they saw as the acceptance of homosexual love in southern Europe, even if later classicists have argued that ancient same-sex practices by no means map seamlessly onto the emergent modern homosexual, whose orientation was exclusively directed toward those of the same sex. In a similar vein, those interested in the arts, like Allerton, would have been well aware that southern Europe held a unique place not just as the supposed origins of civilization and location of much ancient sculpture, but also of male beauty. Johann Joachim Winckelmann, the founder of modern art history in the eighteenth century, emphasized what he believed to be the natural beauty of the Greeks, especially their young men, whose bodies were made even more perfect by virtue of their dedication to athletics. That perfect beauty was the inspiration for those who sculpted or drew their likeness. Aldrich demonstrates that this confluence of supposed acceptance of homosexuality and the emphasis upon the beauty of the southern European youth had made Italy and Greece popular destinations for same-sex-desiring men by the nineteenth century. Some of these men then continued the myth by virtue of their own art and writing. Those who worked in what we would now refer to as the hospitality industry became aware of who was visiting and why; young men who were far poorer than the European and American tourists who visited often did their best to satisfy their comparatively wealthy clientele. Thus, the region, in actuality, did become one that was particularly accepting of modern Western homosexuality, but in large part because modern Western homosexuals made it so.[40]

Some destinations in particular attracted entire communities of wealthy European gay men and lesbians. The city of Taormina on Sicily was one of them. The island of Capri was another. Beginning in the 1890s, a large number of queer Englishmen began coming to the island. These included the writers W. Somerset Maugham, E. F. Benson, D. H. Lawrence, Norman Douglas, and Lord Alfred Douglas and Oscar Wilde. Other wealthy Europeans also summered there, including Friedrich Krupp, a German arms manufacturer who built a large home and invested heavily in the island; in 1900 he was granted honorary citizenship. The fact that he had numerous relationships with young men and boys was either accepted or overlooked because of his generosity. We do not know with certainty where Robert Allerton went on his trips to Italy, aside from Florence, where he and Frederic Bartlett met up one of the summers between years studying in Paris and Munich. Allerton had been traveling with English friends at the time. He returned to Italy a number of times after that early trip. We know also that he had met other gay men during these early years in Europe, so it seems likely that he enjoyed travels in southern Italy with those men, appreciating the reputation the region had for its particular acceptance of queer men like them.[41]

In 1922 Allerton visited Tunisia and Algeria. North Africa had long been held in high esteem by men who sought sex with other men. Beginning with the conquest of Egypt in 1798 and followed, over the course of the nineteenth and twentieth centuries, by imperial ventures in Algeria, Tunisia, and Morocco, French colonial officials had long worried about what they believed were Arab men's predilection for sodomy and the deleterious influence this would have upon French soldiers stationed there. Glyn Philpot, whom we met earlier, traveled regularly to Tunisia and Morocco. On one occasion in Tunisia, he met a man named Amor ben M'rad working on a road; Philpot was so impressed by ben M'rad that he made him his model, and he eventually joined Philpot in London as his servant and muse. The Nobel laureate André Gide wrote at length about his sexual adventures with men, sometimes loosely disguised as fiction. In a series of books, Gide described a world where beautiful brown youths were available for the taking. As Aldrich explains:

Local ephebes had a well-developed practice of offering themselves for sex; their gestures and propositions were well-rehearsed, and they proved expert at seducing European men by approaching them, offering them food, a tour or some small service. There was also a geography of homosexual encounters—hotels where foreigners gathered, gardens where men and boys strolled at twilight, the riverside where youths bathed and rowed.

Aldrich makes clear that an entire commerce revolved around this sort of tourism—as it does in many areas of the world today—facilitated by restaurateurs and shopkeepers. This was not private and clandestine; rather it was open enough that travelers could find what they were looking for, albeit for a price. It is clear that this world existed perhaps in part because societies in the Maghreb had a more accepting attitude toward same-sex sex in the first place, but, secondarily and more importantly, because of the possibilities to profit from the wealthy tourists who came to visit.[42]

Allerton visited the Maghreb just a year after Gide published his autobiography *Si le grain ne meurt*, but Gide and many other writers had been documenting the availability and willingness of supple young Arab men for decades by that point. Indeed, the autobiography recounts one episode in 1895 in Algeria when Gide ran into friends Oscar Wilde and Lord Alfred Douglas, who were staying nearby. This was a coincidence in Gide's telling: one French and two English queer men who happened to be in Algeria at the time precisely because they were queer. Wilde and Gide ventured to Biskra, where the night ended in an apartment, with Wilde having sex with their waiter and Gide with the flautist who had entertained them at dinner. In terms of their mutual friends, Allerton was only separated from Wilde by one degree, and Gide by two. But he need not have known either man in order to be aware of the reputation of the Near East as a site of hedonistic pleasures for men who desired sex with other men. After all, that is how Gide and Wilde ended up there themselves.[43]

No destination in this period of Allerton's travels was farther from home than Tahiti and the other islands of French Polynesia, and perhaps none as celebrated as an escape to the exotic. As historian Ian Littlewood has explained, "'Gauguin's Tahiti' was to become the ultimate twentieth-century tourist destination." Allerton visited at least twice that we know of in the mid-1910s, though he left no record behind of what he did while there. A trip to Tahiti was probably not the most remote location that an American could choose, but it certainly was not a journey that would be undertaken lightly. By the time that Allerton visited, Tahiti and its surrounding islands were a French protectorate, though they had a long history of self-rule before that and also one of English imperialism. The islands are located almost in the middle of the Pacific Ocean, about 2,400 nautical miles south of Hawai'i, and 4,300 miles west of Chile. Allerton had visited his friend Louise Gaylord Dillingham in Hawai'i at least once after her marriage, which occurred in 1910. It may have been this visit that alerted him to the presence of the islands of French Polynesia. That said, Tahiti and other islands of what many people called "the South Seas" had also enjoyed a good deal of publicity in artistic, literary, and queer circles. The painter Paul Gauguin lived in French Polynesia for much of the 1890s, eventually settling in the Marquesas Islands, which Allerton would visit later in life. Allerton could well have learned about Tahiti from Gauguin's paintings or drawings, some of which Allerton was donating to the Art Institute by the early 1920s. But there were other popular accounts of Tahiti, not all related to Gauguin. The bisexual English poet Rupert Brooke spent time in Tahiti and wrote about it. Robert Louis Stevenson began touring the South Seas, including Tahiti, in the 1880s, eventually settling in Samoa. He published widely about these travels, both in fiction and nonfiction. Queer English writer W. Somerset Maugham also traveled to Tahiti, where he was able to purchase a door panel that Gauguin had painted. His travels there served as the inspiration for *The Moon and Sixpence* (1919), his fictionalized depiction of Gauguin's time in Tahiti.[44]

Thanks in large part to the writings of Charles Warren Stoddard, Tahiti also enjoyed a reputation as being especially welcoming of queer men. Stoddard was partially following in the tradition of Herman Melville, who wrote of Polynesian women's and men's beauty and sexual accessibility in *Typee* (1846) and *Omoo* (1847), as well as young men's tradition of taking a bosom male companion who might be a fellow Tahitian or a foreigner. In his 1873 *South-Sea Idyls*, Stoddard discussed couplings with Tahitian men in ways that were much more explicit. Stoddard was born in 1843 and went to Hawai'i for the first time in 1864 to visit a sister who lived there. He returned to Hawai'i in 1870 and visited Tahiti, then Samoa two years later. In *South-Sea Idyls*, which is based on his own experiences, Stoddard is very admiring of the beauty of youthful Polynesian men and also explicit about their desires for white visitors. In one story, "Chumming with a Savage," he recounts his relationship with sixteen-year-old Kána-aná, who claimed the narrator soon after arrival. When he awoke in Kána-aná's bed the next morning, "I wondered what more I could ask for to delight the eye. Kána-aná was still asleep, but he never let loose his hold on me, as though he feared his pale-faced friend would fade away from him. He lay close by me. His sleek figure, graceful and supple in repose, was the embodiment of free, untrammeled youth." Stoddard recounts that Kána-aná was always in the habit of trying to procure for him new and exotic fruits and game. "Again and again he would come with a delicious banana to the bed where I was lying, and insist upon my gorging myself, when I had but barely recovered from a late orgie of fruit, flesh, or fowl. He would mesmerize me into a most refreshing sleep with a prolonged and pleasing manipulation." The message of these stories was clear: moneyed white men could also find this if they made their way to the South Seas. The stories are, of course, racist and ethnocentric in their depiction of the people of Hawai'i, Samoa, and Tahiti, but in this collection and his other writings, Stoddard told the world what they could expect to find in the South Seas and how much they would enjoy it. As Robert Aldrich has pointed out,

FIGURE 3.2 Robert Allerton with Tahitian women. Courtesy of the University of Illinois Archives.

Stoddard also envisioned trips abroad as a means to find oneself, to live as one could not do at home. This was particularly so for those who felt they could not be themselves, sexually, while at home, or simply wanted to live in a world where same-sex desires and eroticism were more normalized.[45]

For the first two decades of the twentieth century, Robert Allerton escaped Illinois during the winter and went abroad in order to find that world where he would be accepted. His enormous fortune allowed him to live an itinerant homosexual existence, meeting a variety of different kinds of men depending on the location of his travels. In major European cities, he mixed with wealthy Westerners, including Americans like himself, his social set containing within it a queer subset of like-minded men and women. And in a variety of locations in the Pacific, the Mediterranean, and the Caribbean, Allerton was able to take advantage of the locales' reputations for being especially amenable to the queer traveler. To speak of Allerton being fully "out" in today's terms would be a misunderstanding of how sexual identities functioned in this period. Among those who shared his proclivities, Allerton was known to be queer. This could well have extended to locals he met in various destinations, even if their definitions of sexual identity were somewhat more inchoate than the emerging hetero/homo dichotomy that was coming to structure identities in the US and Western Europe. Back home and among his non-queer social set in Europe, his sexual identity would have been more concealed, but for many it was an open secret: known but not discussed with Allerton himself. It was Allerton's wealth that allowed for the protection of this kind of open secret. Even if people in power did know or suspect that he was queer, there was little that would come of it. At least in public, Allerton had to compartmentalize his same-sex involvements, a practice that would be tested when he met John Wyatt Gregg.

Chapter Four

Becoming Father and Son

In the early 1920s, Robert Allerton continued to divide his time between Monticello and Chicago, where he could stay with his mother on Astor Street or at the University Club. In early December 1921, the *Tribune* reported that he had hosted a "Chinese party" for debutantes Miss Theodora Winterbotham and Miss Janet Fairbanks at the Fine Arts Club, and later the same month a black and white dance after a glee club performance for Winterbotham, Fairbanks, and Miss Genevieve Carpenter: "Chinese red and silver embroideries were used as decorations." His travels continued, as did his entertaining at The Farms. As much as that decade might have begun like any other, in 1922 his life would change in ways that had probably been unimaginable to him: he would meet John Gregg, who would become his son and partner.[1]

John Wyatt Gregg was an architecture student at the University of Illinois in Urbana-Champaign, about twenty miles to the east of Monticello. Gregg's roommate, Asler Dighton, was Robert Allerton's first cousin once removed (Asler's mother was Robert's cousin). Gregg and Dighton were also in the same fraternity, Zeta Psi, along with Will Lodge and Wendell Trenchard, all local Monticello boys. At some point Asler and his fellow Monticello fraternity brothers invited their friend John Gregg back to their hometown, which included a visit to The Farms to see Asler's cousin, Robert. These visits continued and Gregg and Allerton became closer. Later that year when the young men's fraternity hosted a lunch to coincide with a Dad's Day football game, Allerton agreed to step in as father to Gregg, whose father had died the year before, in 1921. As John Gregg explained many years later, somewhat flippantly, "He didn't have a son and I didn't have a father so we were paired off and lived happily ever after."[2]

It is not difficult to imagine why Gregg and Allerton might have been interested in one another. Physically they were both attractive men. In his twenties, Gregg was quite striking, classically handsome with high cheekbones. And in his late forties, Allerton was distinguished; indeed, newspaper coverage of his bachelor status had always made note of his appealing physical appearance. Given the racial and religious prejudices we know they also had—toward Anglo-Saxon Protestants—their own shared heritage must have been reassuring and appealing. The two also had one overriding interest in common: design. Gregg was in training to become an architect, and Allerton had dedicated the last twenty years of his life to perfecting his own home and estate, all while acting as a patron of the arts. Initial attractions aside, and while their stages in life might have seemed incompatible, they were actually well poised to take on important roles in each other's lives. While Gregg had come from a comfortable middle-class household, both of his parents were deceased and he had no means of support aside from his own capacity to labor; Allerton's vast wealth could not have been anything other than impressive. And Allerton, having experimented with love and courtship in a variety of ways, had come to understand that he wanted a partner who was both local—or at least a resident of the United States—and who could more easily bend his life around the contours of Allerton's own already established life. A handsome and somewhat unmoored young architectural student was as close to ideal as Allerton could have imagined. What Gregg lacked in cultural pedigree—what made him somewhat unformed in his current state—could easily be augmented with exposure to high culture through travel and Allerton's extensive circle of friends. In sum, their respective positions in life combined with the chemistry of mutual attraction made them a fitting match for one another.

How exactly—aside from these initial meetings—Allerton and Gregg decided to become father and son outside of a fraternity banquet remains murky, clouded over by years of stories told and interviews conducted. Because of the uniqueness of their choices, they were asked about the initial meeting during almost any interview or oral history, which themselves became more frequent as the pair became more public about their relationship, increased their philanthropy, and opened their homes to the public. Because the stories they told were covering over a greater truth that always went unspoken, Allerton and Gregg were not always consistent; nor were the news outlets that reported on their meeting. Different reports have Allerton and Gregg meeting for the first time at the fraternity banquet; others are clear that the only reason Allerton was invited to the banquet was because he already knew Gregg, the more convincing explanation. Others emphasize that Allerton was already working on a committee at the University of Illinois charged with establishing a long-term plan for the campus, which had brought him into the orbit of undergraduate students. Some accounts make it seem as if Asler Dighton deliberately set up his fatherless roommate with his childless cousin; others make the

FIGURE 4.1 John Wyatt Gregg in army uniform, 1918. Courtesy of the University of Illinois Archives.

meeting seem more casual. The precise details are long gone, but also less important than the fact that after some initial meeting, the pair decided to pursue a relationship with one another.[3]

Traces of how they came to actually live together are to be found when examining the trajectory of Gregg's life after his graduation from the University of Illinois in 1926. Until that time, we know only that they continued to see each other at The Farms, though whether they had decided to "become" father and son very quickly or were still in the process of "gradually becoming" so, as Gregg put it in an interview much later, is lost to the historical record. Regardless of the specific decisions they made, locating the Allertons in queer history helps us to understand exactly why this decision made sense for them and allows us to see their claims to being father and son as a strategy to preserve their relationship in a social world that would not allow it otherwise.[4]

It also demonstrates just how much the decision was predicated on Allerton's class status, in two specific ways. First and foremost, Allerton's wealth had thrust him into the public sphere in a way that made an explanation for Gregg's presence necessary. Had Allerton and Gregg been working class, they could have rented rooms in the same boardinghouse, for instance. It's possible that those around them might have speculated about why they never married, but they would hardly have been alone in eschewing marriage. No particular explanation would have been necessary, certainly not one that would be printed in newspapers and delivered to inquiring fellow travelers aboard ocean liners. Other men of Allerton's wealth and status also chose to marry women and keep their extensive dalliances with younger men on the side. At this point in Allerton's life, he wanted something more permanent than this and had also determined that he would be unable to marry a woman. It was Allerton's notoriety, itself a product of his wealth, which necessitated a cover story for Gregg's continued presence in his life. Second, that same wealth allowed them to structure their lives fully around the filial dyad that they had created. Neither of them ever worked for pay, at least after the first few years of their meeting. They had the luxury of time to devote to one another and to the homes that they were constantly renovating and redesigning. Their bachelor household survived on the labor of the servants that they employed, no wife necessary to cook or clean because they paid others to do it. In sum, this version of queer couplehood was developed out of a need based in wealth and also survived because of that same fortune. It is for this reason that Allerton and Gregg are relatively anomalous in the historiography of queer life in the United States, few other cases of invented filial relationships being documented. It is difficult to imagine most other queer couples at this time having either the need or the ability to do as Allerton and Gregg did. While their choices remain close to unique, they nevertheless reveal a good deal about the circumstances of queer people in this era more generally and the options available to the wealthiest among them.[5]

But first: Who was the young man who became Robert Allerton's son and partner? John Wyatt Gregg was born on November 7, 1899, in Milwaukee, Wisconsin, the youngest of three children. His parents were Kate Field

FIGURE 4.2 Katherine, John, and Scranton Gregg, 1905. Courtesy of the University of Illinois Archives.

Scranton and James Richmond Gregg. Kate was from Connecticut originally, the daughter of a Bible publisher named Simeon Sereneo Scranton and his wife, Jane. Born in 1861, the eldest of five children, Kate was sent west to go to school, which is where she met James Gregg, who, the story goes, fell in love with the back of her neck in the Summerfield Methodist Church in Milwaukee. When she returned to the East Coast to Martha's

Vineyard, where her family summered, James followed her there, where he proposed.[6]

James Gregg came from less moneyed origins, born in Wisconsin in 1858 to Irish parents (or English and German; census records vary). James's father was a contractor of public works, and James and his brothers (he had seven siblings total) went into the grocery business. By the early twentieth century, James and Kate Gregg and family were doing well; James worked in commerce and flour milling, and they had a Welsh servant living with them, tending to the needs of the family of three children, who had been born in 1888 (Katherine), 1896 (Scranton), and 1899 (John). With cousins and an uncle and aunt next door, John Wyatt Gregg grew up on Franklin Place in a Victorian home on Milwaukee's East Side, just steps from Lake Michigan, at the time the premier address for Milwaukee's elite. John attended East Side High School, Milwaukee's first public high school, graduating in 1917; immediately thereafter he took a job, at least briefly, working on a farm in Pewaukee, about twenty miles west of Milwaukee. In 1918 tragedy struck the family when Kate Scranton Gregg died of breast cancer and the family of five was reduced to four. In the midst of this tragedy, the United States entered what was then known as the Great War. In 1918 both Scranton and John were drafted, but only made it as far as Student Army Training at the University of Wisconsin before the war ended in November 1918. At the close of the war, John and Scranton enrolled there, both in engineering programs.[7]

During his time at Wisconsin, two events occurred that shaped John Gregg's life in important ways. In 1921 his father died of pneumonia, leaving Gregg without parents. His older brother had already graduated from college, and his sister—eleven years his senior—was by this point married. All three Gregg children were now independent, for good or ill, free to make their way in the world however they saw fit. John was left $5,000 in his father's will, almost $70,000 in today's dollars. John had entered Wisconsin to study chemical engineering, but was finding that he did not enjoy the field. As he explained it, "When I began to realize that I wasn't so good at chemistry as my fellow students—they were all eating it up and I was finding it quite a chore. . . . I did briefly work in the chemical laboratory but then I changed and went to work for an architect because it was one of the more practical money making sides of art." John's internship, his junior year at Wisconsin, was with the Eschweiler firm in Milwaukee. He enjoyed the work so much that he decided to pursue a degree in architecture. The University of Wisconsin, however, did not have a major in architecture. After exploring his options, at the urging of his sister to choose a school not so far away as the East Coast (by his telling, Penn and Cornell were then the top programs), he settled on the University of

Illinois, where he decided to transfer. Only some of the more basic classes in mathematics, languages, physics, and chemistry would transfer into his new program, meaning that he would effectively have to start again as a freshman and be a number of years older than his classmates. But at least he would be able to earn a degree in the field in which he now wanted to earn a living. His inheritance from his father would be able to pay some bills, and to make ends meet he could also work part-time in the University of Illinois library and as a teaching assistant in more introductory classes.[8]

In the fall of 1922, John Gregg officially began at the University of Illinois. He had been a member of the Zeta Psi fraternity at Wisconsin, and the chapter at Illinois recognized that membership and welcomed him as a brother. He moved into the Zeta Psi House and became the steward for the fraternity board, planning meals and buying food for them, which also cut down on his own costs. He also became involved in a variety of activities on campus; his final yearbook notes that he was a member of the Architectural Society and the Glee Club (once a particularly popular activity on college campuses), as well as Skull and Crescent, an honorary society, and Gargoyle, an architecture honor society.[9]

He was also a member of Ku Klux Klan, an interfraternity honor society that counted a representative from each Illinois fraternity in its membership. The organization, which was shrouded in some secrecy, regularly hosted roasts and engaged in a good deal of drinking, some of which was reported on by the *Daily Illini*, the school newspaper. Whether or not the University of Illinois version of Ku Klux Klan had any official connection with a newly resurgent national KKK is unclear. A similar group at the University of Wisconsin, founded in 1919 and inspired by the men at Illinois, did not seem to have connections with the national organization, though by 1926, when Wisconsin students revived their KKK chapter, it clearly was affiliated with local Klan members with ties to the national organization. The UI undergraduate group aped some of the traditions of the national organization, including the robes. More important is that its members must have been well aware of the purposes of the real KKK even if they did not participate in all of their activities. They self-consciously chose the name of an avowedly racist, anti-Semitic, and anti-immigrant organization as a way to unite together around their whiteness and their maleness. Given that the group was made up exclusively of men who belonged to fraternities, it is not shocking that the beliefs espoused by the KKK would have appealed to them. During this era, fraternities generally had clauses that restricted membership only to those who were white and Protestant. Some fraternities also staged performances in blackface. The brothers in Gregg's chapter of Zeta Psi all bear Anglo-Saxon surnames.

Whiteness and Protestantism were part of what defined fraternity men's masculinity during this period; that an interfraternal organization should look to the ideals of the KKK is, in light of what we know about fraternities, not entirely surprising. Bowing to pressure from other Illinois students, including the Committee on Student Organizations and Activities, eventually Ku Klux Klan changed its name to Tu-Mas, rumored to be a Native American name of some sort. Unfortunately the records of Illinois's short-lived Ku Klux Klan organization have been lost, making it impossible to know how active its membership was in embracing the virulent racism of the national organization. Knowing that Gregg had no qualms about joining the group does help us to understand the racism and anti-Semitism that animate some of his and Allerton's later actions.[10]

The new relationship with the man who would become his father was also taking up more of John Gregg's time. In the midst of Gregg's college career, tragedy struck the Allerton family, a tragedy that would have both financial and emotional implications for the man with whom Gregg was becoming entwined, as well as their relationship. On December 19, 1924, Robert Allerton's stepmother, Agnes, died, leaving Robert the bulk of her estate, which amounted to about $2 million, approximately $30 million in contemporary dollars. As she explained in her will, "And now, having in mind my affection for my stepson and nephew, Robert H. Allerton of Monticello, Illinois, his affection for me, our living together for so many years as mother and son, and the kindness and filial affection he has ever borne me, the duties and responsibilities he has performed, and that he has ever and always been my son and I his mother," she bequeathed to him a good chunk of the estate that she had inherited from his father, her late husband (and brother-in-law), Samuel Allerton. Included in these bequests were her homes in Chicago; Pasadena, California; and Lake Geneva, Wisconsin. She also left a trust of $400,000 to be divided among five relatives, and numerous smaller bequests to various relatives, employees, and charities. Robert's sister, Kate, now living in Pasadena after separating from her husband following his high-profile affair with an actress, was one of the beneficiaries of the trust that was divided among five relations, which meant that she received far less from the will than her brother. Even Agnes herself, as well as newspaper articles reporting on the will, describe Robert as a stepson and Kate as a niece, even though they both occupied the same roles in the law, if not in Agnes's heart. Aside from the bequests that it articulates, the language of the will also serves as evidence of Agnes's devotion to Robert. She clearly thought of him as her own, even though her sister had actually been his biological mother. Agnes and Robert shared the belief that filial ties could be established outside of the biological parent/child relationship, a belief that Robert was already putting to good use in his developing relationship with John Gregg.[11]

Many years after the fact, Gregg explained what happened in the years following Agnes's death: "My father kept the apartment at 1315 Astor Street and . . . before that time my father always lived at the University Club [when in Chicago]. . . . But then that's when we became closer and he would always introduce me as his son, and of course I had a different name and people . . . It was very confusing so he wanted to adopt me then but I was over age and we did think of going to St. Louis because a jury would allow adults to adopt you. . . ." It remains unclear whether Allerton and Gregg were already publicly referring to one another as father and son in 1925 in the wake of Agnes Allerton's death and just how seriously they pursued the possibility of adoption. It is certainly possible that the pain of loss may have brought them closer together. They now also had a luxurious apartment in Chicago to which they could escape whenever they wished, and while there they likely encountered more people who did not know them personally, as would those in Monticello. In the meantime, Gregg continued to pursue his studies in architecture. In the summer of 1925 after Gregg's third year at Illinois, he traveled east in order to see masterpieces of American architecture unavailable in the Midwest. In the following year, Allerton gave two scholarships to the University of Illinois to fund travel for the two junior architecture majors with the highest averages. While Gregg claimed to have thumbed his way east in search of education, in his honor Allerton would now make it possible for two others to do so on the Allerton tab.[12]

We do not know whether Allerton and Gregg had sex during this period or indeed whether Gregg had sexual experiences with other Wisconsin or Illinois students. Because the pair never publicly talked about their relationship as anything other than filial, one cannot know whether Gregg had already identified as queer prior to meeting Allerton. There is, however, plentiful evidence from many college campuses that those interested in same-sex sex found one another during the 1920s, just as they did beyond the campus walls. There is also evidence that authorities cracked down on it when they discovered it. In 1920 at Harvard University, for instance, a group of administrators conducted more than thirty interviews with students, a recent graduate, and one assistant professor suspected of having sex with one another. Eight of these were expelled or had their connection with the university terminated; two were later reinstated. At Dartmouth College, I found evidence of two separate incidents: one student confessed to homosexual desires in 1918 and was interviewed, quite sympathetically, by Dartmouth's president, in consultation with a specialist in what was then called "mental hygiene," and was allowed to remain on campus so long as he sought treatment and promised to refrain from same-sex activities. By contrast, when a number of male students in a fledgling fraternity called Epsilon Kappa Phi rented a house near campus in 1925 and threw parties where they drank and had sex, other Dartmouth students circulated a petition against them and Dartmouth's president expelled one of them, two others already having graduated. Under duress from the president and their advisers, the fraternity members themselves agreed to "refrain from any activity that may be misrepresented as effeminacy," which included taking women's parts in school plays and, presumably, having sex with one another.[13]

At Sewanee, the University of the South, which was all-male in the early twentieth century, a young William Alexander Percy also experienced a sexual awakening, learning to talk about his experiences in the language of the Greeks, who it was understood placed a high value on the beauty of the male form and engaged in erotic friendships between older men and younger boys. Percy had such a relationship with his Greek professor, Huger Wilkinson Jervey, who was twenty-two, seven years older than Percy. The two formed a lifelong friendship that involved travel abroad to Greece and Italy, known destinations for queer men at the turn of the century, and purchased a summer home together in Sewanee. At Ohio State University in the late 1920s, a young Samuel Steward had sex with many fellow students, both those he met at his aunts' boardinghouse as well those he met on campus, including what seems to be sizable number of brothers in one fraternity. Steward and those men he fellated were aware that in Columbus at the time—as in many other locations across the country—only those who *performed* oral sex were considered to be true homosexuals. As he explained, "'I went to Columbus with the major purpose of bringing pleasure to others, mainly straight men.'" Steward took advantage of this cultural understanding in order to have sex with more people than might otherwise have been available to him. At a moment when definitions of sexual identity were in flux—when homosexuality was still only emerging as a discrete identity category defined exclusively by sexual object choice rather than sexual act or role—Steward had many takers.[14]

Another useful contrast is that of a man named Carter Newman Bealer, exactly the same age as John Gregg and also the son of a grocer. Bealer attended Washington and Lee University in Lexington, Virginia, from 1918 to 1922. He arrived already seeming to know that he was attracted to other men. Soon after becoming friends with a young man named C. C. Dasham, he wrote, "I declare, he is the most beautiful thing I ever saw—so wholesome and healthy, so full of youth." Home on summer holiday in

Washington, DC, he had a brief affair with another man he met in Lafayette Square, then a regular cruising site for gay men. Two years later in 1921, his love still unrequited, he wrote, "I *will* be frank. I am madly in love with C.C. Dasham. 'Sexual inversion,' Havelock Ellis calls it." Two months later, he and a male friend had a frank conversation where Bealer told the friend that while he was similarly inclined—"we came to an understanding" and lent him a copy of Havelock Ellis—"he didn't appeal to me in a certain way." The one who did, C. C. Dasham, was involved with another student named Rutherford Hall. In April 1921, both Hall and Dasham were expelled; in one classmate's telling, "they weren't proper gents"—that is, because of their homosexuality. The next month, Hall drowned in the North River near campus, a possible suicide. During Bealer's final year at Washington and Lee, he regularly had sex with a pair of twins—together—and had minor dalliances and flirtations with a number of other students as well, before finishing out the year (although not graduating due to a failing grade in physics) and returning home to Washington, DC.[15]

A number of points are worth noting about the experience of Carter Bealer. He understood himself as a homosexual, he was not ashamed of it, and he found others—numerous others—like himself at a small, conservative southern college. Some of these fellow gay men had relationships with one another and were understood by many around them as doing just that. And, finally, sometimes there were consequences, occasionally tragic ones as at Washington and Lee, when two students were expelled, and one later died by drowning, a possible suicide. We know of other expulsions—and other relationships and sexual partnerings—at Dartmouth, Harvard, as well as schools like the University of Kansas, where a male instructor's contract was not renewed after several male students claimed that he had kissed them inappropriately. The University of Kansas is also where the playwright William Inge remembers having fumbled sex with a fellow fraternity brother during his time there in the 1920s. Indeed, fraternities at some schools—like the one at Dartmouth—were rumored to be particular hotbeds of homosexual activity. All of this is to say that John Gregg, in all likelihood, encountered other students at the University of Wisconsin and the University of Illinois with whom he could have same-sex affairs or merely transient fumblings in the dark. He also learned the lesson that there could be grave consequences associated with those affairs. By contrast, becoming involved with an older, very wealthy man who provided some protection from surveillance and punishment may have seemed like a particularly appealing prospect.[16]

On June 14, 1926, John Wyatt Gregg graduated from the University of Illinois with a BA in architecture. Immediately upon graduation, Gregg traveled in Europe—England, Holland, and Germany—by his telling alone, though financed by his new patron: "Robert Allerton gave me a nice check to get me going." Upon his return, he began work as a draftsman, and later job captain, for Chicago architect David Adler; he had landed the job through Allerton's connections. At first he lived in Chicago near his friends Paul and Dorothy Schweikher; Paul was a fellow draftsman at Adler's studio. Schweikher recalled: "[John] was a companion to Robert Allerton. Not sure what you would call it at that time ... and he was very social, in the social swim. The rest of us didn't have that— John brought it in." Though this recollection dates from many years later, clearly Gregg's friend recognized that there was something unique— indeed, unidentifiable—about his relationship with Allerton. Even before Allerton and Gregg were publicly identifying as father and son, Gregg was reaping the benefits of being associated with Allerton; his social life had been enlivened in ways that his colleagues certainly did not enjoy.[17]

By 1927 Gregg had been licensed as an architect and had moved into Allerton's stepmother's home at 1315 Astor Street, which Allerton would later sell in favor of an apartment in nearby 1301 Astor, where he lived alongside longtime friends the Potter Palmers and the Tiffany Blakes, just steps from Lake Michigan. Gregg would, years later, explain that he maintained the Astor Street apartments for Allerton, despite the fact that the 1930 census also lists a housekeeper as a resident there, and that he worked at The Farms on weekends; in exchange, Allerton brought him on travels in search of art for his home in Monticello as well as for donating to the Art Institute. John explained, "Robert convinced David Adler that I'd be a much better architect if I went around the world. So we went around the world together just because he was lonesome for a companion." One notes the way that Gregg is attempting to explain to interviewers just why an older man who was not yet his father justified taking such a special interest in him: he was working as a caretaker of his apartments, and the trips abroad were in service of his career. Neither explanation really convinces. Through the late 1920s, Gregg continued to work for Adler, though was given leave to absent himself when accompanying Allerton on his extensive travels. In 1927, for instance, they traveled to Europe and bought at least one sculpture, *The Death of the Last Centaur*, for the grounds at The Farms.[18]

Noteworthy here is how their relationship was discussed in public, precisely because the public discussion was one of the main reasons for calling themselves father and son in the first place. Allerton had grown up in the public eye; he knew that newspapers would report on his comings and goings, just as they had done about his sister, parents, and many of their friends. From the late 1920s, the majority of the reporting on the couple refers to them as some formulation of "father and son." The first mention of the pair together in a newspaper appeared in 1928, two years after Gregg had graduated from Illinois, when the *Chicago Daily Tribune* announced those notables attending a performance of *The Barber of Seville,* cataloging who sat in whose box: "With Mrs. Potter Palmer were Mrs. Barrett Wendell, Mrs. Chauncey McCormick, Prince Galitzen, Robert Allerton, and John Gregg." No explanation is given for Gregg's presence or his relationship to Allerton, though the reporter did note that "the audience at last night's performance of 'The Barber of Seville' was as gay as Rossini's opera itself." It is possible that in using the word "gay," the reporter might subtly have been connecting the relationship of Allerton and Gregg, as members of the audience, with an understanding of opera and theater as connected with a growing homosexual underworld often characterized as "aesthetic." The word "gay," which continued to mean "happy" to most people, often worked to alert readers and listeners in the know, without revealing anything to those who were not.[19]

By 1931 the *Tribune* reported on the two traveling together, but the language of their relationship had become solidified as father and son, despite the fact that this was not legally so: "Robert Allerton, art collector, intensive farmer, and one of our leading bachelors, has recently returned from a trip to China and Siam with his adopted son, John Gregg." The *Tribune* highlighted Allerton's bachelor status and yet simultaneously, and perhaps despite itself, also included the reason that Allerton remained a bachelor, his adopted son. In December of the same year, the *Tribune* covered a charity ball to celebrate recent acquisitions by the Art Institute: "Mr. and Mrs. Potter Palmer will have their son-in-law and daughter, the Oakleigh Thorne-Lewises; Mr. and Mrs. Kellogg Fairbank, and Robert Allerton and his adopted son, John Gregg, with them." Here Allerton and Gregg joined three married couples to make up an even group of eight. In grouping them together in this manner, both their hosts and the *Tribune* called attention to the primacy of Allerton's relationship with Gregg: while others might bring their wives or husbands, Allerton would bring his son. In taking Gregg to these events and calling him his son, Allerton was queering the primacy of couplehood; he was insisting that a biologically unrelated "foster" or "adopted" son could take the place of the wife that was expected of him. And his friends and the newspapers that reported on him acquiesced. Throughout the 1930s, newspapers continued to report on their attendance at various social events as well as their travels. While the variation in ways of discussing Gregg bespeaks an ambivalence about who exactly John Gregg *was* in relation to Robert Allerton, the majority of the time reporters adhered to some version of the "father-son" scenario or simply did not describe the relationship at all, taking it as a given that the two traveled and socialized together. Allerton's wealth, which is what made him worthy of reporting about in the first place, also had the effect of buying the coverage that he wanted.[20]

Understanding why the Allertons decided to become father and son necessitates understanding the emergence of homosexuality as a discrete identity in the United States. While chapter 1 discussed Allerton's friendship with Frederic Bartlett in the context of romantic friendships, and chapter 2 explored Robert's same-sex relationships in Europe and his travels to places like Tahiti, which were thought to be particularly accepting of same-sex sexuality, it bears remembering that by the 1920s, when Allerton and Gregg met and began a relationship with one another, communities of same-sex-desiring men had been making their presence known across the United States for at least three decades. They existed in major cities and, while less organized around a communitarian ethos, gay men certainly met one another for sex, affection, and relationships in rural areas of the country as well, including in male-dominated arenas like farming, logging, and in transient communities that rode the rails in search of work. Gay men and lesbians also found one another at colleges and universities, and Chicago, like other large cities, was home to a wide variety of options for both men and women who desired sex and affection with people of the same sex, including in literary and Progressive reform communities.[21]

One major consequence of this was that some psychologists and specialists in the newly emerging field of sexology developed a discourse of pathology surrounding same-sex intimacy that was then taken up by lawmakers, police, doctors, and others. A number of Chicago doctors and sexologists were active in this movement, occasionally giving lectures on "sexual perversion" that were publicized in local newspapers. Indeed, sociologists at the University of Chicago were national leaders in documenting and theorizing the problems of the denizens of the nation's cities, homosexuals among them. The media also disseminated stories about communities of what were sometimes called "inverts" in major cities, as well as stories about relationships between two women gone awry, where one assumed a masculine role and ultimately took the life of the other. Chicago was the home to the first short-lived gay rights organization in the United States, the Society for Human Rights. Clearly some gay-identified men had begun to identify as a persecuted minority and to organize for their own rights. But what Allerton and Gregg might have seen in Chicago papers like the *Tribune* was a 1925 story of the raid of a Society meeting where its members were carted off and arraigned in police court. Its founding member, Henry Gerber, was fired from his job in the post office as a result of his conduct. They may also have noted the occasional newspaper story about a man found dead in a hotel room, his killer either never found or claiming that the man had made "indecent advances" upon him. Some people could, of course, read between the lines, understanding why two men might have been alone in a hotel room together. The effect of all of these discourses was manifold: It hardened the line between "normal" gender presentation, linking it with heterosexuality and marriage, thereby establishing "the homosexual" as a distinct kind of being who was assumed to be more apt to behave like the other sex. And it paved the way for discrimination and persecution by calling into question the previous forms of intimacy that men had once enjoyed with men, women with women. No longer were these intimacies innocent and honorable; now they were seen as suspect and perverted. This was a lengthy, uneven process that had been well underway for years by the time that Allerton and Gregg met in 1922. And the pair would have been well aware that what they were embarking on together—a partnership between two men—would bring them in for the kind of censure that was now widely applied to same-sex couplings.[22]

The one thing that might save them from persecution was Robert Allerton's fortune. The function of wealth and social class has always occupied a contested place in the narrative of the emergence of homosexuality. The wealthy, particularly in Europe, were at various times shunned or ridiculed for their debauchery, which was often thought to (and sometimes did) include sodomy. But that very wealth, on both sides of the Atlantic, also allowed a margin of protection for the pursuit of those very same-sex practices. When wealth was coupled with fame, however, it could also lead to one's downfall, famously so in the case of Oscar Wilde, whose 1895 trial and conviction was much publicized in the United States and further solidified the stigma around homosexuality.[23] Allerton's wealth both provided the means for the relationship with Gregg but also mandated that he have an explanation for it. The very wealth that might have allowed him to flout society's dictates had also propelled him into its spotlight. And when it really counted, Allerton had little interest in flouting the society that had produced him. Had he wanted simply to have clandestine sex with other men, he would well have been able, but choosing to share his life with one man was impossible for someone like Allerton to do privately. While Allerton liked to retreat to Monticello to live a tranquil existence amid his gardens, he also enjoyed being a public figure like his wealthy friends. In this sense, couplehood, of any sort, needed to be explained. Stories like the one in the *Tribune* calling Allerton the "Richest Bachelor in Chicago" presumed he would marry a woman; if he remained a bachelor and at the same time took up with another man, it would need to be explicated somehow. Calling John Gregg his son was a way of not talking about his actual role in Allerton's life; even if Gregg's relationship with Allerton was an open secret, calling him a son allowed friends and acquaintances to avoid the awkwardness of having to discuss who he really was to Allerton.[24]

The fact that Allerton and Gregg were both men made some sort of explanation doubly necessary. There is a rich literature on the ways that women in the United States throughout the nineteenth century had managed to maintain partnerships with one another, their relationships publicly acknowledged and implicitly sanctioned by their communities. While most anti-sodomy statutes in colonial America had applied equally to men and women, women were prosecuted with incredible rarity. And by the nineteenth century, such laws applied to specific acts between men and men, men and women, or women/men and animals. Same-sex sexual relations between women had legally been erased as a crime. Governed by phallocentrism, lawmakers and many Americans had difficulty conceiving of what two women might do sexually in the absence of a man. It is for this reason that even though most of the early American colonies made sodomy an equal opportunity crime, only men were ever executed.[25]

As we saw in chapter 1, for much of the nineteenth century, women and men had managed to share a good deal of emotional and physical intimacy with one another in ways that did not raise much suspicion about same-sex sex specifically. They did so first as romantic friends. In an era before homosexuality itself emerged as a discrete identity category, pairs of women and of men were emotionally and sometimes physically intimate with one another. For men, however, these friendships tended to end with marriage, whereas women's friendships could last a lifetime. Some women also passed as men and lived in longtime intimate partnerships with other women; many no doubt have escaped their communities' and historians' detection to this day. As the historian Emily Skidmore has recently demonstrated, even when some of what she calls trans men were discovered to have been born female, many of their local communities did not persecute them because they knew these men as community members and valued their participation in the life of the villages and towns in which they made their homes. The history of those assigned male at birth and living as women with male partners is only just beginning to be written.[26]

Finally, some women, generally those who were wealthy and educated, lived in same-sex partnerships with companions that we now call Boston marriages. These women's wealth had allowed them to escape the necessity of marriage, and sometimes their education had made them disinclined toward it at the same time that it made some men uncomfortable enough not to seek them out as wives. Furthermore, many of these pairs of women devoted themselves either to reform work—like Jane Addams of Hull House and her longtime companion, Mary Rozet Smith—or education—like Bryn Mawr College president M. Carey Thomas and her companion, Mary Garrett. All of these were strategies employed by women to be together without explicitly naming their relationships as such; we have little evidence to suggest that men employed them with any degree of success throughout the nineteenth century.[27]

More recently historian Rachel Hope Cleves has documented the case of a female couple named Charity Bryant and Sylvia Drake, who lived in a small Vermont town called Weybridge from 1807 to 1851. They referred to themselves as married and were considered so by many in the town; they were even buried together under a single headstone. Cleves argues that Drake and Bryant were accepted by their community at least in part because they were already so much a part of it and because they contributed in such meaningful ways to the community, economically and spiritually. I would also argue that the fact of their being women made even the suspicion of sex between the two much more palatable than had they been men. They shared a bed together and their community knew it, but in an era when many shared beds, and when many others had difficulty fully imagining the sexual lives of two women, together, independent of a man, Charity and Sylvia were less threatening than two men in a similar marriage might have been.[28]

If we jump forward about one hundred years to when Robert Allerton and John Gregg met and began to live together, even Charity and Sylvia's relationship probably *would* have come in for censure, just as the Allertons would have without an explanation for their partnership. All of this helps us to understand why Allerton and Gregg decided to become father and son. Of course, Allerton's immense wealth would almost certainly have protected them from prosecution—it is, for instance, difficult to imagine the sheriff rapping on the doors of Allerton House with an arrest warrant for either or both of them. But they still had to go about in public together, not just among those who might accept them for who they were, including fellow queers, but also among the Chicago elite Robert knew from his upbringing, or any number of people they might meet while abroad. In London they might well be able to socialize with a cosmopolitan crowd who could nod knowingly at their arrangement, but in the first-class dining room of the steamer that took them across the Atlantic, their fellow passengers and the newspaper reporter covering their journey might not have been as accepting. Becoming father and son was a solution to these other scenarios. Gregg himself hints at this in interviews he conducted near the end of his life. When asked how they became father and son, he frequently placed it in the context of answering people's questions about who, exactly, he was (everyone already knew who Allerton was): "And he began introducing me as his son." "And he would always introduce me as his son." They became father and son so that they could answer this question: who exactly *was* John Gregg in relation to Robert Allerton?[29]

Becoming father and son—instead of some other formulation of being related—probably occurred to them for the obvious reasons: they were separated in age by twenty-six years. Gregg had no living parents. Allerton had no children of his own to object to the arrangement. It was less ambiguous than referring to one another as companions, especially because most companions in their circle were women; it was a feminized role, almost like a servant, taken on by a poorer woman who was presumed to have her expenses paid by a wealthier woman in exchange for serving her. Gregg was not that; he would travel in first class along with Allerton. Making him a son would entitle him to almost-equal treatment, in much the same way that an actual son of a wealthy man would receive. It also made sense to them on a deeper level. Allerton had been adopted, all but legally, by his stepmother-aunt, and they had come to love one another as mother and son. Samuel and Agnes Allerton were also separated in age by twenty-nine years, and they never had biological children of their own despite Agnes's youth at the time of their marriage. In a strange way, Allerton and Gregg were combining the triadic relationship of Samuel/Agnes/Robert—father/spouse/son, but applying it to a dyad: Robert/John—father/spouse/son.

While their arrangement was hardly typical, they were also not the only same-sex-desiring couple to do something similar. While most examples of same-sex couples who employed adoption or father/son relationships in order to secure ties of kinship date from later in the twentieth century—and we will explore them in chapter 7—historians have identified some early examples. From the mid-nineteenth century onward, poet Walt Whitman regularly referred to the young men with whom he associated and had sex as some version of a foster son, adopted son, and occasionally nephew. He sometimes did this in order to explain their relationship to those who might be curious, as in the following letter that he sent to a man who would host him and his companion Harry Stafford: "My (adopted) son, a young man of 18 [Whitman was then fifty-seven], is with me now, sees to me, & occasionally transacts my business affairs, & I feel somewhat at sea without him." Whitman also indicated in this letter that he and Stafford would expect to share a room and bed. More significantly, he and these young men regularly used this language when writing to one another. About a decade earlier, Whitman repeatedly referred to a different young man, Peter Doyle, as a "dear son," "darling son," and sometimes his "young & loving brother" in letters to Doyle himself. Historian

Jonathan Ned Katz argues that, in the absence of a language of homosexuality, "kinship terms—father-son, uncle-nephew, brother-brother—
provided nineteenth-century males several ways to name and define intimacies between otherwise unrelated men and youths."[30]

Not all framed these relationships in filial terms. There is a long tradition on both sides of the Atlantic of men eroticizing the relationship
between two asymmetrically aged men. Nineteenth-century men trying
to understand their attractions for other men often looked backward to
the Greeks and Plato's *Symposium*, particularly, wherein he extolls the virtues of spiritual and erotic love between men that was capable of inspiring courage and valor. Others highlighted the explicitly sexual world of
classical Athens, whereby citizen men might take younger male sexual
partners, glorifying in their exploits. Nineteenth-century English literary critic John Addington Symonds, for instance, who had a penchant for
sex with younger working-class men, attempted to come to terms with
these desires by studying the Greeks. The result was *A Problem in Greek
Ethics* (1883), which defined Greek love as "a passionate and enthusiastic attachment subsisting between man and youth, recognised by society
and protected by opinion, which, though it was not free from sensuality,
did not degenerate into mere licentiousness." We do not know whether
Symonds's desire for younger working-class men was shaped by his reading of the Greeks, or whether he used the Greeks to try to justify to whom
he was attracted (not just men, but men who were different from him in
terms of age and class). For our purposes, the point is that attempting to
understand (and practice) same-sex attraction and sex via generational
asymmetry was well established, often by reference to ancient Greek culture, by the time Robert Allerton and John Gregg first met. Historians
of the early twentieth-century United States have also shown that many
same-sex-desiring men structured their relationships around age asymmetry: wolves and jockers taking up with lambs, punks, and preshuns, the
youth of the latter category sometimes, but not always, standing in for
femininity. Or wealthy married men who sought out sex with younger
men, the difference in their ages and statuses defining their roles in the
relationships. To a degree, that tradition lives on among those gay men
who pair off as daddies and boys, the age asymmetry providing part of
the erotic charge in their relationship. We do not know whether Allerton and Gregg were attracted to one another despite or because of the
difference in their ages. Both were handsome men, and however much
their relationship was structured by a twenty-six-year age gap and a vast
difference in wealth, they may have found those differences incidental to
their attraction to one another. Or perhaps the tradition of generational
asymmetry among same-sex-loving men suggested a model to them, not

just for their own mutual attraction, but also for how to talk about it with the rest of the world.[31]

Whitman, Symonds, and many others prior to the 1890s were living at a moment when homosexuality had yet to be named explicitly. Even if Whitman himself clearly understood his attractions as being almost exclusively geared toward men, many other men did not, engaging in sexual relations and flirtations with other men and with women without necessarily thinking of themselves as abnormal or even bisexual, the word itself not yet used in this sense. Filial analogies and homages to the Greeks were thus approximations for what the men felt about one another, ways of making sense of what did not yet have a name. By the 1920s, however, adoptive or foster son/father relationships could be a deliberate cover for what would otherwise be condemned and understood explicitly as the newly named category of homosexuality. This was especially the case when one partner was young, handsome, and relatively impoverished by comparison to his wealthy older partner. The age asymmetry that some might have understood as a model for queer relationships was precisely what demanded an explanation. In one similar case, historian Katherine Parkin demonstrates that Edgar Apperson, a wealthy Indiana automobile innovator, used the fiction of adoption to explain how two different (and not overlapping) men became his live-in companions from the 1910s through the 1940s. While Apperson was also married twice, he carried on a seventeen-year relationship with Ralph Polly, described variously in newspapers as an adopted or foster son, as well as a driver, fishing guide, and caretaker. A year before Polly's death in a car accident, Apperson, fifty-seven, met twenty-five-year-old Gilbert Alvord, who would go on to live with Apperson and his second wife for decades, staying on after her death in 1942. When Apperson died in 1959, he left his estate to Alvord, whom a local newspaper described as a companion. Apperson and Allerton were different in one important way in that Allerton never married, but they were similar in that their wealth allowed them to do as they pleased, effectively creating an identity for their younger partners. In Apperson's case, his two younger companions seemed to be more often publicly identified as his employees in one way or another. This may have been because that is actually how they came to know Apperson in the first place, and also because of their own socioeconomic backgrounds. While John Gregg's background was certainly far humbler than Allerton's, he was solidly middle, if not upper-middle, class, and he possessed a college degree. In the duration of their time together, it is also clear that Allerton wanted Gregg to be treated by others as a classed equal, not as a lesser.[32]

Even if we were to entertain the possibility that Allerton and Gregg were *not* engaged in an intimate same-sex partnership, the fact that they were two single men—who would remain so legally for the rest of their lives—demanded that they come up with some explanation for why they had both decided to eschew courtship and marriage in favor of spending all their time together. Even without the newly emerged category of the homosexual, this would be difficult to explain. Claiming to be father and son went some way toward doing so, but only so far. Recall how Gregg explained their meeting and note how jarring it actually is: "He didn't have a son and I didn't have a father so we were paired off and lived happily ever after." Why, people might ask, would becoming a father or a son foreclose the possibility of marriage? For biological fathers and sons, it certainly did not. Why would a father and son continue to live together even as the son grew up, graduated college, and earned a living?

The closest correlate to this type of relationship would be the custom of the spinster daughter remaining at home to devote herself to the needs of her aging mother or father. But Gregg and Allerton are clearly different from this model. First, Gregg was not Allerton's son to begin with, but rather became so after their meeting. In other words, Gregg chose to structure his life this way, rather than have it become so by default and because no other options existed. Second, Gregg's relation to Allerton is different as well because the dutiful daughter was herself proof that her mother or father had already been married and produced children. While she may have been substituting for her deceased other parent, her very existence was a testament to that other parent's existence once upon a time. Third, Gregg was male and so his companionship, his devotion to Allerton, is different from the subservient femininity expected of the single daughter toward her parent, in large part because she was presumed to have no other options, a career being inappropriate and marriage having eluded her. A daughter was financially dependent on her parent, and her companionship was the price exacted for that dependence.[33]

These were the obstacles that faced Robert Allerton and John Gregg when they first met in 1922 and as they came to be a couple over the course of the 1920s. They wanted to be together, but they could not do so openly without some sort of explanation, however implausible it might have seemed for those around them. Even if their cover was not at all times and in all places believable—and in some places it was clearly altogether unnecessary—at least it existed. It gave them something to say when a new acquaintance asked who precisely John Gregg was. The rest of the acceptance they enjoyed we can attribute to Robert's enormous fortune.

Chapter Five
Lord of a Hawaiian Island

In the early 1930s, at the beginning of the Great Depression, Robert Allerton and John Gregg traveled to Thailand and Angkor, which, the *Chicago Tribune* informed its readers, "was the distinctly chic thing to do these days," as well as to Samoa and the Marquesas Islands. While in China on another trip, they donated funds to help restore the ancient imperial Chinese palace in what was then called Peiping. In 1935 the *Tribune* reported, "Armed with everything except guns, they are going into Africa, to Mombasa of the thunderous sound, to Zanzibar and Madagascar, then back across the southern ocean to South American capitals and the West Indies." Like many of their wealthy friends, and despite the crippling poverty all around them, the Depression was clearly not standing in the way of Allerton and Gregg's desire to see the world.[1]

It was on one of these trips, in 1937, that Allerton and Gregg stopped in Hawai'i and first ventured to Kaua'i, where they would eventually live. They were on their way back to the mainland United States from Australia by boat and were planning to stay in Honolulu, where they could visit friends and recuperate before continuing back home. But the hotel manager had overbooked and could only house them for nine days and their ship left on the tenth. They decided to visit Kaua'i, known then and now as "The Garden Isle," the northwestern island in the Hawaiian archipelago (Ni'ihau, farther west than Kaua'i, is privately owned and only accessible to Native Hawaiians). They could stay there for a night with enough time to be back to board their ship by the next day. Many years later, Gregg recounted that first visit:

Mrs. Walter Dillingham, whom my father had known since childhood, suggested that while we were on Kauai we might look at the McBryde place near the Spouting Horn. Alexander McBryde had died four years before and the house was empty (and incidentally for sale). Louise [Dillingham] contacted Philip Rice who was executor of the McBryde estate, and he opened the place for us. The charm and beauty of the spot struck us dumb, and we hardly spoke to each other although we stayed there almost an hour. We left to continue in our rented car to see the rest of the island but got only as far as Kapaa when my father suggested we return for a second look, suggesting it might be a wise idea in our travels to return to the same place each winter instead of going far and wide.

We did go back, and a few months [later?] we were the owners of Lawai-Kai. I designed a new house to our needs and taste, and in the fall we returned to Hawaii with a set of plans under our arms. The first of April 1938 we moved into the house completely ready with furniture we had used in other places.

This brief account contains within it not only the history of Allerton and Gregg's entrée into Hawaiian society but, more intriguing still, the colonial origins of those who introduced them to Hawai'i, as well as to the land that would become their home.[2]

The story of Allerton and Gregg's move to Hawai'i has been told before in ways that emphasize the increasingly chilly climate for gay men in Chicago and elsewhere in the United States. Persecution of gay men and lesbians in public places was indeed on the rise in the 1930s as the "pansy craze" of the 1920s had given way to a crackdown on gender nonconformity and same-sex desires in public. A 2007 write-up in the glossy gay monthly *Out* explains that Allerton and Gregg's neighbors in Kaua'i accepted this gay male couple in a manner that was increasingly impossible in Illinois and elsewhere in the United States—in part, some claim, because Hawaiians were naturally accepting of homosexuality itself. This explanation not only employs stereotypes about tropical locations and sexual hedonism that do more to sanction Western desires than anything else, but it also makes little sense because the two men were no more visibly "out" as a gay couple in Hawai'i than they had been in Illinois.[3]

Perhaps most importantly, there is little actual evidence to suggest that the wealthy and connected couple ever experienced much in the way of discrimination. Rather, it makes more sense to see their decision to buy a winter home in Hawai'i in light of Allerton's aging. By the late 1930s, he was pushing seventy and had a number of health problems that made traveling around the world every year increasingly challenging. Settling upon one tropical destination that was closer to all the other ones they wanted to visit during the winter made more sense. Like other wealthy "snowbirds" who wintered in warmer climates, they could permanently say goodbye to the Illinois snow. They also had friends nearby in Honolulu: rich white friends who descended from the earlier European colonists in the islands and who could introduce them to other such descendants in Kaua'i. Allerton and Gregg's half-time move to Kaua'i was thus entirely in keeping with their wealth, their connections, and their position.[4]

Focusing on the couple's supposed persecution elsewhere also has the effect of erasing the colonizing they did in their new home in Hawai'i, casting them as victims or refugees escaping homophobia in Illinois and achieving acceptance in Hawai'i. In truth, Allerton and Gregg were rich white imperialists on the island of Kaua'i, just like others before them and many who would follow. They used their wealth and connections to exploit the land and remove indigenous Hawaiians from it, impinging upon communal land management that had existed for centuries. Bear in mind that Hawai'i was not yet a state and that many of the land claims of indigenous Hawaiian people were still very unsettled in the 1930s and '40s, when Allerton and Gregg first made their home in Kaua'i. Hawai'i was also not regulated by US law when it came to wages and labor practices, meaning that they could hire Native Hawaiian, Japanese, Chinese, and Filipino laborers (many of them children) and pay them wages far below those mandated on the mainland. Allerton's and Gregg's wealth and whiteness, which they shared with the descendants of Hawai'i's earliest colonizers, allowed them to ingratiate themselves with those very descendants. They did not have to worry about whether they would be accepted by the people of color, including Native Hawaiians, who made Kaua'i their home, precisely because the social lives of whites and nonwhites were already thoroughly bifurcated and class-segregated by the time the Allertons arrived in the late 1930s.[5] They hired those same nonwhite people—who had long ago become part of an Asian and Pacific Islander working class largely centered around sugar and pineapple plantations—to build and service their home and gardens; their acceptance of the couple as queer outsiders was beside the point.

For these reasons, it makes more sense to see Allerton and Gregg's decision to move to Hawai'i in the context of their class status, rather than their sexuality. While they never publicly identified as gay or as a couple on Kaua'i, gay publications, in particular, tend to speak about them in that context, highlighting the acceptance they supposedly achieved there and comparing Hawai'i favorably in contrast to Illinois in that regard. This has had the perhaps inadvertent effect of erasing Hawai'i's own long-standing traditions of same-sex eroticism that differ from modern Western notions of sexual orientation. Because Native Hawaiians had long sanctioned sexual relations between older and younger men, Allerton and Gregg were, oddly enough, much more in keeping with these ancient traditions than they were with the publicly recognized gay couple they are often remembered as being.

Returning to John Gregg's description of their first glimpse of the Lawa'i Valley helps us to understand just how intertwined the land was with colonialism in Hawai'i. Gregg recalled that their friend Louise Dillingham alerted them to the presence of the land then known as the "McBryde property." Allerton and Gregg regularly socialized with Walter and Louise Dillingham when they docked in Honolulu after a trip abroad and before sailing for the mainland. As a child in Chicago, Allerton was friends with Louise Gaylord, who married Walter F. Dillingham in 1910 at her parents' estate in Florence, Italy. Dillingham, born in 1875 in what was then the kingdom of Hawai'i, was the son of Benjamin Dillingham, who founded the Oahu Railway and Land Company as well as a number of sugar plantations, and was grandson on his mother's side of Lowell Smith, a prominent missionary in the Hawaiian islands beginning in the 1830s. Walter Dillingham, founder of the Hawaiian Dredging Company, was responsible for the construction of a dry dock at Pearl Harbor, which would eventually become part of the US naval base there; he also enlarged ports at Kahului and Hilo to allow for greater shipping access. His sister was married to Walter Frear, one of the first governors of the Territory of Hawai'i, once it had been annexed into the United States. Through Allerton's own pedigreed birth, the couple was intimately connected with one of Hawai'i's oldest colonizing families; it was only fitting that they should be introduced to the land that they would purchase through the Dillinghams.[6]

Louise Dillingham introduced them to Philip L. Rice, scion of another of Hawai'i's "founding" families. Rice, the executor of the estate from which they would buy their land, was the grandson of William Harrison Rice, Protestant missionary and later the manager of the Lihue Plantation on Kaua'i. Philip's father, William Hyde Rice, became one of the greatest landowners on the island and served in the Hawaiian House of Representatives 1870–72 and 1882–84 and the Hawaiian Senate 1886–90. Seemingly beloved by natives and *haoles* (whites or foreigners) alike, he was also the last of the royal governors of Kaua'i, appointed in 1891 by Queen Lili'uokalani. With the overthrow of the monarchy in 1893, Rice adapted quickly, serving the new president of the Republic of Hawai'i (and his childhood friend), Sanford Dole. One of his eight children, Philip Rice, was an attorney on Kaua'i; his brother William was sheriff and also ran the Lihue Inn, where Allerton and Gregg stayed while in Kaua'i. Philip and his wife, Flora, would become their good friends. Thus the couple arrived at Kaua'i not only with the Dillinghams paving the way, but under the auspices of one of the most powerful haole families of Kaua'i as well.[7]

The colonial roots continue. As Gregg makes clear, Allerton purchased the land in the Lawa'i Valley from the estate of a man named Alexander McBryde. The land itself had originally belonged to Hawaiian Queen Emma, widow of King Kamehameha IV (and before that to her uncle, an adviser to King Kamehameha I). Emma retreated to the Lawa'i Valley in 1870 following the deaths of her son and husband in the 1860s. She built a home in the upper portion of the valley and stayed there only a year, during which time she planted tropical vegetation, including rose apples, bougainvillea, bamboo, ferns, and mangoes; much of that vegetation remains growing in the Lawaʻi Valley to this day. In 1876, having returned to Honolulu, Emma leased the land to a Scotsman named Duncan McBryde. McBryde was a district court judge who hired others to cultivate sugarcane in the upper portion of the land, in the tradition of Hawaiʻi's first sugarcane plantation, founded up the road in Kōloa. After Emma's death in 1885, McBryde's wife, Elizabeth, purchased much of the land outright. In 1899 the McBrydes' son Alexander lowered Queen Emma's home into the valley floor so that he might live in it further from the sugarcane that was planted in the upper portion of the valley. In 1917 he built a home of his own and, in consultation with a horticulturalist named Dr. Gerrit P. Wilder, planted a variety of palms, gingers, ferns, and plumerias in the valley, many of them imported from elsewhere in the southern hemisphere. He remained there, living with his companion, a young Hawaiian man named Gabriel I, until his death in 1935, when the lower portion of the valley in which he had made his home was first offered for sale. Years later, John Gregg likened McBryde and Gabriel I's relationship to being like "a father and son arrangement, you might say." McBryde's brother Walter, also a bachelor with a male Hawaiian companion, lived nearby at Kukuiolono Park. Apparently the Lawaʻi Valley was conducive to non-biologically related wealthy fathers and their sons.[8]

Bringing our story full circle, in 1899 Benjamin Dillingham worked with William A. Kinney and Walter McBryde to consolidate the McBryde plantation and two others into the McBryde Sugar Company, which retained control of much of the upper portion of the valley, where it continued to cultivate sugarcane. Dillingham's daughter-in-law Louise—and through her Robert Allerton—was thus also connected to the first haole owners, the McBryde family, of the land that Allerton would purchase. The story of Allerton and Gregg's acquisition of the cove at Lawaʻi, then, is one steeped in the colonial history of Hawaiʻi, tracing back to the earliest arrivals of white missionaries, who then became sugarcane planters, and extending tentacle-like into the twentieth-century exploitation of the land. Far from a narrative of two gay men fleeing persecution who just happened upon a deserted beach that they came to occupy by courtesy of accepting locals, Allerton and Gregg found their home as the end result of almost two hundred years of European colonization.[9]

Gregg's explanation above also makes clear how quickly the couple purchased and then set about transforming their plot of land in Kauaʻi. By June 1941, the *Chicago Daily Tribune* reported that "[Robert Allerton] farms half the year in Illinois and is lord of a Hawaiian island for the other six months. He has built there in beautiful Hawaiian style, as has Doris Duke Cromwell, suitable to a Sybaritic life up in the tropics." This was an exaggeration—Allerton was not lord of the entire island—but it does capture a sense of how Allerton and Gregg came to occupy the land and their relationship with those indigenous to it. Gregg described one of their first tasks upon arrival: "The tenants that were raising watercress, lotus root and cattle up the valley were dismissed, and my father and I started organizing that part of the land which had at one time belonged to Queen Emma. We discovered old walls, house sites and many burial caves." Some of these, of course, would have to be removed to make room for their home and accompanying gardens, as the couple bent the land and its history to suit their own needs.[10]

The estate, which tourists can visit on a tour of the National Tropical Botanical Garden, is indeed stunning and a testament to the designs of Allerton and Gregg. They named it Lawai-Kai, roughly translated from the Hawaiian as "Lawaʻi by the ocean." While locals—including Native Hawaiians—had usually referred to the spot as Lawaʻi Beach, Gregg explained that he and Allerton thought "it sounded too much like Atlantic City or some place like that," so the new haole arrivals christened the beach with a Native Hawaiian name. The original purchase, about eighty acres in total, includes a cove on the southern shore of Kauaʻi where the waters of the Lawaʻi Stream flow from above and mix with the Pacific at a beautiful sand beach. On either side of the cove, steep walls, now covered by bougainvillea planted by Queen Emma, rise up so that the cove is contained within an exceedingly private valley. The cove and the gardens are accessible by boat and by a narrow switchback road on the east side of the valley that only allows for one car at a time, a road that remains gated, barring those not granted access from entering. Alongside the road, one can see the remnants of the train tracks that used to carry sugarcane down into the valley. The Lawaʻi Stream snakes through the Allerton land and up the hill at the north end of the property, where taro used to be cultivated by Native Hawaiians and where Europeans later planted sugarcane.[11]

While Allerton and Gregg built their small one-story home in proximity to the beach and the cove, they designed a series of garden "rooms" in the land farther away from the beach, primarily on the east side of the stream. In order to access the home and the beach from the main road that descends down into the north side of the valley farthest from the ocean, one passes through many of these rooms, which is only possible on foot. As Gregg explained, even in a thoroughly constructed series of garden rooms, they "wanted to keep the Polynesian atmosphere here by not allowing cars to drive to the house." Most rooms feature a fountain or statuary, and all are designed with meticulous attention to the plants and flowers. One room has a long rectangular mirror pool with a white latticed pavilion at one end, complete with a bench for contemplation and a statue of the goddess Diana at the other, whose image is reflected in the water. The statue is a reproduction of one featured in their gardens in Illinois. In another room, an elevated and undulating art deco stream flows between statues at either end, gurgling quietly as it moves down a very slight grade. A grove of bamboo trees provides protection along the southern side of this room. Another room features walls of tall palm trees. Alongside the east cliff walls, one sees Asian statuary hidden among the tropical vegetation, and man-made streams and waterfalls emerge in the foliage, all carefully planned by Allerton and Gregg. Along the stream stand towering Moreton Bay fig trees, with their enormous exposed roots rising as high as a person and made famous in the movie *Jurassic Park*, which was filmed there after their deaths. On the west side of the river is a grove of various species of trees from around Micronesia and Polynesia, all planted by the couple's chief gardener.[12]

As they were building the gardens, Allerton and Gregg sought to make their home as private as possible. Residents of Kaua'i had for some time been in the habit of visiting the beach at Lawa'i, so Allerton told their new lawyer, Philip Rice, to announce in the local paper that the beach would now be closed to the public. Gregg explained: "We got a very bad name by being stuffy Illinoians coming here and taking our beautiful beach away from us but anyway it worked and we put up gates with a chain on it and things of that sort to get a little privacy because my father did not want to live in a public park." In early December 1938, just after Allerton and Gregg had arrived to assume ownership, Philip Rice responded to student correspondents from the nearby Waimea High School government who hoped to take representatives of the Ninth Territorial High School Government Association Conference on a sightseeing tour that would include Lawa'i Beach: "Visitors at Lawai, presently, would be unwelcome and it would be an intrusion for anyone to visit there who is not a personal friend or expressly invited. The present owner purchased the property at quite a high figure and with a view to making it as much his private residence property as is any privately owned residence of any of us." While earlier owners, including McBryde and Queen Emma herself, did not object to occasional visits from their neighbors, Allerton and Gregg were intent on creating as much privacy as possible at Lawai-Kai.[13]

The couple continued to expand their holdings, buying up land not included in the original purchase. In 1940 Allerton reported, "I'm happy to say we are in process of making a deal with the old Hawaiian woman who owns the 2 pieces of land in our midst—it will be a great relief to own them as one of them is right in the center of what we want to develop next

FIGURES 5.1 AND 5.2 A garden room and detail of mermaid statue at Lawai-Kai. The statue is a replica of one designed by Italian sculptor Libero Andreotti in 1931.

year." The purchase of these tracts, as well as trades Allerton made for land in exchange for water rights with the McBryde Company, increased the overall land to just under one hundred acres. In these instances, we see Allerton and Gregg expelling tenants who subsisted on the land, forgoing customary land practices that had allowed for local residents to visit the beach at Lawaʻi, and buying out Native Hawaiians in order to make the Lawaʻi Valley their own. This is straightforward colonizing, and yet

most accounts of the couple—which highlight the oasis they found at Kaua'i, where they could be themselves—end up discounting these very practices because they do not jibe with the narrative of two men who were themselves supposedly persecuted in other settings. As latter-day story-tellers focus on Allerton and Gregg's queerness and their escape from the homophobic mainland in favor of an oasis of tropical acceptance, what becomes lost are the power and connections wielded by Allerton in the service of colonizing his new island home.[14]

Most accounts of the couple in Kaua'i make note of the truly stunning garden estate they created there, but almost all make it seem as if this were something that they not only designed but also built themselves. This was not the case. Lost in the usual telling are the countless underpaid men and women, boys and girls, who actually built Lawai-Kai. The stories often make it seem as if Lawai-Kai was the retirement idyll of two men with time on their hands, rather than a full-scale outdoor renovation. In order to build their home, maintain it in the style to which they were accustomed, and develop the ambitious garden they had planned, they needed laborers. Throughout their time there, Allerton and Gregg employed a multitude of Chinese, Japanese, Filipino, and Native Hawaiian men and women both to develop their estate and to cook and clean for them. In their first months living there—December 1938 to May 1939—they had one servant working in their home, a young man named Richard Wong, and three others working outside in the garden: Iwao Daida, who had worked for Alexander McBryde since 1933; Gabriel I, who had been McBryde's companion; and Abraham Palacy, who was injured in early 1939 while on the job. It was during these months that their home was also constructed by laborers hired by their contractor.[15]

Allerton and Gregg returned to Illinois in the spring of 1939 but continued to employ these laborers both to maintain their home and develop the garden. When Philip Rice reported to them that Wong had absconded from his duties, Gregg wrote back at length, giving us a sense both of Wong's schedule as well as his relationship with the Allertons:

When in residence we demand Richard to work from 5:30 A.M. to 9 P.M. with no days off, when the other boys work from about 7 A.M. to 4 or 4:30 (I forget) with Sundays off. I always felt the difference came in with easy time in the summer [when the couple was absent].

We both like Richard and he likes us and I thought he was loyal to us but we haven't the experience you have with orientals. He's young and can be excused on that count occasionally, first if it doesn't upset the other boys and second if he is sincere and honest about it. It is hard for us to judge now.

Wong was subsequently fired when he neglected his duties and became surly toward Flora Rice.[16]

When Allerton and Gregg returned to Kaua'i in the winter of 1939, they hired additional laborers to work on the garden. The two referred to the workers, often with little regard to their actual ages, as "boys." Immediately upon their return, Allerton and Gregg were pleased to see that "the boys have taken wonderful care." The next year, Allerton again wrote, "Our 4 boys here have done a wonderful job. Everything is in perfect order. They are all 4 of them such nice boys." In this account, Allerton was describing a number of grown men. Sometimes, however, the boys were just that.

The couple hired schoolchildren to tend to the gardens on weekends, for instance. At times they employed upward of twenty laborers in building and excavating. Gregg reported of their own efforts in 1940: "We work like Filipinos all day." In this observation, he highlighted their own purported labor, foregrounding the degree to which labor itself had become synonymous with Asianness for the couple. In the same vein, Gregg groused about the difficulties of replacing their cook when the previous one was drafted for the war in 1942: "Our new 16 year old cook is learning fast and will be as good as Edward soon but it takes a lot of my time. I get a vacation from my defense job to teach for a few days or the boss [that is, Allerton] would have had a hard time breaking him in." In the same year, Gregg reported: "I am trying to train a 12 year old girl to do our house cleaning and the result is I do a great deal myself." In these instances, it was the training of the nonwhite children that he portrayed as the real work, not the labor that the boy and girl themselves performed cooking and cleaning for the couple.[17]

While Allerton was certainly forced to recognize that labor through remuneration, he often griped about that as well. Particularly during the war years, both men complained about the difficulties not just in finding labor but in the competition they faced in terms of wages, both from the defense industries and from the nearby pineapple and sugar plantations. In 1943 Allerton was asked by the governor to sit on a labor board for the island of Kaua'i. He wrote of his refusal: "did not accept as am too opinionated & think every one too highly paid & wages keep steadily going up." At the time, he was paying some men at the rate of $2 per day. Average national earnings of those in nonsupervisory positions in 1943 ranged from an hourly high of $1.10 (in mining) to a low of 61 cents (in retail). In other words, the most generous reading is that Allerton was paying about half the average national hourly rate, a rate he believed to be too high. That said, Hawai'i was not yet a state, and rates in Kaua'i were lower than those nationwide, so what he paid was usually in keeping with local wages. This, of course, is only to say that Allerton, like the neighboring plantation owners, was in a position as an outsider to take advantage of lower pay rates in Hawai'i.[18]

It is not surprising, of course, that the wealthy couple might have employed other people to execute the actual building of their estate or that those workers might have been underpaid men and women of color. Nor is it shocking that two white wealthy men in the mid-twentieth century might have been casually racist in speaking about their nonwhite employees. It is not even particularly surprising that those laborers would receive so little credit for the work they did in constructing the estate. But precisely because the Allerton Garden is a tourist destination that garners a good deal of attention, the narrative of how Allerton and Gregg came to build their estate is circulated with some regularity. In all of these narratives, the couple themselves "built" the gardens, "created a private paradise," and "transformed a dusty valley into a verdant hideaway with tropical plants from around the world." The *Christian Science Monitor*, for instance, claimed that Robert Allerton did the latter "with the help of his partner John Gregg," making their relationship the generative one in creating the gardens, not the work of the laborers who actually built them. In *The Out Traveler Hawaii*, a gay tourist guidebook, Matthew Link goes one step further, explaining that "most tourists are told Robert Allerton and his son developed the property, not his homosexual lover." This account even further obscures the real laborers by putting the couple's homosexuality at the center of the story, as if that was the causal agent in building the gardens. The story of the creation of Lawai-Kai is partially correct—two Illinoisans did design the estate—but it was the sweat of Kaua'i's workers that actually "built" it. While no one at the time would have pretended otherwise, that the couple's queerness has become so central to their story has made the erasure of that labor all the more complete.[19]

Hawaiians' supposed acceptance of the two men's homosexuality is also curious, not just because the couple's money is what bought them that acceptance, but also because they were never open about being gay. Just as in Illinois, their claims to being father and son helped to ease any discomfort that those around them might have experienced had the truth been more open. The latter-day insistence by gay journalists, however, has had the unfortunate consequence of erasing traditional Hawaiian forms of same-sex sexuality that predated European arrival in the eighteenth century. These traditions did not abide by modern Western notions of binary sexual identities (homo/heterosexual) and instead were predicated upon asymmetrical relationships of power between older and younger men with no fixed homosexual identity being assigned to either party, a practice called *aikāne*. Older men might have relationships, sexual and otherwise, with younger men, while also maintaining long-term partnerships with women; those same young men might themselves grow up to do the same. Understandings of this queer practice were obscured by the emergence and spread of the late nineteenth-century medical category of the homosexual, based on the notion of a fixed and abiding desire for a particular sexed object choice. It is homosexuality that Hawaiians supposedly accepted in the 1930s, in the form of the Allerton and Gregg, not the islands' own indigenous forms of queer sexuality. The pair never publicly identified as gay and, because they were an asymmetrically aged couple, actually bear some resemblance to Native Hawaiian understandings of same-sex sexuality. However, because they are often written about in the gay press as being accepted by locals, their version of queer sexuality eclipses that which came before them. In this way, Hawai'i became known as a place that accepted gay people, not a place with a long, varied, and continuing history of same-sex practices that are not gay by modern Western understandings. In this double move, not only did Allerton and Gregg colonize the island itself, but their supposed version of homosexuality also eclipsed the native queer traditions that predated it.[20]

From 1937 to 1941, Robert Allerton and John Gregg spent half the year in Kaua'i and half the year in Illinois, the place whose inhospitality to gays they had supposedly "escaped" by moving to Kaua'i. That all changed with the attack on Pearl Harbor on December 7, 1941. They did not actually know about the attack until late that afternoon, when a friend phoned to tell them about the blackout planned for that night. "Not being radio listeners we hadn't heard any word and we hadn't seen anyone all day, it being Sunday," reported Gregg. While they had just arrived for the winter, it was soon apparent that they would be unable to leave in April, as they usually did; all journeys via passenger ships had been canceled because of the US entrance into the war. That said, Allerton did describe the decision to stay on as their own, and no doubt they could have pulled strings in order to make an exit if they had really wanted to: "We have decided to stay here the duration of the war. There is much more we can do in real service than if we were on the mainland." Allerton had almost immediately made a donation to the Red Cross, and Gregg was made an assistant to the sheriff: their lawyer, Philip Rice, replaced his ailing brother, Willie, in that position. Gregg would later become a lieutenant in Kaua'i's Home Guard, leading a troop of forty Filipino men. Allerton headed up the local Red Cross relief project and regularly entertained soldiers on the estate through the Red Cross and United Service Organization. If the couple had primarily kept to themselves their first two winters, socializing mainly with their friends the Rices and others (like the Dillinghams) in Honolulu, it was during the war years that they emerged among the leading white citizens of Kaua'i. They used their wealth and whiteness—Gregg was only able to lead the Kaua'i Home Guard because he was white—in order to establish themselves more firmly on the island.[21]

While it is unclear exactly why, their decision to live on Kaua'i year-round also prompted Allerton and Gregg to acquire land on the northern shore of the island, where they built a home on Ke'e Beach that they used as a getaway from Lawai-Kai.[22] In June 1943, in the midst of World War II and their involvement in island life, Allerton wrote to their office manager in Chicago that he and Gregg were attempting to make a purchase of some land on the northern shore. He explained that they had sent an emissary

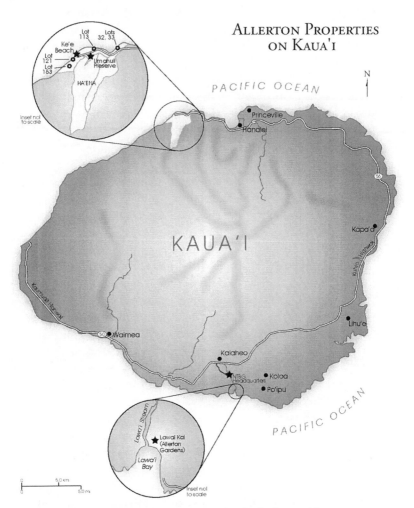

FIGURE 5.3 Allerton properties on Kaua'i. Map by Elisabeth McCalden.

to Honolulu to "interview the heirs + to make them a cash offer if they decide to sell." A year later he again wrote that they had been presented with the opportunity to acquire yet more property on the northern shore, "the choicest on the island aside from Lawai Kai," and that he wanted the office manager to set aside money for the purchase. On July 27, 1944, Allerton reported that the deal had gone through successfully. In the spring of 1945, the two men finalized the purchase of yet more land, this from the estate of Charles Augustus Brown. Over the course of two years, they had purchased land in two different ways in the neighborhood of Hā'ena: designated plots of land owned outright by those who sold them, as well as shares in a *hui*, or collective of owners. In purchasing land from the Brown estate, Allerton and Gregg were amassing one of the greatest stakes in the hui, and in the process of later claiming that land as exclusively their own, they would help to destroy what had amounted to a hundred years of collective ownership and the last gasp of indigenous communal land management on the island. In a complicated series of land deals, Allerton and Gregg ensured that land long held in Native Hawaiian hands would be privatized and later turned into a park that is now popular with tourists from the mainland.[23]

Indigenous Hawaiians had not understood land to be privately owned. Instead, they worked the land communally, governed by a reciprocal yet hierarchical relationship between *mo'i* (royalty or supreme rulers), *ali'i* (chiefs), and *maka'āinana* (commoners). The maka'āinana tended the land of their communally managed plot of land, or *ahupua'a*, taking from it what they needed and supplying the mo'i and ali'i, the latter operating as middlemen between the two other groups. This system of land management began to change with the arrival of Europeans in the early nineteenth century. Encouraged by notions of private property, Hawaiian leaders both instituted a new form of government, a constitutional monarchy, and a new system of land ownership that was designed to be equitable but that in practice disenfranchised the vast majority of maka'āinana. In what came to be known as the Māhele of 1848 and the subsequent Kuleana Act of 1850, large tracts of land were awarded outright both to the mo'i (the government) as well as to ali'i. By contrast, the maka'āinana were required to make individual applications to claim land (what would be called kuleana lands), even if they had been living there for generations. Unlike the ali'i and mo'i, and because they had to make individual claims for their land, the maka'āinana had to employ Western surveying methods to document their land claims and produce two witnesses to prove that they had occupied that tract of land since at least 1839. They were given two years to do so. For a variety of reasons, most maka'āinana failed to register their claims. Many did not have the funds to pay for the surveying; some simply did not understand what was now required of them; many resisted the notion of Western-style privatization of land; and still others may have believed that, if they limited themselves to bounded tracts of land, they would no longer have access to the fishing and water rights traditionally granted them through residence and belonging in the ahupua'a. In any event, less than one percent of Hawaiian lands were awarded to maka'āinana, and they effectively became tenants on land that their ancestors had been occupying for generations.[24]

The ahupua'a of Hā'ena, where the Allertons would eventually purchase land, was initially typical of most land apportioned during the Māhele.

While some maka'āinana filed for and were awarded kuleana lands in the ahupua'a, the majority of the land was awarded to an ali'i named Abner Pākī. The land passed to his daughter, Bernice Pauahi Bishop, at his death in 1855, and she sold it eleven years later; it was sold a second time, to William Kinney, in 1871. It was at this moment that the thirty-eight Native Hawaiian residents of the ahupua'a regained control of their land. Coming together in a collective called a *hui kā'ai 'āina* (in this case, the Hui Kū'ai 'Āina o Hā'ena), they purchased the land from Kinney in 1875 in a counteroffensive designed to allow them to stay on the land but also to manage it communally in the spirit of their ancestors. While most hui lasted only until the 1920s, the Hui Kū'ai 'Āina o Hā'ena remained intact through the 1960s, almost a hundred years after its founding.[25]

Hui were difficult to maintain because individual shares (thirty-eight in the case of the hui at Hā'ena) were subdivided between heirs at the death of an original member, and not all heirs continued to reside on the ahupua'a. Some original members or their heirs also sold their shares to others, some of them haole who had little interest in communal ownership. The situation was exacerbated when Hawai'i was annexed by the United States and became a US Territory in 1898; it then became subject to American laws of property. In 1923 the Territory of Hawai'i passed legislation allowing for any member of a hui to sue the others for the right to partition one's portion of the property, either to sell it or to occupy one's distinct piece of property outright. It was to be the end of the hui, but only if co-owners chose to exert their right to partition. For thirty years, no one in the Hui Kū'ai 'Āina o Hā'ena did so—until Robert Allerton and John Gregg started buying up shares.[26]

While the couple had already bought land on the northern shore of Kaua'i, it appears that their earliest purchases were pieces of land that they owned outright (likely kuleana lands). In any event, the designation of that land as private property had occurred at some point before Allerton and Gregg became involved. Not so with the land in the hui at Hā'ena. In this case, in 1945 they purchased just over five out of thirty-eight shares of the Hui Kū'ai 'Āina o Hā'ena that had gone on the market as part of the estate of Charles Augustus Brown. Brown, a native of Massachusetts who had come to Hawai'i in 1877, had married Irene Kahalelaukoa 'Ī'ī, daughter of John Papa 'Ī'ī, chief justice of the Hawaiian Supreme Court; they had two sons and a daughter (who died in infancy) before divorcing. At some point (at least by 1909), Brown had acquired these shares of the hui, and when he died in 1937, they passed to his heirs. Those heirs, perhaps because they were themselves indigenous Hawaiians, had allowed the hui to remain intact.[27]

In buying shares in this hui, Allerton and Gregg must have been aware of the legislation, dating from the 1920s, that would allow them to sue to partition their shares from the other owners. And this is what they did, joining with Paul G. Rice, nephew of their friend and former lawyer Philip Rice, to disband the collective. In 1954 they initiated a suit in the Fifth Circuit, where now-Judge Philip Rice presided, to partition the land. A commission was then appointed to devise a plan to divide the land. Hawaiian studies scholar Carlos Andrade explains what came next: a valuation of the land based on its perceived use (wet, pasture, etc.) and its location (beach, interior, road), as well as a provision that allowed those who had lived on land and improved it (either by farming or by constructing a home) a greater claim to those particular plots. Allerton and Gregg had 12.3651 percent of the hui (making them the second-largest shareholders; Paul Rice was third), including a house near Keʻe Beach, on land that was part of the ahupuʻua. After much squabbling, pooling of shares, divisions, some donations of land to the county, and annexations, all based on the need to assign value to individual plots of land, the partition was completed in 1967. Land that had been worked collectively for thousands of years had now been divided and privatized. While Allerton and Gregg were certainly latecomers to the process as a whole, they had been instrumental in destroying one of the longest running hui on Kauaʻi.[28]

There is one final wrinkle. In 1974, ten years after Allerton's death, the state of Hawaiʻi, which had plans to develop a park on the northwestern shore of Kauaʻi, set its sights on Gregg's land at Hāʻena. At the same time, he and others associated with the then-named Pacific Tropical Botanical Garden (PTBG) became interested in an additional plot of land owned by the state just north of Lawai-Kai and the PTBG; according to a friend, Gregg had long recognized "the importance of somehow acquiring the waterfalls and surrounding land to make this part of the PTBG." When the state approached him to buy his property at Hāʻena, he "quickly seized the opportunity to exchange part of his Haena land for the waterfalls, conveying this by bequest to the PTBG." For 170 acres of his Hāʻena land, he gained approximately 104 acres for the Pacific Tropical Botanical Garden. Most of the Allerton land in Hāʻena then became part of a state park. The land that Gregg had brokered for what became the National Tropical Botanical Garden (NTBG) is home to its headquarters and research library.[29]

The end result of all of these land deals is that a majority of Allerton and Gregg's northern shore land is now owned by the state, while the land on the southern shore is owned by the NTBG and by the Allerton Gardens Trust. The northern coast land is open to visitors, and numerous tourist guides and websites include it as one of Kauaʻi's most popular beaches; this means that its use by Native Hawaiians has diminished as its popularity has increased with tourists. Much of the Allerton land on the southern shore is either inaccessible to residents of Kaua'i or open for a steep fee. (Those wishing to see the Allerton Gardens [Lawai-Kai] may book a tour online for $60.) While the NTBG is dedicated to the preservation of native foliage, in choosing to make the land available for those purposes, Allerton and Gregg denied Native Hawaiians the right to make their own decisions about their home. Guidebooks to Hawai'i highlight the gardens. And the Allertons, whose name is affixed to them, are celebrated for their generosity. This anti-conquest, to use a term coined by literary scholar Mary Louise Pratt to characterize how colonizers have been able to represent their colonialism as benevolence, erases the Native Hawaiians whose homes Allerton and Gregg helped to steal, along with the long history of colonialism they marshaled in order to do so.[30]

Allerton and Gregg spent much of their time on Kaua'i developing their gardens, just as they had done in Illinois. But their vision for this new garden included plants not indigenous to the Hawaiian islands. When not gardening, they traveled throughout Asia and Oceania, and in an era when this was still poorly regulated by US customs, they brought back cuttings, seeds, and plants. In this, they were following in the tradition of Queen Emma herself, who planted the bougainvillea and tamarind trees that still grow at Lawai-Kai; Alexander McBryde, Dora Isenberg (also a Rice descendant), and other early haole residents of the island did the same, planting the land with much of its non-native foliage. Allerton and Gregg brought plant samples back from trips to Ceylon (now Sri Lanka), Siam (now Thailand), the Philippines, Tahiti, Puerto Rico, and from other islands in the Hawaiian archipelago. As Gregg explained many years later:

My father thought the only thing that he could do for the island, to repay it for the good life it gave him was to bring in other things [from other] parts and introduce them to the island, much against the dislike of Dr. [Harold] St. John and some of those people who want to keep the island pure. We brought that small-growing heliconia—I don't remember the name of that. It's the one that we brought in. It's a South American one and we brought it in from that Pennock's Nursery in Puerto Rico.

He here acknowledged his recognition that some, including famed horticulturalist Harold St. John, believed that importing non-native species might choke out those plants indigenous to the island, and yet Gregg framed Allerton's insistence on doing so as a service to the island itself— the purported reciprocity of Pratt's anti-conquest—rather than as a way to enhance the beauty of his own land. Those non-native plant species have made Hawai'i—and the island of Kaua'i—one of the most horticulturally diverse places in the world while simultaneously making it the extinction capital of the United States. The very plants imported by Allerton and Gregg (among others) have been suffocating indigenous species since their introduction. While the National Tropical Botanical Garden is now in the business of abating the extinction of native flora, the fact remains that some of what the couple themselves imported to the island brought about that very sort of extinction, a fact usually obscured by reports of their benevolence in funding the NTBG in the first place.[31]

Robert Allerton and John Gregg's visit to the island of Kaua'i in 1937 profoundly altered their lives, as it did those of the residents of the island. Rather than seeing their arrival in Hawai'i as an escape by persecuted gays, however, the two men were simply recognizing their own desires for a more permanent settlement in a tropical location, a decision they could make because of their wealth and whiteness. Upon arrival, they set about transforming the land into what eventually became the National Tropical Botanical Garden, upsetting native land claims and established horticultural patterns in the process. In much of this, including their casual racism, Allerton and Gregg were, it must be said, no different from other wealthy haole settlers from the mainland. They arrived at an auspicious moment, where plentiful land was still available at relatively low prices (certainly compared to today), and they had the funds to transform that land. But the couple went beyond simply making purchases, employing locals, and undergoing renovations. In their importation of non-native plant species and their efforts to eliminate the Hui Kū'ai 'Āina o Hā'ena, they fundamentally disrupted long-entrenched ways of living on the island of Kaua'i. At Lawai-Kai and in Hā'ena, they also made homes for themselves, homes where they showcased queer domestic space and invited the world to visit, the subject of the next chapter.

Chapter Six
Queer Domesticity in Illinois and Hawai'i

In 1939, soon after Robert Allerton and John Gregg had commenced splitting their time between Kaua'i and Monticello, Allerton explained in correspondence to Philip Rice, his friend and lawyer: "This Jeckyll [*sic*] and Hyde life we are leading now is new to us and hard as we are always thinking of two things at once. Our Kauai life and Illinois life get all mixed up together sometimes. How lucky we are to be able to live in two such heavenly places when so much disturbance and unhappiness is blowing around." Knowing what we do about Allerton and Gregg, one might think that the "Jekyll and Hyde" existence to which Allerton referred was that between their gay selves and the straight version they presented to others, but as I will demonstrate, their life as "father and son" was more than just a charade put on for observers. Rather, living as father and son, and financed by substantial capital, allowed Allerton and Gregg to create two homes that showcased their queer domesticity. It was the shuttling between the two that Allerton found confusing, not his contented life with his son and companion.[1]

Until 1938, Allerton and Gregg continued to live at The Farms. From 1938 to 1946, they split their time between The Farms and Lawai-Kai. And from 1946, once they had donated The Farms to the University of Illinois, they lived exclusively at Lawai-Kai, making shorter trips back to Illinois each year. They also continued to take extensive trips to various destinations within the United States and abroad, usually in Europe, Asia, and the South Pacific, but occasionally to the Caribbean and Latin America as well. When they had lived together at The Farms, we have less evidence to document what their day-to-day lives were like because they had little need to correspond about it between themselves or with anyone else. That changed in Hawai'i. In order to manage their finances, oversee The Farms while away, and also ensure that they were able to live on Kaua'i in the manner to which they had become accustomed, they corresponded extensively with a woman named Helen Murphy, and later a man named Herbert Gorsuch, both of whom worked for Allerton out of an office in the First National Bank of Chicago, which had been founded by Allerton's father in the prior century. That correspondence allows us a window into Allerton and Gregg's relationship with one another that we would not have otherwise. The correspondence demonstrates that Allerton and Gregg fashioned a queer domestic life for themselves in Hawai'i, living in a much smaller home than Allerton House, and with a greatly reduced staff, none of whom lived in.

During this period—the 1930s through the 1960s—most Americans understood male homosexuals, via the popular press, as shady lurkers of back rooms and bars, diseased and damaged men who were arrested in parks and highway restrooms for soliciting sex. Following a 1920s heyday when homosexuality was both pathologized by medical men and lawmakers, but also fetishized and celebrated by slumming city dwellers out for a night in the city, most historians see the 1930s through the early 1960s as the nadir of twentieth-century American gay life in terms of persecution. When the news media covered homosexuality and police attempts to "clean it up," much of that coverage portrayed gay men as essentially existing in public, without private homes to which they might retreat and be among their own kind. There is some truth to this representation because many gay men did meet one other in bars, parks, and public restrooms, but newspaper and magazine reporting focused almost exclusively on those locations because that is where gay men came into contact with the law, neglecting the fact that of course queer people also had private homes. By contrast, the Allertons fashioned a queer life that centered around the home. Their letters show us what life was like for one same-sex couple during the mid-twentieth century: their daily routine and its interruptions, their socializing, and the ways that they structured their relationship in a manner that had little precedent in the homes in which they had grown up or in American culture more broadly. This life was made possible entirely by Allerton's fortune. Their socioeconomic class accounts for their ability to fashion such elaborate queer domestic spaces, the publicity surrounding them, and their concomitant need for a filial cover to explain their relationship with one another, especially as they opened their home up to others, both friends and strangers.

Just as importantly, it is clear that Allerton and Gregg's relationship was not simply one of two men who lived together—a same-sex couple— but also one that was profoundly shaped by their asymmetry in wealth and in age. In that respect, Allerton and Gregg actually did resemble the father-and-son pair that they publicly proclaimed themselves to be. The Allertons are therefore useful not just for showing us one example of what queer domesticity looked like in midcentury America, but also for demonstrating that couplehood has historically taken many different forms. Especially in the wake of the now successful fights for same-sex marriage rights in the United States, we are familiar with the argument that same-sex couples are just like heterosexual couples but for their genders. If anything, some proponents of marriage equality made it seem as if same-sex couples would achieve an egalitarianism in couplehood that married straight couples, with the expectations of traditional gender roles, could never hope to achieve.[2] Allerton and Gregg did not live this particular same-sex ideal. Because Allerton controlled the purse strings, he was able to dictate the financial choices that they made. But as Allerton aged and grew increasingly frail, Gregg came to occupy the role of caretaker. Their asymmetry in age and wealth really did make them behave in ways that appear filial. They are instructive, then, not just for historians of queer sexuality, but for all historians who study couples and how they have negotiated their relationships. The most obvious parallel to Allerton and Gregg is the archetype of the married heterosexual pair under coverture, where women's and men's roles were distinct, hierarchical, and presumed to be complementary. In the case of the Allertons, very different roles structured their partnership, but not in a manner that brought with it the subservience that was often a part of marriage under coverture. As we will see, however, they were far from an equal pair.

For many years historians of homosexuality, especially for those studying the period before gay liberation and the rise of self-proclaimed lesbian and gay subjects, found evidence for men's queer lives in public and women's in private. Gay men were understood through the prism of sex, for which records of arrest and criminal prosecution were usually available. Lesbians were much more visible in the form of the couple, which occupied a home. These divergences in queer history were based both on the actual lived experiences of queer men and women, as well as their own cultures' blind spots. For instance, history shows us more examples of women living in long-term partnerships with other women, those relationships being understood in a variety of ways by their peers depending on the era and the couple involved. It is also demonstrable that queer women seem not to have engaged in public sex with the same frequency as queer men (in part for reasons of safety and access to the public in the first place), but it is also the case that police and lawmakers did not *believe* that women did such things and did not pass laws barring them, which meant there would be no arrests and prosecutions left behind for the historian. As a result, we are left with an incomplete picture of how and whether queer men and women are different in their relationship to the home and the domestic sphere. As scholars Matt Cook, Stephen Vider, and Sharon Marcus have argued, this has led us to see lesbians as fundamentally contained within the home and gay men as being anti-domestic, despite much evidence to the contrary. As Marcus amusingly put it, gay male desire has been "the love that dare not go indoors."[3]

As much as some of these omissions are ones of evidence and oversight, there were also real reasons that gay men had an ambivalent and equivocal relationship to the home, and not just because they might have had a challenging time growing up in their natal homes. As Matt Cook explains, because they have been feminized, gay men have been seen as being particularly adept at the domestic while at the same time they have been conceived as being a threat to the home and the heterosexual family that is meant to be contained within it. For this reason, many gay men, especially those sharing a home with another man, have felt like they were inventing a particular form of queer domesticity from whole cloth, especially so in the early twentieth century when there were few models to emulate. The historian John Ibson has referred to queers of this generation forging relationships as "men without maps." Scholars have demonstrated that pairs of queer domesticated men certainly did exist—including those whom Allerton knew, like John Borie and Victor Beigel, or Charles Shannon and Charles Ricketts—but the majority of examples from this period are either to be found in Europe or are couples that scholars have unearthed in the contemporary moment, not ones to which Allerton and Gregg would have had access. Because of this, I argue that Robert Allerton and John Gregg asserted kinship with each other not just because it was a plausible way of explaining their relationship with one another, but also because kinship made their relationship seem fit for a home. That is, claiming to be related made their occupation of a domestic space together more acceptable to those who might have questioned their co-residence at The Farms or Lawai-Kai. And the fact that they were public figures who might have need of an explanation not just for their relationship, but also for the fact of their sharing two elaborate homes together, once again owes everything to Allerton's wealth.[4]

Because Allerton and Gregg were almost always with one another, at least once they moved in together in 1929, we have no surviving correspondence between the two. If earlier correspondence existed, and it is likely that it did, it has since been destroyed or remains in private hands. What does survive, however, is the correspondence between Allerton, Gregg, and their bookkeeper, Helen Murphy. Murphy worked for Allerton in an office in the First National Bank of Chicago. Her role was to see to Allerton's accounts, make sure he had enough money at the ready, and, with the assistance of an accountant, Herbert Gorsuch, do his taxes. But she ended up being much more than that, becoming a friend to both Allerton and Gregg. She regularly made personal appointments for both of them with dentists and doctors. After the move to Hawai'i, she also shopped for them, sending them items they could not find on the islands. Gregg and Allerton tended to correspond with Murphy separately, and she had different relationships with each of them. Generally the letters between Murphy and Gregg are more casual, and in these letters both are clearly working to ensure that Allerton is pleased with whatever arrangements they are making.

Despite the fact that these are business letters—many are filled with endless columns of numbers related to yields at The Farms or transfers of stocks—Allerton and Gregg were also genuinely fond of Murphy. Gregg and Murphy usually signed letters to each other with "Best love." At one point when Gregg believed that she had misconstrued his anxiety about firing an employee as delight, he wrote to her: "It grieved me very much to know that you interpreted my letter of last Sunday to read that I was elated over Richard's discharge. More serious and disheartening to me was for you to think me capable of deriving pleasure from any one else[']s misfortune." Gregg clearly cared what Murphy thought about him, even if she was effectively in his employ (via Allerton). Indeed, while Gregg and Murphy regularly referred to Allerton as "our boss" in their correspondence (a practice I will return to presently), Gregg often wrote to Murphy as if she were simply performing tasks for him out of the goodness of her heart. In 1940 he wrote to her, "You are too good to me Helen and I can't show you my full appreciation for your kindness to me. I continually am reminded of it even when I blow my nose on my new handkerchiefs, sew on a button and now when I take a bath. You're much too good but I thank you just the same and send you much love." While there is clearly some performative gratitude going on here between an employer and his proxy employee, there does seem to have been genuine affection between the three. They all regularly exchanged birthday and Christmas presents (Murphy often asking Allerton and Gregg for advice on what to get the other one), talked politics in their letters (all were Republicans), and gossiped about their relatives and friends. Murphy wrote to Allerton in regard to a friend who had recently died, and in doing so conveyed something of the truly personal nature of the bond she shared with the pair: "You remember Jen, my short, fat friend—well, she is still with me in my mind and thru all these years I have never discovered anyone who can fill the void she left." They met up for lunch when the pair was in Chicago, and sometimes Gregg would attend the opera with Murphy; at other times they would give her tickets from a season's subscription they did not plan to use. She visited

them at The Farms, sometimes bringing her own relatives, and Allerton and Gregg made it possible for Murphy and her husband to travel to
Hawai'i and stay at Lawai-Kai at one point when they were absent.[5]

Also noteworthy here is just how much Murphy did for Allerton and
Gregg. She regularly ordered books for them, among them the latest titles
by many writers, including queer authors Vita Sackville-West, W. Somerset Maugham, Gertrude Stein, and Carson McCullers. While it was not
beneath her to pop out to Marshall Field's to pick up another set of sheets
to mail to them in Hawai'i, she was also fully responsible for most of Allerton's sizable fortune. Allerton sold stocks, liquidated assets, and moved
money around at her recommendation. She not only did Allerton's bid-
ding in terms of making money available to him; she clearly helped him
earn the money that he was spending. Murphy was their only employee
with access to a safe deposit box, and she had power of attorney for both
of them so that she could execute financial transactions on their behalf
when they were in Hawai'i. This was a remarkable career for a woman in
the 1930s and 1940s, especially a married woman. As Allerton wrote her in
the wake of the bombing on Pearl Harbor, which kept Allerton and Gregg
on Kaua'i indefinitely, "Sometimes I fear you don't realize dear Helen how
much I appreciate all you do & the responsibilities you have but I do." As
a woman taking on these responsibilities in this era, Murphy truly was
unusual. Also noteworthy, however, is that we know as much as we do
about Allerton's and Gregg's private lives thanks to their ability to employ a private bookkeeper and accountant cum friend, truly a testament
to their immense privilege.[6]

Helen Murphy suffered a stroke in June 1943 while vacationing at
French Lick Springs, Indiana. With effort, she was able to sign documents
that relinquished power of attorney to the accountant Herbert Gorsuch,
but getting into the vault was another matter: only Murphy knew the
combination and she was too incapacitated to remember it. By late that
summer, it was clear that Murphy would not be able to return to her job,
and Gorsuch, who had been working with her for twenty-two years, took
over full-time with the assistance of his wife, Ruby, as bookkeeper. Allerton made sure that Murphy's salary would continue for as long as she
lived. A year after her first stroke, Murphy suffered a second in June 1944,
and Allerton and Gregg visited her in October of that year in Chicago.
Helen Murphy died on March 2, 1950. She was seventy years old. While the
correspondence continued between Allerton, Gregg, and Gorsuch, it was
never quite the same. They simply were not as friendly, and all three maintained something of a distance in their correspondence. Further, by the
later 1940s onward, almost all of the correspondence was between Gregg
and Gorsuch, Allerton relegating that duty to Gregg as he aged. Our best

window into the queer domesticity of this father-and-son pair thus comes during the decade-long period between the early 1930s and 1943, when Allerton and Gregg were corresponding with Helen Murphy.[7]

In writing about queer domesticity, historians Matt Cook and John Potvin are clear that there is no one element that can define a home as queer. The very word "queer" defies such precision, denoting the non-normative, in this case to be at odds with general expectations for the arrangement of a household. Potvin does go further, however, and names "seven deadly sins" that characterize the homes of what he calls "bachelors of a different sort": queerness, idolatry, decadence, askesis, decoration, glamour, and artifice. While Allerton and Gregg may not have been disposed to idolatry (of a female diva in Potvin's reading) or askesis (the "unnatural training of the self"), in all other ways they adhere nicely to Potvin's schema. Allerton and Gregg fashioned two homes for themselves where men were at the center and where aesthetic taste and refinement ruled supreme. They also embraced particular forms of artifice (especially in the mimicking of statuary) and lived lives that could easily be characterized as glamorous and decadent; indeed, there was often a self-consciousness to the glamour of their estates. Their queer father/son couple relationship was generative of much of the design at Lawai-Kai (and, to a lesser extent, the gardens at The Farms). While Potvin is primarily concerned with the physical space of the queer interior, in a more quotidian manner we can see queer domesticity at work in the everyday lives of Allerton and Gregg and how they made a home and shared it with one another.[8]

As we have already seen, in the days both before and after the arrival of Gregg, Allerton and The Farms played host to many weekend visitors, invitations to which were coveted by Allerton's social set in Chicago. These parties continued through the 1930s after Gregg was in residence at Allerton House, and were as much about a display of the residence as they were about socializing. One visiting couple, friends of the Allertons named Mary and Ambrose Cramer, composed a poem in commemoration of their time at Allerton House:

At Allerton let me abide
And watch the hybrid dancers glide.
See Robert with a Chinese prance
Invite Brunhilda for a dance.
Hear Ambrose's merry bursts of banter
Admire Sylvia's girlish cantor
While John upon the radio's pyre
Plays music till the room's on fire.

Clearly the celebrations had not diminished in fun since the arrival of Gregg; if anything, they had become that much more spirited. But during the weeks when just Allerton and Gregg and their staff were in residence, the estate was much more private. As Gregg described it:

Well, no one ever came here [The Farms] or was allowed to come here unless it was the garden clubs or the local neighborhood came in or something like that, and so it was a very private place. Now, when people applied to come—groups—the Mattoon Garden Club or something like that came—they weren't entertained, but they were allowed to walk around and that's the only time we ever saw people here. It was isolated, and we didn't want any ballyhoo about it, because then the curious would come. So it was a very private place. . . . We used to walk around here in our underpants and there wasn't anybody to see because we worshiped the sun . . .— took sunbaths as we walked.

This privacy—except at well-coordinated times—was one of the reasons that The Farms earned a reputation as being the home of eccentrics, but it also allowed Allerton and Gregg to create a private queer oasis of their own, sunbathing and walking the grounds in various states of undress. Even within the house itself, it was clear that certain parts of it were private, for Allerton and Gregg alone. The attic was one of those spots, according to chauffeur and farm manager, Elmer Priebe.[9]

Over the course of Gregg's residence at Allerton House, he and Allerton also renovated many of the gardens and "garden rooms" that Allerton had first laid out when he designed the original house and grounds. Among these was a garden dedicated to a statue called the *Sun Singer*, by Swedish sculptor Carl Milles. Allerton and Gregg had ordered the statue from the sculptor in 1929 on a trip to Stockholm. They had admired the *Sun Singer*, which looked out over Stockholm's harbor, but wanted a small version, more akin to another statue that was in Milles's own garden. Working with a translator, they asked for a statue that resembled the one in the harbor but at the size of the other statue in the sculptor's garden. They planned to place it on the terrace outside the library at Allerton House. When it finally arrived in Monticello, it became clear that there was a misunderstanding: the statue was much larger than Allerton had asked for, the full fifteen feet tall, just like the one overlooking Stockholm's harbor. The size of the statue necessitated an entirely new location, which is how the present garden came about, the statue finally being placed a much greater distance from the house. As Gregg explained it, "Carl Milles said that it was the best setting of any of his works. We'd go out there a lot, especially around the sunset time in the fall. It was incredibly private. We tore down a house or two, including an old lady on a pension who

FIGURE 6.1 Unpacking the *Sun Singer*, 1931. Courtesy of the University of Illinois Archives.

wouldn't sell at first." It was in the same year that Gregg and Allerton finished work on the garden for the Fu Dog statues, which had been imported from China. The staff referred to the practice of adding sculpture, replanting, and rearranging as "putting velvet on the garden." During the times they lived at Allerton House, Gregg explained that "the gardens were mostly for floriculture to decorate the house, so it was one of my jobs to do all the flowers for the house. My father planned all the meals, but it was a busy enterprise here." This was their normal division of duties, though things would change somewhat when they went to Hawai'i, in part because they could not find the same kind of staff that they had in Illinois and this meant more actual cooking on the part of one of them, which Allerton was not really skilled at doing.[10]

From the first, and unlike the plan for Allerton House, the design for Lawai-Kai was very much a joint effort. Even before they had formally acquired the property, as Gregg explained it, "I had drawn up plans for a house and with the use of the photographs [that they had taken on their first visit] I made a model of the house and put all the photographs around it and even now it looks pretty good." They planned much of that house around Biedermeier furniture from their Astor Street apartment, an apartment they would no longer need if they were going to be wintering in Hawai'i. When they arrived back in Hawai'i in December 1938, Gregg wrote to Helen Murphy:

I can't start telling you about the joys of this place. We hardly exist we're so daffy and gay. The new home is starting and there are so many other things to do that we're fairly tongue-tied and just sort of look at each other like Cheshire cats. Don't expect too much in the way of description. It is beyond words.

About a week later, he wrote, "It seems, and gets, more beautiful here every day, Helen, and we have to pinch ourselves that it is real. Such a wonderful thing that we bought this place. We're daffy as kids and fit as fiddles." This is when they were in the initial stages of planning the home, when they had hired a contractor to pour the foundation and a number of local boys to do work in the garden. They also had hired Richard Wong, "a young Chinese-American boy," to do their cooking and housework for them, even if it was not always up to snuff. Later they would fire Richard and bring a young man named Lyman Watts with them from Illinois, importing someone from the mainland because they could not as yet find someone to meet their standards, even if those had been loosened somewhat in the tropics. As Murphy saw the situation, "Lyman is a very fine boy and undoubtedly will fill in nicely, and it makes a more homey atmosphere for you and John." Allerton was quick to confirm that this was so: "The Rices came for luncheon & Lyman did beautifully. He & John concoct very appetizing food. Lyman is so clean & understands our ways, seems to be very happy[,] gets on well with our boys." By boys, he meant the young men who were working on the gardens, clearing land and planting.[11]

Just as they were in Illinois, the pair continued to be quite precise in their expectations for how their home should appear, not just in the matter of the architecture and the gardens, but everything that went into the house as well. Both Allerton and Gregg wrote separately to Murphy in February 1941 to extol their flower-arranging classes. Allerton explained, "We learned a lot at our flower arranging lessons very much. Mrs. Peterson is a real genius." Because they had to rely on Murphy to send them some things that were unavailable in the islands or could not wait until they returned to the mainland, they often had to be quite precise in explaining their vision. In this instance, Gregg was running interference between Murphy and Allerton:

About the napkins. I think your material sounds very fine. I wrangled an expression of opinion about monograms, initials [?] and crests out of the boss and found he liked just a plain A about three quarters of an inch high just like the A in "Lawai-Kai" that is on the <u>pillow slips</u> you had made for his bed.

Similarly, after moving to Lawai-Kai permanently, they designed a doubled set of stationery for both homes that allowed for use no matter the location. The achievement of a particular vision was one way that Allerton and Gregg expressed their senses of self. Their queer domesticity was bound up in adhering to a very exacting aesthetic sense, from the architecture to the landscaping to everything that filled the house.[12]

Allerton and Gregg had two separate bedrooms at Lawai-Kai, as they also did in Allerton House. While they sometimes shared double rooms or cabins while traveling—or occasionally adjoining rooms in a suite—we simply cannot know whether they used the separate beds in these rooms or whether they shared a bed. Even if they did in fact sleep apart, that was not particularly unusual. For much of the nineteenth and first half of the twentieth century, many married heterosexual couples had separate beds, and sometimes separate bedrooms. This was, of course, possible only for those who could afford to do so, but it was especially necessary for Allerton and Gregg because they employed staff who observed the living arrangements of their employers and could easily report back to others about who slept where at Lawai-Kai or Allerton House.[13]

Entertaining continued to be a high priority for Gregg and Allerton in their new home in Hawai'i. They had their first real party in early 1940: "We had 35 people for an egg nog party New Years afternoon. Our first general party & show off & we have done a lot since we came to the path & back in the jungle it all looks pretty crude & rough but wait a couple of years!" This would not be their last party. They regularly entertained friends from Honolulu, including Louise Dillingham, who had introduced them to Kaua'i. In January 1941, Gregg reported:

We are in a flutter today getting ready for Mrs. Dillingham who arrives by plane tomorrow. Her friend, Mrs. Kennedy, comes on the Saturday plane for the week-end. We are busy airing the guest house bedding and laying in supplies and planning meals to make everything run smoothly. We've been trying out a few new recipes to spring on the guests.

They also had many guests from overseas who made a point of visiting their estate or who knew friends of friends who directed them to visit, especially once the landscaping was fully complete. Georgia O'Keeffe visited them in 1939 while they were only beginning to transform the Lawa'i Valley. Yale University president Charles Seymour visited them in 1947.[14]

There were also activities galore to do on the island, as well as on their own property. As Allerton recounted to Murphy in 1940, "We are well & happy & having a wonderful time planting and gardening to our hearts content & also making all day picknicks to remote beauty spots."

FIGURE 6.2 Picnicking at Lawai-Kai. Courtesy of the University of Illinois Archives.

He elaborated about those picnics: "We go once a week on all day excursions horse back usually and have now been in all the canyons & difficult spots. One does not get the full beauty of the island until one penetrates into such places." Within only a couple of years of purchasing the land on Kaua'i, they had not only made a home for themselves, but were also continuing to find new places to explore on the island.[15]

When the Japanese bombed Pearl Harbor and Allerton and Gregg were stuck in Kaua'i for the duration of the war, they both became involved in the war effort—Allerton volunteering with the Red Cross, and Gregg at first as assistant to the Kaua'i sheriff and later as a lieutenant for the Kaua'i Home Guard, where he commanded a platoon of forty soldiers, drilling them three times per week. All of this meant that Gregg was away from home for longer periods of time, and clearly Allerton missed him. He was forthright about this in his letters to Murphy. Soon after Gregg's duties started, Allerton wrote, "Of course I miss John. He is gone all day." By Christmas, Allerton was grateful: "It was a treat to have John home for the daylight time. He is gone at 9 & not back till 5 so we have very little time to enjoy the beauties of Lawai Kai together. . . . It is a quiet peaceful life. One is very busy from 7:30 until 4:30. John gets back about 5. We have dinner in the pantry & the evenings reading in the stone room early to bed." Even Murphy was chiding Gregg for abandoning Allerton during the days: "Undoubtedly you are very happy to be engaged in useful war work, but it is hard on our boss to be alone so much of the time for I can realize how much he misses your company." A month later, she returned to the theme: "I think it is a pity you can't devote more of your time to our beloved boss, who must [miss] your companionship very much." What is astounding here is that Gregg's leaving during normal working hours—just to do his job for about two years—was probably the most time they had spent apart since they had moved in together in 1929. They were so used to being around one another, whether in Illinois, Hawai'i, or traipsing around the globe, that Gregg's absence over the course of the working day was enough to seriously disrupt Allerton's equilibrium. Within about a month, Allerton happily reported: "John's job for the moment has petered out. There wasn't enough to do. It is grand to have him home & to help in our garden work."[16]

After being trapped on Kaua'i during the Second World War beginning in 1941, they found that they liked living there and decided to make it their permanent home. This was likely also a consequence of Allerton's age—he was in his seventies by the mid-1940s—and the hospitable climate in Hawai'i. No doubt it also had something do with the welcome they had received by their neighbors and by Hawaiians more generally, a welcome that had everything to do with their wealth and connections. In October 1946, Allerton and Gregg completed paperwork to donate their estate at Monticello to the University of Illinois at Urbana-Champaign. Fifteen hundred acres, including the house and gardens, was transferred to the university and renamed Robert Allerton Park. Allerton also designated an additional 250 acres north of the home to the 4-H Club. A third area, comprising 3,775 acres made up of eight farms north of the Sangamon River, was provided so that money generated on the farms could be used to support Robert Allerton Park. From that point onward, the University of Illinois maintained Allerton Park and Allerton House as a conference center, which could also be rented out for weddings and other events. Allerton and Gregg were free to return to visit whenever they liked and would stay in a small house on the grounds designated for them.[17]

Allerton and Gregg shipped about 30,000 pounds of household possessions from Illinois to Hawai'i: at least fifty-eight barrels, seventy-five boxes, and six crates arrived by steamer. While that shipment included some of their costumes, they also gave away much of that collection to friends at the time of the move; soon thereafter Mrs. Kellogg Fairbank Jr. was seen at a costume ball in Chicago in a "magnificent green skirt and gold threaded shocking pink sari which was draped over her head," a gift from Allerton. The *Chicago Tribune* also announced an exhibition and sale of the Robert Allerton Collection, with this reminder: "Remember that this collection was assembled years before today's enthusiasts started flocking abroad and before antique prices began to climb during the last war." Allerton and Gregg had been well ahead of their time in pursuing the queer aesthetic that had so defined their home at The Farms.[18]

Gregg and Allerton always portrayed their relationship as one of almost perfect harmony. Their day-to-day correspondence with friends and employees through the 1940s and '50s certainly also leaves this impression. Whether or not this was actually so or simply the way they chose to depict themselves remains open to debate. If one took them at their word, however, it would be difficult to imagine a biological father and son, one financially dependent on the other for more than forty years, living together without conflict and strife. While some couples achieve that level of peaceful coexistence, it is by no means a guarantee of couplehood. Instead it makes more sense to recognize the uniqueness of their relationship: neither biological father and son, nor a straightforward couple either. They may have achieved a happy coexistence not only because Gregg had chosen to be with Allerton in a manner similar to couplehood, but also because he was always beholden to him. Their union, voluntarily entered into by two adults, more resembled the bond between a couple that does not share a common lineal history, than it did a typical father-son dyad. And yet, because they actually did structure their relationship in ways that more resembled that of a father and son, it was not couplehood as we know it, either. The relationship came with strings attached, in a manner not dissimilar from that of an older and wealthier man and his younger wife. Gregg was always provided for, but with the expectation that he would work to make Allerton happy. Those duties increased as Allerton aged.

The very language of the letters with Helen Murphy also demonstrates a relationship other than simply lovers or that of parent and child. While the letters were often dry monetary discussions, they also belie an intimacy borne of many years of friendship. Gregg and Murphy usually referred to Allerton as "the boss" (Gregg), "our boss," or occasionally "our beloved boss" (Murphy). In September 1939, for instance, Gregg wrote to Murphy: "The cord in the boss's ankle is limbering up in fine shape and he enjoys the massage." And in December of the same year, Murphy relayed that "it was a great joy to get a few lines from our boss this morning." While neither ever referred to Allerton as Gregg's father, only rarely did they call him Robert, Murphy leaning more toward "Mr. Allerton." While it is possible to imagine a scenario in which a father might be considered the "boss" of his son, it seems less plausible to posit a man as his lover's boss. In the end, neither analogy really works: Murphy and Gregg both seemed to be acknowledging that the relationship between Allerton and Gregg was something either more akin to that between Allerton and Murphy or altogether unique. While the correspondence can be read both ways—to mean that they were "really" lovers or that they more resembled father and son—what is most clear is the degree to which Gregg and Allerton's relationship was one defined by the differences in their ages and their roles. Murphy's repeated calls upon Gregg to ease up on his war work in favor of devoting more time to Allerton are certainly evidence of this; she saw it as Gregg's primary duty to care for Allerton, not the other way around. Allerton cared for Gregg financially and, especially as Allerton aged, Gregg cared for him physically. In this, they are noteworthy not for whether they most resembled a pair of lovers or a father and son but for what they also were: two men divided asymmetrically by wealth and age who structured their relationship around these two fundamental axes. Murphy acknowledged the uniqueness of their relationship when she wrote to Allerton, "You are indeed fortunate to have so devoted and faithful a companion as John has proved to be." On a different occasion, Allerton himself used similar language in describing the happiness he had with Gregg: with a friend like Murphy and "an ideal companion & friend such as John is my cup of happiness is very full."[19]

There are a number of other ways to explore the filial aspects of the relationship between Allerton and Gregg. The first of these is financial. Over the years that they were together, Allerton controlled the finances, but he also continually worked to make Gregg financially independent by giving him money or bestowing property upon him. Their financial relationship was vastly unequal because Gregg came into it with almost nothing, and Allerton's wealth only increased over the years as his inherited wealth reproduced itself and after he inherited even more when both his parents died. In this respect, they resembled the father and son that they were claiming publicly to be, with Gregg not having access to funds until and unless Allerton allowed him to do so. But like many other wealthy parents who have more money than they can possibly spend on their own and who also desire the best for their children, Allerton went out of his way to make sure that Gregg would have some financial independence prior to Allerton's demise. While many parents who act in this manner offer their children homes (or money toward the purchase of those homes) or perhaps trust funds, in theory Gregg had no need for a home of his own, because *unlike* most parents and their children, he continued to live with his father. Nevertheless, Allerton did make it possible for Gregg to buy a number of plots of land and a house on the northern shore of Kaua'i on the Nā Pali coast, and this despite the fact that they almost always used this house together, not separately. Allerton was following in the footsteps of his own father, who had set him up with land starting at a young age and eventually The Farms once he reached maturity.

From Gregg's earliest days moving to The Farms, Allerton had been giving him jobs to do to keep him occupied and to make him a contributing member of the household. While Gregg designed and redesigned large portions of the gardens at The Farms (and later the house and gardens in Kaua'i), Allerton also gave him additional responsibilities when he moved from Chicago to Monticello in 1929. As Gregg explained it, "He said now you take over managing the farms with Elmer and you manage the gardens (whether he was just tired of doing it or just wanted to give it to me I don't know which, probably both, he had plenty of other interests. He did plenty of reading. He didn't care too much for the business side of farming.)" While Gregg's assumption of farm management would not generate income of his own, the farms certainly did sustain much of what happened at the estate, and so it was a real responsibility, especially for a young man who was educated and trained to a profession he had only so recently lost. It was not unlike what a wealthy father might do for his son, again their relationship so structured by Allerton's wealth. As Gregg put it, "My father gave me jobs because he was not satisfied with the way things were, and so that I wouldn't feel that I was wasting all the talent that I'd been trained for. He wanted to give me my head to try things out."[20]

In 1936 Allerton made his first substantive move to give Gregg some financial independence. He gave him $100,000—almost $1.8 million in today's dollars—which Helen Murphy promptly began investing in securities. She had also opened a safe deposit box for Gregg and was transferring some bonds from Allerton to Gregg. At the same time, Murphy assumed power of attorney for Gregg, giving her the ability to manage his finances, just as she did for Allerton. This was now a full fourteen years after Allerton and Gregg had met. Gregg had moved to The Farms about seven years before. Clearly Allerton believed that Gregg was fully committed to the relationship by this point. Murphy then proceeded to give Gregg periodical updates about the progress of his accounts. Allerton continued to pay for most day-to-day expenses, which meant that Gregg's money only grew, with him having no real need to spend it on anything other than gifts for Allerton and Murphy, and small gifts that he made to some of his own elderly relatives. As Gregg wrote to Murphy in March 1940, "Its laughable the big bank balance to report. No chance to use it for labor here!" On another occasion, he wrote, "It's nice and disturbing to have such a big bank balance. It's nice to have 'money in the bank.'" In part, Gregg's discomfort may partially be because he knew that Murphy was aware of how he came into the money in the first place, via an enormous revenue-generating gift from Allerton; but Gregg also seems to have been adjusting to the fact that he was not just surrounded by money at all times in this new life, but that he actually controlled some of his own as well.[21]

That ability to control his own money also allowed him to manage his relationship with Allerton in different ways, and Allerton's relationship with other people as well. In June 1940, Gregg wrote to Murphy that he had loaned a man named Wayne Peck $500. Peck was an elderly man who had been born on Allerton land and still lived near The Farms but had fallen on hard times. "The boss and I have always liked him very much and he came to ask the boss for money but talked to me first to see if I thought he had a chance[.] I thought it wiser to let him have the money myself and not mention it to the boss and have him feel differently about him than he does now." Gregg would not have been able to make this loan without the original gift from Allerton, a gift he was now using to protect Allerton from having to know that one of his tenants might have lost his way financially.[22]

One of the most significant ways that Allerton provided for Gregg was through the house and associated lands they purchased on the northern coast of Kaua'i that were part of the hui at Hā'ena, discussed in the previous chapter. As Allerton explained to Murphy their plan to purchase this land, he also told her of their "plan to buy this in John's name." By the summer of 1944, they were able to make an offer on a number of pieces of property that they could combine into what they then referred to as the Na Pali House. The deal was still not set by December, but was looking more and more likely. They began to stay in the house occasionally that year through early 1945. In February 1945, Allerton wrote to Herbert Gorsuch, "You see from the enclosed that John at last is owner of the Brown properties which gives us both great satisfaction after such a long wait." Gregg wrote to Gorsuch in April, "Robert gave the check and the deed is made out to me. I suppose that constitutes a cash gift to me, doesn't it. I will pay the employees there and will have real-estate holdings to report in 1945 and territorial taxes to pay." The fact that the deed would be registered in Gregg's name made little difference in their day-to-day existence or maintenance of the property. By the 1940s, Gregg was already assuming many of the managerial duties of their other property as well. Instead, this gift was both a symbolic act—Gregg could have some property of his own—and likely one effected for tax purposes as well. When Allerton died, the house would not be taxed as part of his estate because Gregg would already own it. But in subtle ways, it was clear that this was Gregg's house, not Allerton's; they always referred to it as being so, for instance. Thus, Allerton offered Gregg a modicum of independence in a manner that was not dissimilar from what Allerton's own father had done in deeding him portions of his farmland.[23]

Allerton revised his will a number of times as his relationship with Gregg solidified and as he made other financial transactions that altered the composition of the estate that he would leave behind. In 1941, for instance, he wrote to Murphy that he would need to revise his will and inquired about what Gregg's income would be after he was gone. "If he is to live here [The Farms] or at Lawai Kai as I want him to do and as we live now it seems he will need more than I figure out to me now." Murphy responded that he would earn about $15,000 annually in revenue from The Farms, about $256,000 in current funds. She then went on to detail the various trusts that Allerton's previous will had designated for Gregg so that he could make up his mind about how best to proceed with his new plan. Soon thereafter he began to contemplate leaving The Farms to the University of Illinois, which would exclude it from the will he would write in favor of Gregg.[24]

In addition to the monetary consequences of their filial relationship, being father and son also allowed Allerton and Gregg to interact with family who disapproved of what they perceived as homosexuality, but could accept in the form of this open secret. Allerton and Gregg regularly visited Gregg's hometown of Milwaukee to see his sister and brother and their families. Gregg's niece, Jane Gregg Schowalter—daughter of his brother, Scranton—recalls these visits from when she was a child, at the time not realizing exactly who Allerton was in relation to Gregg. She does not remember how she found out, but she knows that her father understood them to be a couple and that he very much disapproved of what he believed was his younger brother's homosexuality. Nevertheless, they were welcomed back to Milwaukee year in and year out. Allerton and Gregg also regularly entertained and visited Gregg's sister, Katherine Gregg Courtenay. By the time they had relocated permanently to Hawai'i in the 1940s, many of Allerton's uncles and aunts had already passed away. His nephew Allerton Johnstone had died in 1929, having jumped from the fifth floor of a Los Angeles hotel to his death, reportedly the result of excessive drinking. Robert's sister, Kate, having finally divorced from her husband in 1930, died in late 1937, after a battle with brain cancer. But Vanderburgh Johnstone, Robert's surviving nephew and closest relative after the death, regularly visited Allerton and Gregg, bringing with him a series of different women with whom he was involved, and eventually his twin sons, Crane and Vanderburgh. Aside from their disapproval of some of those women, Allerton and Gregg got on well with Johnstone, and he was among the largest beneficiaries in Allerton's will when he died.[25]

While Allerton and Gregg might have been forthright about their relationship with some of these relatives, it seems more likely, given their reticence in almost all other facets of their life together, that they maintained their identities as adopted father and son even with their relatives. And those relatives, no matter what they might have personally thought about homosexuality, were able to welcome Gregg and Allerton into their home—and be welcomed by them—precisely because they need not ever explicitly acknowledge why and how the pair had come to live together. This was, of course, easier on Allerton's side of the family, not just because he was wealthy and many of his relatives may have had expectations of inheritance after his death, but also because Gregg was not replacing anyone else in becoming Allerton's son. Not so in the case of Allerton's relationship to Gregg. Both Scranton and Katherine, Gregg's siblings, had known their own father just as well as Gregg had done. To have Allerton replace James Gregg as John Gregg's father but not their own must have been strange. It made sense, of course, only if one understood that Allerton and Gregg were not *really* becoming father and son, even if that cover was useful for them in navigating the world around them.

Allerton and Gregg were, as we know, separated by twenty-six years. When they moved to Hawai'i full-time in the early 1940s, Allerton was in his late sixties. He turned seventy in 1943. That year he wrote to the accountant that "being 70 I want to live as long as I can be healthy + well." He did indeed live a long life, into his early nineties, but during the last decades of his life, he became increasingly dependent on Gregg for help in managing the world around him as his body became decreasingly reliable. Allerton was also partially deaf and suffered from asthma, conditions that were nearly lifelong ones for him, and neither of which made aging any easier. The asymmetry in their ages and Gregg's duties as caretaker actually did make him akin to the son that he had always claimed to be, or like a younger wife who increasingly has to manage the health of her aging husband; both comparisons are apt. It was during these years that Gregg became more active in corresponding with their accountant, Herbert Gorsuch, effectively taking on the role of managing their lives together in a way that had been much more coordinated between the two of them (and Helen Murphy) during the 1930s. Even during those years, however, Allerton's health was always a subject of conversation in the letters that went back and forth across the ocean between Chicago and Hawai'i.[26]

In March 1946, for instance, John reported:

Mr. Allerton seems very well now that he takes his digitalis every day and isn't bothered with night coughing unless he works too hard during the day. He sometimes does very strenuous work like moving heavy potted plants around for several hours or trimming trees but he says he prefers to cough a little at night and have some fun in the daytime. The doctor says he must avoid taking cold which is a strain on the heart and I hope we haven't planned to get home too early [to Illinois in the winter].

Gregg saw himself as overseeing some of Allerton's health needs, even as the latter still pushed against the doctor's orders occasionally. The next year Allerton underwent surgery for hemorrhoids, and Gregg reported to Gorsuch: "He is wonderful about pain and didn't complain at any time and except about nuisance of it, he has taken it in his stride." In 1951, when Allerton was almost eighty, Gregg reported that his asthma was growing worse on Kaua'i, though sometimes let up when they traveled (they had just been to Honolulu). By the early 1950s, the number and frequency of times that Gregg mentions Allerton's asthma or related coughs and colds increased. It was clearly getting worse, and they were having to do more to manage the condition. After returning from a trip in 1953 to Fiji, Samoa, and Tahiti, where it had rained a lot, exacerbating Allerton's asthma, Gregg wrote: "He feels the effort was well justified although it lowered his morale to know he can't go plunging ahead as he is used to. The many happy experiences we had, though, make pleasant recollections in the future." Allerton required some surgery in his final years, which further incapacitated him in its wake. That said, he and Gregg continued to travel, meaning that during those periods, he was even more dependent on Gregg in terms of mobility and access while abroad.[27]

Allerton and Gregg took lengthy trips domestically and internationally every year right up until Allerton's death in 1964. Allerton's travel as a single man had regularly taken him to destinations known to be friendly to queer visitors. Gregg and Allerton returned to some of these locations, but visited a large number of other places as well, effectively circling the globe many times over. Gregg wrote to Murphy in 1938 about why they loved to travel so much: "But travel is wonderful in what it does to oneself. The memories it stores up and the interest it creates in the news and the daily life one leads, the movies, the papers, the novels and in the broadening it gives one in the solution of ones [sic] own daily problems. What a lucky fellow I am to have had the opportunities I've had." In March 1932, for instance, Gregg sent his sister, Katherine, a postcard from Hamburg, what he called the "annual birthday picture and the third one taken in the Ratskeller." The next year he and Allerton were on a trip around the world, which would include a stop in China. There, Gregg explained, "Allerton expects to call on Mrs. William J. Calhoun. . . . She has interesting people constantly around her in her home, and prominent visitors from the States always make a point of calling on her at least once." Calhoun was the widow of a former US special envoy to China. The next year they were off on a cruise that would take them to various ports in Africa, Europe, then South America and the West Indies. In total, "Robert Allerton and his foster son, John W. Gregg," spent about three months on the cruise with other noted Chicagoans, reported the *Chicago Tribune*.[28]

FIGURE 6.3 Gregg and Allerton in Hamburg. Courtesy of the University of Illinois Archives.

Until the mid-1940s, when commercial aviation made travel by air much more convenient, all of these trips were taken by boat. Allerton, Gregg, and all of their fellow passengers would have spent anything from a few days to a number of months on a ship together. On cruises around the world, this meant they had plenty of time to get to know one another and crew members. Especially after they began to travel back and forth to Hawai'i regularly (and before that as well when venturing anywhere in the South Pacific or Australia), Allerton and Gregg traveled on the Matson line. As historian Allan Bérubé has shown, many of those who worked on the Matson line—as waiters, pursers, cooks, room stewards, bartenders, bakers, and butchers—were gay men, primarily white because of racial exclusion in hiring. A gay cook and steward who worked the very ships that the couple took during the 1930s, and later went on to publish what he called *The Gay Cookbook* in 1965, explained that of the five hundred men working in the steward's department in the Matson company, "Probably 486 were actively gay!" Another former steward estimated the percentage somewhat lower at 65 to 70 percent, still a remarkably high figure. The gay stewards referred to the ships that Allerton and Gregg regularly took—the *Lurline*, the *Matsonia*, and the *Mariposa*—as the "Queer-line," the "Fruit-sonia," and the "Mary-posa" or the "Fairy-posa." Matson ships were more generically called fruit boats or fruit ships. Imagine for a moment what all of these gay employees must have made of Allerton and Gregg. While the pair did not book a single with only one bed on these cruises, they usually booked a suite with rooms that adjoined one another. In the late 1930s, Gregg was still a very handsome young man in his late thirties. Traveling with a father with whom he did not share a last name, one wonders what this large population of gay men who cooked for and served Allerton and Gregg thought of their relationship. By the 1930s, many gay men had also long embraced the notion that they could determine who among them was a fellow queer by voice, mannerism, and gesture. While calling themselves father and son might have allayed questioning by their fellow guests—at least those who did not want to appear rude—one suspects that there was a good deal more conversation belowdecks.[29]

We do not know what Allerton and Gregg thought of being surrounded by so many working-class gay men—their peers in one way—at precisely the same moment that they were also surrounded by so many of their social peers in the first-class cabins and dining rooms. Allerton and Gregg did comment about other aspects of their travels aboard the "fruit boats," however. At one point, Gregg complained that he found that women on board the ships did too much drinking. On another occasion, in November 1941 when the United States was gearing up for a possible war with Japan, he groused about other passengers on the ships:

We are loaded up with defense workers on this ship. They're all over the place and make the decks look like a cargo ship. We have 170 of them. Just laborers, traveling 1st class, under government contract. Also we have 70 army flyers in uniform and altogether, with no tourist to speak of, gives the ship a queer look. Poker games and men in shirt sleeves etc. everywhere. But otherwise a mostly delightful trip with warm sunshine and the sea full of flying fish.

"Queer" in this context likely did not mean "gay" for Gregg. Instead what he found most disturbing is that the soldiers on the *Lurline* should be sailing first class with himself and Allerton, rather than in some lesser class or, better yet, on another ship altogether. It seems likely, then, that Allerton and Gregg kept to themselves, avoiding socializing with the queer stewards all around them, especially if they feared their fellow passengers commenting upon their own relationship, which might have come into relief in the presence of so many other gay men. That said, there is a long history of middle- and upper-class gay men "slumming" with queer working-class men sexually. It is not beyond the realm of possibility that Gregg, in particular, might have arranged assignations with an attractive young waiter or purser while on board the "Fruit-sonia" or the "Mary-posa."[30]

Their travels often involved visiting other people or arranging to meet them in faraway locations. In Angkor, for instance, they toured with

Louise Dillingham and her son, Lowell. They traveled around Japan in 1952 with their Honolulu friends Marjorie and Robert Griffing. Of that trip, Gregg reported: "The last half of the trip we went completely Japanese, went to Japanese style hotels where we left our shoes at the door, slept on the floor, ate our meals in our rooms, Japanese food and even talk. It was great fun." They often visited Florida to see Frederic Bartlett, who had moved there permanently with his third wife, Evelyn. They visited other locations on the East Coast with regularity as well. In 1944 Gregg reported back from a trip to New York: "We saw the Atlantic Ocean and all the gay metropolitan life of the East which is quite different from the quiet of our Pacific." By the mid-1940s, Gregg could not have been unaware of the double meaning of the word "gay," especially as it related to New York's nightlife. In June of the same year, the *Chicago Daily Tribune* included them in an article devoted to Father's Day: "Among the many well known men balletomanes in the audience the most eagerly welcomed were Robert Allerton and John Gregg barely off the Clipper from Hawaii where they were spending the winter when the fateful Dec. 7, 1941, changed the way of life and thought of every American." Long after donating their Monticello home to the University of Illinois, they continued to return for visits, often combining them with other trips on the mainland, as in the summer of 1947, when they went on an extensive driving tour of the West Coast. Without a ballet to attend in Hawai'i, they often took in performances when they were back on the mainland. As Justin Spring has argued, midcentury queer men's love of ballet was as much about the art as it was "an opportunity to admire male beauty in a public setting, and at the same time to mix with others who shared [one's] taste for art, music, theater, and dance. . . . [A]t a time when the public gathering of homosexuals in bars and nightclubs was essentially forbidden by law, the lobby of the Civic Opera House was one of the better places in Chicago to meet a friend or find a date." While Allerton and Gregg were unlikely to be looking for dates, going to the ballet would have allowed them to socialize with their peers, both the Chicago elite like the Palmers and Bartletts and other queer men who flocked to the performances.[31]

In 1946 Gregg announced excitedly, "The Pan American is putting on a new flight of planes beginning today. Just 9 hours between here and the coast!" The advent of commercialized air travel revolutionized their vacationing, as it did the travel of all who could afford it. No longer would they travel on the "Queer-line"; instead they took Pan Am and other airlines in increasingly complex itineraries to all sorts of new destinations together. In April 1948, Gregg wrote back to Chicago from Fort Lauderdale, where they had been to visit Frederic and Evelyn Bartlett: "We have had a lovely visit here and leave in the morning for Nassau and then back to

FIGURE 6.4 Allerton and Gregg at the Great Buddha of Kamakura at the Kōtoku-in Temple, Japan, 1930s. Courtesy of the University of Illinois Archives.

Miami before going on to Cuba. Florida has been an eye opener to me and makes me realize how much better off we are in the Hawaiian islands. Too many people here to suit me. And most of them Jews." After Cuba they went on to the Yucatán Peninsula, then to San Francisco, before flying back to Kaua'i. Gregg here (and elsewhere) demonstrated his prejudice toward all the other people who were also making pilgrimages to sunny climates in his dismissal of the preponderance of Jews in Florida. Air and road travel had increasingly made it so that the vacations he was used to spending only with those of a certain class were now open to people from many more walks of life. They did, however, have a predilection for the islands of the Caribbean. Gregg explained of Port-au-Prince, Haiti, "It is a revelation to us that these places are so large and progressive. Such fine hotels and wonderful food and drink." In April 1949, they planned a trip to Bermuda for that summer by instructing their accountant, Herbert Gorsuch, to telephone "Mr. Olson at the Chicago Motor Club and ask him the name of the snappiest (not the biggest) hotel in Bermuda suitable for two gentlemen of refined habits." Gorsuch wrote back with recommendations, assuring them, "Both these hotels are restricted." During the 1950s and '60s, they would also venture to other destinations much closer to Hawai'i but farther away from the mainland United States: Fiji, Siam (Thailand), Ceylon (Sri Lanka), Hong Kong, Singapore, the Philippines, Japan, and India. They also continued travels to Europe, in the spring of 1956 visiting Ireland, Scotland, England, Sweden, Norway, and Denmark.[32]

Being able to call themselves father and son—no matter what any of those around them believed them to really be—was a convenient way not to have to talk about their relationship with the countless strangers they met on their journeys. These included the staff who served them on cruise ships, hotels, and airlines and the locals in any of the places they visited who toured and chauffeured them. It also applied to all the people of their own social class—fellow Americans as well as Europeans, Asians, and Latin Americans—that they met on tour, at dinner, and on deck when they were sailing. Regardless of whether these new acquaintances believed that Allerton and Gregg really behaved as father and son—and surely many of them did not—speaking of their relationship in these terms would have diminished the awkwardness that might otherwise have characterized conversations between the two men and those they met on their travels.

Being father and son also helped them in their day-to-day lives at Lawai-Kai. As we have already seen, Allerton and Gregg liked to entertain. Their guests included people they knew from Chicago and other parts of the mainland, as well those they had met in the islands, sometimes through connections back home. But they opened their home to other visitors as well, including people they had not previously known, including US soldiers during the war and the actors and crews making films and using Lawai-Kai as part of their set. Word of their hospitality clearly spread, and they welcomed friends of friends who happened to be in the islands for a vacation. They were proud of the home they had created on the southern shore of Kaua'i and were often eager to show it off. While their status as hosts in these situations allowed them to set the terms by which their guests would be welcomed and able to interact with them, once again being father and son proved helpful in situations where they did not already know their visitors. Though Lawai-Kai remained a private residence, it was already on its way to becoming the public park that they would make it after their deaths.

On one occasion in 1942, Allerton and Gregg played host to soldiers stationed in Hawai'i during World War II. As Allerton wrote to Murphy, "The multitude of soldiers stationed all around us think this place Paradise, especially swimming in the river & eating our coconuts. They are a wonderfully fine lot of boys from every where all very serious & anxious to do their job." While historians have demonstrated that the Second World War represented a watershed moment in queer history for how it brought queer people together in unprecedented ways, it was still the case that the United States military explicitly discriminated against homosexuals, screening for homosexuality in recruitment and conscription, barring them from serving, and sometimes discharging those suspected of homosexuality from the ranks with a "blue ticket" that was neither honorable nor dishonorable but was often read as proof of homosexuality.[33]

That Allerton and Gregg lived as father and son allowed them to entertain members of the military, just as it allowed Gregg to serve in that military, albeit in a voluntary capacity as a lieutenant for the Kaua'i Home Guard. Without the father/son cover, no matter how flimsy, it is unlikely that he would have been chosen for this position or that the US Army would have consented to have a photographer from *Life* magazine take pictures of soldiers at Lawai-Kai, as it did in October 1942. As Gregg explained, "We had fun last Sunday when the correspondent and photographer from LIFE were here to take pictures of the Army boys in swimming. The boys have invented a new way to ride the waves." Apparently they inflated canvas bags and then rode the breakers in toward shore as if they were on surfboards. A crew of shirtless young American soldiers frolicked on the beach, swimming and picnicking while a magazine photographer took their picture and two bachelors looked on, presumably admiring the nation's finest from their front-row seats. This is a queer spectacle that was made possible by the fact that Allerton and Gregg presented themselves as father and son. Similarly, in April 1945, Gregg and Allerton were treated to a tour of military readiness in Honolulu when they were visiting the territorial capital. "We had a good time and stayed a week instead of the two days we had planned. Everyone was good to us and feted us and showed hospitals, jungle training centers, air bases, plane motor assembly lines etc that were far beyond our wildest dreams." Their queerness as bachelors was trumped in this instance by their class, the cover of father and son providing all that was necessary for them to be welcomed by the US military.[34]

Both of their homes in Kaua'i were used as movie sets. They allowed the film *Naked Paradise* to film at the Hā'ena property on the north end of the island in 1956. The film, released in 1957, starred Richard Denning, Beverly Garland, and Leslie Bradley and told the story of thieves trying to escape from a tropical island after a botched robbery. *South Pacific* was partially shot at Lawai-Kai, with the whole movie filming over a total of nine weeks in various other parts of the island of Kaua'i, including the beach at Hā'ena. In 1963 *Donovan's Reef*, starring John Wayne and Lee Marvin, also filmed part of its storyline on the Allerton estate.

In the midst of all this attention to Lawai-Kai, Allerton and Gregg again welcomed a *Life* photographer and his wife for a ten-day visit in 1957, during which they hosted a tour for forty "ladies and gentlemen" affiliated with the Honolulu Garden Club. A full-page spread covered the visit in the *Honolulu Star-Bulletin*, which noted that "luncheon for the more than 40 guests was served in the 40-foot, white-walled dining room and on a portion of the lanai." The accompanying photographs show Allerton leading the ladies of the Garden Club on a tour of the estate. Lawai-Kai was subsequently featured as the inaugural garden in a series of articles in *Life* dedicated to great gardens. The eight-page photo spread, entitled "Great Tropic Garden: A Hawaiian Landscape Is Made into an Ordered Jungle," primarily focused on foliage, as well as statuary and architecture, and contained little in the way of commentary, but a small picture of the pair on the last page explained that Robert Allerton "and his adopted son John Gregg" had also developed Allerton Park in Monticello. It is unlikely that *Life* would have chosen to feature the estate had Allerton and Gregg been more open about their relationship; this was, after all, six years before *Life*'s 1964 infamous feature story on "Homosexuality in America" with the byline: "A secret world grows open and bolder. Society is forced to look at it—and try to understand it." While that story was not entirely unsympathetic, it certainly treated homosexuals as tortured and abnormal creatures unable to speak with expertise about their own lives. By contrast, the story about Allerton and Gregg's tropical garden treated their relationship as incidental to the story; they were relevant only as creators of the garden, not because of who they were to one another. Their filial claims made this coverage possible, as it had operated in so many other aspects of their lives together.[35]

From the 1920s through the 1960s, Robert Allerton and John Gregg fashioned two queer domestic spaces: The Farms and Lawai-Kai. As two single men devoted to a life of beauty, they developed homes and gardens to suit their tastes and those guests they chose to invite inside their world. Without an established tradition of what a queer domestic space might look like, they relied on their own aesthetic, architectural, and horticultural training to craft places that were pleasing to the eye and that met their exacting standards. All the while they publicly identified as father and son, relying on filial claims in order both to move about the world unscathed and to invite that world into their homes. Their class position allowed for the full flourish of their aesthetic sensibilities, and that same privilege also necessitated an explanation for why they chose to share a domestic space with one another.

At the same time, the way that they structured this relationship between two men separated by age and wealth really did resemble that of a wealthy father and his son, or an older and wealthier husband and his devoted younger wife. Allerton was fully in charge of the finances, even as he worked to grant Gregg a modicum of fiscal independence, especially as he grew older. And Gregg cared for Allerton as he aged, assuming greater responsibility for him as he reached his eighties and nineties, as we will see in the final chapter.

Chapter Seven

Legally Father and Son

By the late 1950s, Robert Allerton's and John Gregg's lives had fallen into a predictable rhythm: they spent their winters at Lawai-Kai, entertaining friends, family, and other visitors, and they traveled during the spring and summer: back to the mainland to see friends in Chicago, check in at The Farms, further afield to Europe, Asia, and the Caribbean. In 1958 Allerton turned eighty-five and it is clear that he was experiencing more health problems as he aged and was generally becoming frailer. Friends of Allerton's generation also began to die. Frederic Bartlett, his exact contemporary in terms of age, had died in 1953 at age eighty. Potter Palmer Jr. had died a decade earlier. Countess Ethel Beatty (née Field), also Allerton's exact age and his childhood playmate, had died in 1932. Walter and Louise Dillingham would die in 1963 and 1964, respectively. Because of his advanced age, Allerton and Gregg began to solidify plans for the fate of Allerton's estate and Gregg's inheritance after his death. While the pair had been transferring property into Gregg's name for some time and Gregg had been included in Allerton's will for many years by this point, Allerton was in the habit of revising his will to include others or modify the terms of various inheritances. Allerton's last will was finalized just eight months prior to his death. Another step in their plan was for Allerton legally to adopt Gregg, to secure in the law what they had been claiming for decades. This had not been possible in 1922, when they first met, but Illinois changed its law in 1959 and the adoption was completed in 1960. They also planned for what would happen to Lawai-Kai, when Gregg, too, had passed away. Neither had a direct descendant, though both certainly had siblings with children, and they needed to be sure that their wishes would be followed after their deaths.[1]

This period—the late 1950s and early 1960s—was also a crucial one for gay and lesbian people in the United States, and for same-sex couples. After a period of relative openness and self-discovery fostered by the Second World War, the early years of the Cold War brought renewed persecution of those discovered to be gay or lesbian, who were fired from jobs in the federal government and across the country in other fields, especially education. Psychiatrists and psychologists pathologized same-sex attraction in their writings and their treatments, recommending conversion and electroshock therapy. And police entrapment and raids targeted the men who frequented gay bars, clubs, and cruising areas like parks and public bathrooms. The media paid more attention to homosexuality during the 1950s, even if most of the coverage was negative. Gregg and Allerton could not have been immune to reading about popular perceptions of homosexuality, even as they continued to live within the insular cocoon of their wealth and their filial cover story. They would have been well aware that increasing numbers of people would suspect them of being homosexual, even if most people were unlikely to say anything about it.[2]

In 1948 Alfred Kinsey and his team of researchers at Indiana University published *Sexual Behavior in the Human Male* (the volume on the human female followed in 1953), which demonstrated, among other things, that 37 percent of American men had engaged in sexual relations with another man to the point of orgasm. Approximately 8 percent identified as exclusively homosexual in their behaviors and fantasies. While the reports caused a nationwide scandal, they also proved reassuring to many gay and lesbian people who increasingly learned that they were not alone, and that many of their behaviors were quite normal, at least statistically speaking. In 1951 Edward Sagarin, writing under the pseudonym Donald Webster Cory, published *The Homosexual in America: A Subjective Approach*, in which he advocated for the civil rights of gay people, for their fundamental humanity, and against their continued persecution. At the same time, a wide swath of other commercial publishing enterprises—from physique magazines, to book club services, to newsletters and semi-secretive dating services—were developed throughout the 1950s and '60s catering primarily to the needs, both erotic and intellectual, of gay men. While conversations about what constituted homosexuality were hardly new at midcentury, it was a pivotal moment during which homosexuals were coming to understand how commonplace they were and were beginning to speak on their own behalf.[3]

Nothing illustrates this phenomenon better than the birth of homophile activism. Precisely because many gay and lesbian people had formed communities as a result of the Second World War, they were also in a much better position to fight back against persecution and discrimination. Forming together in a number of different organizations—beginning with the Mattachine Society in 1950 and the Daughters of Bilitis in 1955—so-called homophile activists began to publish newsletters, exchange information, stage protests, and work to educate the public about homosexuality as actual homosexuals understood their lives. These activists asserted that there was nothing wrong with being gay; the problem lay with societal persecution of homosexuals, who, after all, were not harming anyone by being gay. While historians have demonstrated that some of this initial activism was limited in scope and not particularly confrontational, by the 1960s a number of chapters of various organizations had taken their protests to the streets and were becoming increasingly insistent about their rights as US citizens to live without persecution.[4]

By the late 1950s, then, Robert Allerton and John Gregg bore witness to mounting evidence not only that there were queer people all over the United States—which they had known anyway—but also that more and more gay and lesbian people were choosing to publicly self-identify as such. Their choice to live as father and son was becoming increasingly anachronistic; it had made sense in 1922 when they first met, but was starting to look like a product of its time by 1960. I do not want to overstate the case here: gay couples and queer people met with enough persecution that it is likely that most remained closeted at work and with their natal families. However, unlike in earlier eras, midcentury America was much more cognizant of how widespread the phenomenon called homosexuality was. A pair of men, even ones asymmetrically aged like Allerton and Gregg, would have been far less likely to try to begin presenting themselves as father and son in the early 1960s, precisely because it would have been less believable. Indeed, increasing numbers of queer couples availed themselves of the option of legal adoption, but without the pretense to those around them that they *really* were father and son, mother and daughter; instead it had become a legal workaround in the absence of civil partnerships or marriage. Allerton and Gregg's solution to same-sex couplehood was beginning to seem like one of an earlier era. And yet they persisted because it was how they had always publicly presented themselves and also because they were about to pursue legal adoption and did not want to call their relationship into question. Being father and son remained a compelling narrative that allowed them to navigate the world beyond Lawai-Kai.

Throughout the 1950s and '60s, Allerton and Gregg entertained a number of gay couples at Lawai-Kai or made the estate available to these couples if they were traveling elsewhere. We know this because letters from these visitors survive in the archives of the library of the National Tropical Botanical Garden. It is entirely possible that Allerton and Gregg socialized quite regularly with other gay people throughout their lives, as we know that Allerton did abroad before he met Gregg; if that was the case, the evidence has not survived, likely because Allerton and Gregg were discreet. Associating openly with gay people made them more likely to be seen as gay themselves. But inviting them into the privacy of their home was another matter altogether. These visits are also worth considering because they were some of the rare occasions that Allerton and Gregg would be treated *as* gay people. While relatives and friends understood the open secret that was their relationship, they abided by its fiction when they visited and socialized with the Allertons. All of that was unnecessary with other same-sex couples, some of whom were much more publicly gay than the Allertons ever felt they could be. The conversations that could be had with other queer men would have been close to unique for Allerton and Gregg. Not only could they speak about queer culture and shared interests in opera and the arts, but they could also speak about what it was like to move about in the world as a same-sex couple and the strategies that they employed to do so.

Among these visitors were Howard Greer, a fashion and costume designer based in Los Angeles, and his partner, Max. In 1954 Greer wrote to thank Allerton and Gregg for their hospitality when he and Max had visited Hawai'i and the gardens at Lawai-Kai. Greer had met with much success in Hollywood, working for studios like Paramount and as a fashion designer making clothes worn, on- and off-screen, by Shirley Temple, Katharine Hepburn, Rita Hayworth, Joan Crawford, and others. In 1949 he published *Designing Male*, about his years in the business. We don't know how Greer and his partner were introduced to Allerton and Gregg, but their correspondence makes it clear that they had known each other for some time. In writing to thank them for their hospitality, Greer gave them advice about where to visit on their upcoming trip to Portugal, and to urge them to be in touch as they passed through Los Angeles en route to Europe: "Couldn't we corral some of your friends for drinks on that evening . . . or will you be up to your ears in other people??"[5]

At some point during this period (the letter is undated), Allerton and Gregg hosted another Hollywood costume designer, Walter Plunkett. In writing to thank them, Plunkett explained, "I've tried to describe some of the wonder and beauty of your place—but find I cannot. It is most certainly the loveliest I've ever seen." He, too, hoped that they would be in touch when next they were visiting the mainland. It is also unclear how Plunkett had come to know Allerton and Gregg, though it is certainly possible that Greer had put them in touch. The two likely knew each other; both were very successful gay men working in the same industry. Plunkett's letter does not say whether his partner, Lee, had accompanied him on this trip, a partner he would later legally adopt in order to insure his inheritance rights. It would be difficult to believe that the two pairs of men did not discuss the strategy that both couples used in order to secure their same-sex partnerships.[6]

Around the same time, another man named Raymond wrote to thank Allerton for his hospitality, expressing much gratitude for the tour of

Lawai-Kai and for Gregg showing Raymond and his (male) friend Whitney around the island. He confirmed that he expected Allerton and Gregg for dinner when they were in San Francisco to see Lily Pons at the opera. Like Plunkett, we don't know how Raymond had come to be a visitor at Lawai-Kai. Historians have demonstrated that many gay men formed informal networks of contacts to introduce one another to other gay men with whom they might socialize when they visited new places. While some of these contacts were explicitly sexual, in others they were simply friendly. In the case of Allerton and Gregg, it is likely that gay men and others who appreciated landscape design (sometimes overlapping categories) were aware of their presence in Kaua'i, especially after magazine articles began to feature their estate. Indeed, as Raymond explained, "I have been singing your praises in Honolulu and here at home, only to find many people know about you and your fabulous gardens, so you see you are famous."[7]

In 1956 Allerton and Gregg received a lengthy letter from a male couple who referred to themselves as the "Swissers" because they lived in Zurich. The letter demonstrates that at least one of them had spent considerable time in Honolulu, which is perhaps where they had met Allerton and Gregg. They also had a friend in common. The four men shared a love of art and music, and the writer of the letter, Hugh (no last name given), told them a good deal about what had been exhibited at the Zurich Art Museum over the last year and what shows had played at the opera and the symphony. Hugh and his partner, Ernest, may or may not have been to Kaua'i; Allerton and Gregg definitely had been to Zurich to visit them. In imagining a visit to Lawai-Kai and the dinner party—perhaps Japanese themed, he hoped—Hugh wrote: "We wonder what costume we would select for the evening, what to put on, or take off—and how much? It's fun to imagine oneself in such surroundings, partaking of that which is quite impossible in person but possible in imagination." Like Allerton and Gregg, Hugh had earlier alluded to his fondness for nudity in his garden in Zurich: "In fact the seclusion is greater than one can even find in any vacation-place, for where, please tell me, can one or could one strip completely and take in the sun, where there IS sun to take in?—save in one's own garden."[8]

These four letters are both revealing and frustrating, simultaneously. They demonstrate that Allerton and Gregg, for all of their involvement in the mostly heterosexual social scenes of Kaua'i, Honolulu, and Chicago, also had gay connections that spanned the globe. This is not terribly surprising, given that Allerton had been socializing with other queer men since the later nineteenth century, and also because, for all of their claims to filial status, they remained two biologically unrelated men sharing a home together. They were read as queer no matter what they called themselves. This would have been particularly so when they socialized with other queer men. The letters are tantalizing, however, for everything that they do not reveal: how the couples all met one another; whether they had many friends in common who had facilitated the introductions; the invisible queer network of wealthy and well-connected men that arranged for these contacts at a moment in US history when homosexuality was persecuted and men and women in a variety of fields were losing their livelihoods because of their sexual predilections. These friendships and the details they reveal about the correspondents' lives also highlight the security of wealth and the ability to work in certain industries—like Hollywood costume design—where homosexuality was either ignored or quietly tolerated if it remained discreet. Allerton and Gregg had met when being together publicly necessitated a cover story; increasingly gay men, especially those who enjoyed similar wealth and privilege, could opt not to disguise the nature of their relationships. Allerton and Gregg, because they had relied on the cover of kinship for so long by midcentury, felt unable to abandon it. Indeed, it was during this era that they legally secured their filial ties.

In the late 1950s, at the same time that they were entertaining queer friends at Lawai-Kai and traveling to the mainland and abroad to see yet others, Allerton and Gregg, in consultation with a lawyer, began the process of securing in law what they had been publicly claiming for many years. Allerton would adopt Gregg as his legal son. When the two had first met in the 1920s, the legal adoption of an adult child was not an option in Illinois, though it was possible in some other states. At least initially, the pair may not have known that this was something they wanted to pursue, regardless. Allerton could not have known in 1922 how devoted Gregg would prove himself to be. By the late 1950s, however, they had been together for almost four decades. Legal adoption would secure in law what they already knew to be true.

As historians of adoption have documented, informal adoption was remarkably common before and after the advent of legal adoption in the mid-nineteenth century. Many children throughout American history have been raised by people, often kin, who were not their biological parents. When legal adoption was first developed in the 1850s in Massachusetts, it was a vehicle explicitly designed to give adopted children the legal—and not just the social—benefits of kinship. First among these was the right to inherit in the same manner as biological children. Until legal adoption, and barring a will that explicitly named them as beneficiaries, adopted children would have had no inheritance rights to a parent's estate if that parent died intestate, that is, without a will. Legal adoption was radical in one sense in that it declared the adopted child to be legally the same as biological offspring.[9]

In using adoption law, the Allertons may thus not have been all that uncommon, if indeed protecting Allerton's inheritance for Gregg was their primary purpose via the adoption. But in another way, they were certainly atypical. The vast majority of adoptions have concerned minors, and even adult adoption, which became available in selected states in the 1920s and increased by the mid-twentieth century, has generally been employed retroactively to legitimize a relationship that began with actual parenting of a child by an adult: a stepparent, for instance. Allerton and Gregg, while not unique in employing the practice to unite one person who did not actually raise the second, were certainly uncommon. After all, Gregg had *already* been raised by a set of parents from whom he had also already inherited.[10]

They were also on the front end of a tiny but growing movement of same-sex couples who used adult-child adoption in order to legally secure their relationships. Historians have demonstrated that in nineteenth- and early twentieth-century Italy, which had a longer history of recognizing adult-child adoption, same-sex couples employed the device to validate their ties. It is possible that Allerton, who had traveled throughout Europe, including Italy, at the turn of the century and beyond, had been inspired by this model of family when he invited Gregg to be his son in the 1920s. In later years, other same-sex couples asymmetrically separated in age also entered into adult-child adoptions. It may be that they were partially inspired by age difference to consider the strategy, or the elder partner's more foreseeable demise led them to consider adoption as a way to secure an inheritance. Civil rights leader Bayard Rustin, for instance, adopted his longtime partner, Walter Naegle, in 1982. The two were separated by thirty-eight years and had met in 1977. As Naegle explained of the reasoning behind their entering into an adoption, "'Well, I think because of our age difference—it was just assumed if we lived out our natural lifespans he was going to die before I did.'" Rustin was concerned about protecting Naegle's rights following Rustin's passing, particularly his right to stay on in the rent-controlled apartment that was in Rustin's name as well as the right to inherit his estate uncontested by Rustin's relatives. Both were explicitly monetary concerns. Naegle recounted the process by which Rustin was able to adopt him in 1982:

"We actually had to go through a process as if Bayard was adopting a small child," [Naegle said]—even though he was in his 30s at the time. "My biological mother had to sign a legal paper, a paper disowning me. They had to send a social worker to our home. When the social worker arrived, she had to sit down with us to talk to us to make sure that this was a fit home."

There is no evidence to suggest that Allerton and Gregg underwent any such similar process, in part because they were not even in Illinois when the adoption took place, the location being chosen because they had maintained Illinois as a legal residence and because Illinois had finally amended its code to allow for adult-child adoption.[11]

Recall that Allerton and Gregg's friend Walter Plunkett and his partner, Lee, who visited Lawai-Kai, also used adoption in order to secure inheritance rights and gain legal recognition for their relationship. Others also considered this strategy. Francis Rose, a wealthy English aristocrat who was involved sexually with both men and women (and had married a woman), had considered adopting his younger lover, Luis, as a means to ensure that Luis would inherit his titles. Instead, he began to insist that Luis was actually his illegitimate son, born of a brief liaison with a Spanish woman named Pilar. While most in their circle did not believe what was likely a fiction, the impulses that propelled some couples toward adoption also governed Rose's efforts: employ the law in order to grant a younger partner certain rights following the death of the elder.[12]

In 1971 Jack Baker, a gay rights activist and law student at the University of Minnesota, was adopted by his lover, Michael McConnell, after they had been denied a marriage license. In their case, the adoption was partially used as a means to attract publicity to their cause, but a reporter for *Time* magazine also explained that "McConnell and Baker were basically trying to legitimize their association as best they could, but they say they also had inheritance rights in mind." The reporter also predicted that the pair would be eligible for a residential tuition discount and a head-of-household tax deduction. In 1977, famed midcentury writer Christopher Isherwood adopted his longtime—and much younger—partner, Don Bachardy, after they had been together for about twenty-five years. The pair had always lived publicly as a gay couple, even though Bachardy was sometimes taken by strangers to be Isherwood's son, given Bachardy's youth when they met (he was eighteen) and their age difference (thirty years). While they were using adoption only for its legal benefits, it was also the case that both Isherwood and Bachardy—like Allerton and Gregg—sometimes compared their relationship to that of a father and his son. As Isherwood wrote early on in their relationship, "This sense of responsibility, which was almost fatherly, made me anxious, but full of joy." Isherwood paid for four years of art school for Bachardy, who became a painter. At Bachardy's first art show, in London, Isherwood described himself sitting off to the side watching Bachardy interact with attendees: "I put on a rather disparaging expression, like a parent who fears to show his pride." As Bachardy recounted after Isherwood's death, "He often said he'd never been denied any of the pleasures and satisfactions of a parent because he met me when I was young enough that he could still have an enormous influence on my development and this was

our crowning achievement." Because Isherwood and Bachardy were separated in age enough that they really could have been father and son—
unlike some same-sex couples who only used the legal tool of adoption to
secure an inheritance—they analogized their relationship to one of filial
kinship, much as Walt Whitman did with his younger male companions
in the nineteenth century.[13]

The reasons that Allerton and Gregg chose adoption are open to debate,
but they are all suggested by the motives of other couples who also used
the strategy of adopting a same-sex partner, albeit in adoptions that occurred after Gregg's by Allerton. Four reasons seem possible: to reduce inheritance taxes; to safeguard Gregg's inheritance; to make legal what the
couple already lived in practice, one consequence of which was to allow
Gregg to make medical decisions on Allerton's behalf should he be incapacitated; and to declare publicly and symbolically through the law and its
attendant publicity the filial feelings they shared. All may be valid. While
the federal government would claim taxes on the value of the estate, not
each individual legacy, at the time Illinois (where the will was probated)
also had an additional inheritance tax on each bequest to an individual.
In the two years after adult adoption was made legal in Illinois, an official
at the Cook County court explained that "most adult adoptions are conducted for the purpose of saving on the state inheritance tax. A legal heir
can exempt the first $20,000 of an estate while a 'stranger' can exempt
only $100." As a legal son, Gregg would have been taxed at a lower rate and
allotted a greater exemption. It is possible that Allerton and Gregg sought
adoption to avoid these higher taxes, but considering the size of the estate, these savings would have been relatively minimal.[14]

When the adoption took place in 1960, four years before Allerton's
death in 1964, Allerton had been planning for how to provide for Gregg for
twenty years. His final will, dated April 1964, distributed some $21.5 mil-
lion to many people and institutions, and while Gregg was certainly
named, he was not the chief beneficiary; the Art Institute of Chicago and
the Honolulu Academy of Arts were. While a legally executed will could
have declared Gregg a beneficiary regardless of his relationship to Allerton, the adoption would have made the will less contestable and more
securely protected Gregg's inheritance: $3 million in trust and all of Al-
lerton's property on the island of Kaua'i. Legal scholars have seen inheritance as the primary reason that people have sought legal adult-child
adoption.[15] It remains unclear, however, whether anyone would have contested the will in the first place. Allerton's closest biological relative at
the time of his death was his surviving nephew, Vanderburgh Johnstone.
Johnstone was also named in the will and was already a rich man, having
inherited his mother's share of the Allerton fortune. He had also spent a

good deal of time with both Allerton and Gregg; it thus seems unlikely that the person in the best position to contest the will would have done so. That said, he had standing as an heir at-law and there was certainly precedent for contesting a will on the grounds of "undue influence," especially in the case of a nonrelative inheriting a substantial portion of an estate. We cannot know whether Allerton believed Johnstone (or another relative) would have contested the will, particularly given the long-standing filial claims of Allerton and Gregg. As legal historian Lawrence Friedman puts it, "Wills that violated social norms were certainly vulnerable; but the word 'vulnerable' is not a synonym for 'doomed.'"[16]

All of this is to say that it is quite possible that Robert Allerton adopted John Gregg because he saw it as an opportunity to actualize in the law the status that they had claimed for their then-thirty-eight years together. The Illinois legislature had made adult-child adoption legally possible at the end of 1959, and so they became father and son because that is what they believed themselves already to be; courts and other state statutes since then have also recognized this desire to publicly legitimate a relationship as a basis for adult adoption.[17] It may also be that as Allerton aged, the pair sought to legally recognize Gregg as a son so that he might make medical decisions on Allerton's behalf if Allerton himself was not able to do so. This is certainly possible, but given the widespread acceptance of their relationship as father and son by many, some of whom did not actually know that it was not legally so until 1960, it seems unlikely. After all, their wealth and long-standing relationships with various doctors and hospitals in Kaua'i and Illinois had already paved the way for Gregg to make decisions on Allerton's behalf. At the moment of the adoption, the First National Bank claimed it was one of Allerton's "greatest dreams," and Allerton himself, writing to friends, said: "Our lawyer has taken advantage of the new Ill. Adoption law + at last John is my legal son. I am very happy." The third and fourth reasons for the adoption converge here: the law made real the status that the couple had already claimed for thirty-eight years. It created a father and a son. But the law may also have legitimized the way the two men already felt about each other. The latter two reasons were certainly those emphasized by the Allertons themselves and thus complicate any understanding of the pair as straightforwardly "gay"; their legal actualization of the claims to being father and son further demonstrates the queerness of their union. Even as more and more gay men and women were coming out of the closet during this era—either by choice or by force—Allerton and Gregg were only becoming more firmly entrenched in their identities as father and son.[18]

On March 5, 1960, the *Chicago Tribune* announced that Allerton had adopted Gregg in the Piatt County Courthouse in Monticello. Judge Henry Timmons Dighton, who shared a surname with some of Allerton's cousins, oversaw the decree. Dighton must have long known about Allerton's relationship with Gregg—indeed, everyone in Monticello did. Allerton and Gregg were not present in court when the adoption decree was issued. Forrest N. Williams, vice president of the First National Bank of Chicago, represented the two there because the new father and son were in Hawai'i.[19] Williams issued a statement on behalf of the pair explaining, "Under a recent change in the Illinois law which became effective the first of this year, [Allerton] has finally been able to legally adopt John Wyatt Gregg who has stood in the relationship of a son for thirty years." It was this announcement that prompted papers in Illinois and Hawai'i to write their own stories, discussed in the introduction, in which they tried to parse out what it meant for a man to adopt someone he already claimed as his own son. Was he a companion? A friend? Or something else entirely? In 1960 the public announcement of a legal adoption of one man by another made the relationship look much queerer than it already had been perceived, precisely because it called into question the beginnings of the relationship itself and the reasons for its existence. The 1920s origins of the relationship, understood in a transformed midcentury world, seemed more suspect than they would have forty years earlier.[20]

In order to ensure their legacy, there was one last step that Robert Allerton and John Gregg wanted to take. Having already donated The Farms to the University of Illinois, they now set about determining the fate of Lawai-Kai and the rest of Allerton's fortune. In June 1963, Allerton gave an additional half a million dollars to the Art Institute of Chicago, making him its greatest living benefactor. In recognition of his generosity and his service as a board member, in 1968 the AIC would name the entrance wing on Michigan Avenue in his honor.[21]

Allerton and Gregg had long welcomed visitors at Lawai-Kai, and they wanted to be able to ensure that the garden paradise they had developed on the southern shore of Kaua'i would live on, not just as a legacy to their own design aesthetic, but in order to ensure the appreciation and survival of the flora of Hawai'i. And yet neither of them had a direct descendant to whom they could entrust the property and the task of its maintenance. Allerton's wealth and connections presented him with numerous options, however. In the early 1960s, he and four other wealthy philanthropists—Henry Francis du Pont of Delaware, Deane Waldo Malott of New York, Horace Marden Albright of California, and Paul Bigelow Sears of Connecticut—petitioned the US Congress to establish the

Pacific Tropical Botanical Garden as a federally chartered nonprofit botanical garden to serve the public's interest. As Section Three of that charter reads, the PTBG's original mandate was

to establish, develop, operate, and maintain for the benefit of the people of the United States an educational and scientific center in the form of a tropical botanical garden or gardens, together with such facilities as libraries, herbaria, laboratories, and museums which are appropriate and necessary for encouraging and conducting research in basic and applied tropical botany.

The Pacific (renamed National in 1988) Tropical Botanical Garden remains the only tropical botanical garden with a charter—issued August 19, 1964—from the US Congress. The act established the PTBG as a corporation to be run by a board of directors, including its five founding members, of up to fifteen people. In order to get the garden up and running, Allerton made an initial gift of $75,000, and when he was unable to attend the first official meeting of the board of directors, he made an additional gift of $1 million in December 1964, just months after the official establishment of the PTBG. In order for the PTBG to function, it would need to have a home, and gifts like the one made by Allerton would ensure that the board of trustees would be able to buy land for that home and construct offices to manage the garden. The board was also cognizant that a number of its most generous supporters—including Allerton and Gregg—would make donations and posthumous bequests of land in the future that would constitute the actual gardens that future generations might visit and where the horticultural work of the organization would be carried out.[22]

Almost as if he knew that he could finally rest easily now that the Pacific Tropical Botanical Garden had been established, Robert Henry Allerton died on December 22, 1964. He had fallen and broken his hip, after which he had been transported to the Wilcox Hospital in Līhu'e, where he died after succumbing to coronary thrombosis. Obituaries ran in most of the major newspapers, including the *Washington Post*, the *Chicago Tribune*, and papers in Hawai'i and downstate Illinois. All of the obituaries detailed his lifelong history of philanthropy—especially gifts to the Art Institute of Chicago, the Honolulu Academy of Arts, and the Pacific Tropical Botanical Garden. The *Chicago Sun-Times* closed its obituary by noting that "Mr. Allerton never married. He is survived by his adopted son, John Wyatt Gregg."[23]

Allerton's will, dated April 1, 1964, was probated in the Piatt County Circuit Court, where both Allerton and Gregg still claimed legal residence. The will distributed approximately $21.5 million in assets, about $175 million in today's dollars. Of this, Allerton left all real property—including the house and its contents in Kaua'i and any real estate in Illinois—to Gregg, as well as $3 million in trust. He left a number of trusts and bequests in amounts ranging from $100,000 to $1,000 to his closest relation, nephew Vanderburgh Johnstone, and to other relatives, as well as to friends and employees in Kaua'i and in Illinois. The remainder of the estate, which was approximately $15 million, was to be divided, two-thirds going to a trust for the Art Institute of Chicago and the remaining third into a trust for the Honolulu Academy of Arts. Gregg and the First National Bank of Chicago would act as trustees. Allerton had left Gregg with more than enough money on which to live out his days in the home on Kaua'i. In consultation with Gregg himself, he had also left the bulk of his estate to two of the organizations to which he had been most dedicated throughout his life.[24]

At Allerton's request, there was no funeral. His body was cremated and the ashes scattered in the ocean off the coast of Lawai-Kai. As Gregg explained: "He didn't want any part of him in Monticello." "He said when you look out at the ocean think of me." Robert Henry Allerton had lived an extraordinary life of ninety-one years, one made possible by the wealthy family into which he had been born. He had circled the globe countless times, entertained lavishly, and collected and donated millions of dollars' worth of precious artwork to many institutions. Perhaps most notably, he designed and eventually bequeathed to the public two stunning estates that combine Western and Eastern design aesthetics, especially in the many garden rooms that surround the two very different structures. He had also left behind an adopted son to carry on his legacy.[25]

Conclusion
John Wyatt Gregg Allerton

On January 15, 1965, just a few weeks after the death of Robert Allerton, John Gregg filed notice in the Piatt County, Illinois circuit clerk's office that he was intending to change his name to John Wyatt Gregg Allerton. The hearing on Gregg's petition was conducted on January 25 of that year, just one day prior to the probate of Allerton's will. According to Gregg, Allerton had suggested the name change at the time of the adoption, but Gregg had resisted because "I had become established with [the name] John Wyatt Gregg and [Allerton] said that it didn't make any difference" to him whether Gregg changed it or not. Later, however, Gregg said he "saw the wisdom of his idea and I changed my name right after he died because if I was going to carry on all the things that he had started I didn't want to have the Gregg name and the donations that I would give with the Allerton money, I didn't want them to be Gregg donations." Like a son—or a wife—who carried on the legacy of their wealthier father or husband, Gregg had fully become an Allerton, albeit after the death of his father/ partner. In explaining his choice to a woman interviewing him a number of years later, he said: "After all, you are going to change your name after you get married, aren't you, so I didn't find it difficult." Gregg here analogized himself to the position of a wife, eliding the differences between his same-sex partnership and that of the heterosexual union he expected of his interlocutor.[1]

In the years following his father's death to his own, in 1986, John Gregg Allerton did continue to make gifts in the Allerton name to a number of the institutions that Robert had always supported. In 1975 the Board of Trustees of the University of Illinois honored John Gregg Allerton with its Distinguished Service Medallion. He continued to travel the world, spending considerable time in East Asia in particular. Most years he also returned to Allerton Park for a visit. As he explained on one of those annual visits, where he stayed in a small cottage on the grounds, "I feel closer to my father when I'm here than I do any other place, because he created

In accordance with the joint wishes

of my adoptive father,

ROBERT ALLERTON

and myself, commencing March 1, 1965

my name will be

JOHN WYATT GREGG ALLERTON

FIGURE C.1 John Wyatt Gregg Allerton name-change announcement. Courtesy of the University of Illinois Archives.

this place. So I feel his spirit is still zooming around here. So I really come back to be with my father also."[2]

When he was not in Illinois or abroad, Gregg Allerton lived at Lawai-Kai, where his paid companion, Toshio Kaneko, saw to his everyday needs (Kaneko also traveled with him). John also continued to work on behalf of the Pacific Tropical Botanical Garden. As we saw in chapter 5, in 1974 he exchanged a portion of his land at Hā'ena, which the state wanted to turn into a park, for land owned by the state of Hawai'i that abutted the PTBG land that had been purchased with Robert Allerton's initial donation. John was continuing the stewardship that he and Robert had begun years earlier. He remained dedicated to the land at Lawai-Kai for an additional twenty-one years following the death of Allerton. When Hurricane

Iwa hit Kaua'i in November 1982, for instance, it caused major damage, and John rebuilt and replanted in its wake.[3]

John Wyatt Gregg Allerton died at the Kaua'i Veterans Memorial Hospital on May 1, 1986, having undergone elective heart surgery a few weeks earlier. He was eighty-six years old. Like his adoptive father before him, he was cremated and his ashes were scattered over Lawa'i Bay without a ceremony. John's will left $400,000 in trust to the Honolulu Academy of Arts and numerous bequests, small and large, to friends and family members. Toshio Kaneko received a good deal of John's personal property and a cottage in Hā'ena in which to make his home. Gregg bequeathed land that he had acquired in recent years from the state of Hawai'i to the Pacific Tropical Botanical Gardens. But the bulk of his estate, which included Lawai-Kai and about $9 million, was designated as the Allerton Gardens Trust, to be administered by the First National Bank of Chicago. While the Pacific (later National) Tropical Botanical Garden would manage Lawai-Kai beginning in the 1990s, and eventually open it to paying visitors, the Allertons were effectively controlling Lawai-Kai and their estate from beyond the grave, leaving it in the hands of the bank established by Robert's father in the nineteenth century.[4]

I first heard about the Allertons from an archivist at the University of Illinois at Urbana-Champaign, which holds most of their personal papers and, of course, owns Allerton House and The Farms. She told me about the Allertons and their house because she thought that someone studying queer history would be interested in them. She understood them as queer, and many gay people in the area also believed that the Allertons were "family." The official word at The Farms—in the form of its docents and all printed literature—was consistently that they were adopted father and son. Similarly, the first time I visited the National Tropical Botanical Garden in 2009, the tour guide at the Allerton Garden told their story with no mention of their relationship being anything other than that between an adoptive father and son. As one longtime NTBG employee noted, by the late 1990s on tours of Lawai-Kai it "became taboo to mention the Allertons" or their relationship. This is hardly surprising. The Allertons had become father and son precisely so that people would have a language to talk about them. And, no small matter, the stewards of their two homes, many of whom knew the couple personally, may have felt duty-bound to talk about the Allertons in the language they themselves had chosen. Their relationship was an open secret: their claim to being father and son—which also was legally true after 1960—allowed those who preferred not to think of them as queer to interact with the pair or, in later years, tour Allerton Garden in Hawai'i or get married at what is now the Allerton House conference center and wedding venue without thinking about them as gay.[5]

Many queers, however, have dismissed their filial claims as just a cover. Gay guidebooks to Hawai'i consistently refer to the pair as gay, as chapter 5 shows. At least one history of Chicago's gay community, called *Out and Proud in Chicago*, includes the Allertons, despite the fact that they were certainly never out or proud, at least not of their homosexuality. *Out* magazine, the glossy gay monthly, did a story about the pair. And queer people around Urbana-Champaign who grew up being told the official version of the Allertons, even as they suspected a more complicated story, are often excited to talk about them as being queer. I was told by one local who had been an undergraduate at the University of Illinois in the 1970s that he had written to John Gregg Allerton, asking for support for a fledgling gay student group, but had received no reply. In other words, much like how it was for Robert and John themselves, in the years since their deaths there was an official story and a story for those in the know.[6]

In more recent years, the official narrative has shifted significantly, even among those who are not queer. A book about Robert Allerton's philanthropy and public impact by historians Martha Burgin and Maureen Holtz fully recognizes his relationship with Roger Quilter and explores his relationship with John Gregg in detail. Lucinda Fleeson's memoir of her years on Kaua'i working at the National Tropical Botanical Garden discusses the Allertons, somewhat disparagingly, as closeted homosexuals. Other NTBG staff referred to the Allertons as gay when interviewed for the story in *Out*. While the websites of both the Allerton Park and Retreat Center and the Allerton Garden at the National Tropical Botanical Garden at the time of this writing both refer to Gregg as Allerton's adopted son (and protégé, in the case of Allerton Park), tour guides no longer insist that Allerton and Gregg were father and son and nothing more. When I toured the NTBG again in 2017, my guide, while never actually using the word "gay," referred to Allerton and Gregg as "lifetime companions" and explained that the adoption took the place of a civil union "because there was no such thing at the time."[7]

The increasing tendency at both estates and in non-queer media to talk openly about the partnership of Allerton and Gregg is a product of the remarkable strides forward in gay rights in the last two decades alone, when sodomy was decriminalized (in 2003), the Defense of Marriage Act found to be unconstitutional (in 2013) and marriage equality became the law of the land (in 2015). While I do not want to overstate the degree of equality now enjoyed by lesbian, gay, and bisexual people—against whom it is still perfectly legal to discriminate in terms of housing or employment in a majority of US states—there is no question that in the media and among Americans more generally, acceptance of homosexuality has grown by leaps and bounds in recent years. The new telling of the Allerton story is a reflection of that growing acceptance. No longer is everyone in agreement that their secret needs to be a secret any longer.

My hope, however, is that this doesn't lead us to analogize Allerton and Gregg's partnership to a civil union or to a same-sex marriage, or indeed to liken all past queer companionship to marriage. As this book has demonstrated, in some ways Allerton and Gregg's relationship did resemble that of the father and son they always claimed publicly to be. Their partnership was not a union of equals, even though the inequality in their relationship did not seem to adversely affect either of them. In the struggle to legalize same-sex marriage nationwide, many LGBT activists have made the not unreasonable claim that gay people are just like straight people in their relationships and deserve to have them recognized as a consequence of this. But that argument presumes that *straight* marriages and relationships are also all the same. And they aren't. The Allertons demonstrate that there are numerous ways that people in history, and in the contemporary world, act out couplehood, and many of these ways are not the idealized egalitarian relationships most celebrated by the gay rights movement.

This matters for our study of history. In recent years, some historians have taken to retroactively referring to same-sex historical partnerships as marriages, even though many of the people involved in these so-called marriages never referred to them as such. In at least one case, Rachel Hope Cleves has argued persuasively that one community did accept a same-sex marriage as such, if only socially, because of course legally it was an impossibility. And it is clear that by the mid-twentieth century, some gay people referred to their partners as husbands and wives, analogizing their relationships to marriage, albeit sometimes inflected with camp. But many same-sex partnerships were not marriages at all, not only because they lacked any of the rights and privileges of marriage, but also because the participants structured their relationships in ways that did not resemble the marriages of their heterosexual contemporaries.[8]

To think about the Allertons as if they were like a married couple is not only to ignore the manner in which they structured their relationship, but it is also to consider them outside of their moment in history. Not only was marriage or a civil union unavailable to them because of when they lived, who knows if they would have taken advantage of it had it been available. To do so would have been to admit to homosexuality, which they never publicly did. Had they lived at a time like ours with greater acceptance of homosexuality, perhaps Allerton and Gregg would have been more likely to live openly as a gay couple. But in that case, it seems likely that Allerton might have found a partner long before he met Gregg. And Gregg might not have found the idea of being with Allerton so appealing in a world where he could live openly with another man his own age. There is obviously no way to know. But it is worth noting that historical circumstance shaped the very possibility of this relationship as much as either man's actions, or the incredible fortune of Allerton, did.

The argument I am making is partially political and echoes those who see the pursuit of same-sex marriage as homonormative. By this I mean that entering into legal marriage reinforces the notion that the proper way to be gay—or straight—is to abide by the dictates of a lifelong, monogamous partnership. I also agree with the historian William Kuby, who has recently argued that when nonconforming couples fight for access to marriage, marriage itself is what gains strength, acting as the ultimate arbiter of citizenship and adulthood, and regulating which people (at least in the United States) are entitled to all kinds of benefits, most notably health care. This is a real problem.[9]

But in the realm of history, and outside of biography, often marriage and couplehood are such easy shorthands that we don't think all that much about how different couples structured their relationships, which has the effect of making it seem as if all marriages or conjugal pairings really were the same.[10] Robert Allerton and John Gregg are just one example of a decidedly non-married couple who organized their relationship in an unconventional way, their asymmetry in age and wealth providing the very scaffolding on which their lives unfolded together. They were, simultaneously, intimate partners *and* father and son, and that makes them a very queer couple, indeed.

And almost all of their choices can be traced back to the wealth into which Robert Allerton had been born. The Allerton fortune is what had thrust Robert into the public eye and necessitated an explanation for his relationship with John, but it also provided enough insulation that those around them were effectively forced into accepting that explanation, even when it was less than believable. As characters in the last one hundred years of American queer history, Allerton and Gregg are spectacularly unrepresentative. They could do things that other queer people could not. But for all of their privilege, they also expose the limits of acceptance. Even a couple this wealthy, with almost every advantage, could not do completely as they pleased. Their ability to live openly as father and son is surely a testament to their wealth, and yet their need to do so simultaneously demonstrates the intolerance of the society around them.

Acknowledgments

More than a decade ago, when I was working on another book in the archives at the University of Illinois at Urbana-Champaign, archivist Lisa Renée Kemplin casually asked me if I'd ever heard of the Allertons. In the years since, no one has helped make this book a reality more than Lisa Renée, who even drove me out to The Farms on my next research trip to UIUC. I am very grateful. Also at UIUC, I'd like to thank Ellen Swain for inviting me to campus to talk about the Allertons, and Katie Nichols at the Archives Research Center, who helped with the photographs. At the Juliet Rice Wichman Research Center at the National Tropical Botanical Garden on the island of Kaua'i, Rae Matthews gave me access to materials related to the Allertons. The late Rick Hanna answered my many questions and also made that visit possible.

I am grateful to my former institution, the University of Northern Colorado, for funds that allowed me to travel to Illinois and Kaua'i on those research trips, and my current employer, the University of Kansas, for funds used to secure images in this book. My high school friend Libby McCalden just happens to be a talented cartographer and produced the map of the Allertons' estates on Kaua'i that appears herein. Thanks to Jane Gregg Schowalter and David Fletcher for talking about their memories of John Gregg and to Valerie Langfield for sharing her research on Roger Quilter. Thanks to Joey Orr for pointing me in the direction of sources on the decorative arts, and to Chris Mitchell for a research lead. My debt to the former keepers of records at Allerton House and to Allerton historians Martha Burgin and Maureen Holtz should be evident in the notes. Thanks, especially, to Maureen for sending me copies of Robert Allerton's letters to Ellen Emmet. Thanks also to Ashley Sims for the tour of Allerton House.

I am grateful to friends who read drafts of chapters and of the articles and conference papers that those chapters once were, including Colin Johnson, Erin Jordan, Aaron Lecklider, Jen Manion, and the editors of *Genders* and the *Pacific Historical Review* and those journals' outside readers. Thanks to Carlos Andrade, who answered my questions about land claims in Hāʻena. I am especially grateful to Marie Grace Brown and Ai-mee Armande Wilson, who joined me in a writing group in the summer of 2018 that gave me the encouragement and feedback necessary to write this book, and to those who gather weekly to write in the Hall Center conference room. Thanks to my former colleagues in the Department of History at the University of Northern Colorado and my current colleagues in the Hall Center's Gender Seminar at KU; with both groups I workshopped drafts of chapters. The external readers for the University of Chicago Press read the manuscript carefully and offered many astute suggestions. At the Press, the late Doug Mitchell was enthusiastic about this book from the get-go; I am sad that he did not live to see it in print. Taking over after Doug retired, Tim Mennel has been an excellent editor, pushing me to figure out the point of the story, and always reading thoroughly and thoughtfully. Susannah Engstrom guided me through the editorial process, and Erin DeWitt has saved me from careless errors and improved the prose with her careful copyediting.

I am especially grateful to colleagues in KU's Department of Women, Gender, and Sexuality Studies, family, and friends, who asked me questions about what I was working on and made me think that returning to the Allertons after many years might not be a bad idea. Thanks finally to Michael Pahr, who is always supportive, even when I ignore his advice about sunk costs.

Notes

INTRODUCTION

1. "Companion Adopted by R. Allerton," *Champaign-Urbana Courier*, March 5, 1960; "Robert Allerton Adopts Friend," March 5, 1960; "Robert Allerton, Piatt Park Donor, Adopts Companion of Many Years," March 4, 1960, clippings from unknown newspapers, all in John Wyatt Gregg Allerton (hereafter JWGA) Adoption and Name Change folder, box 5, Allerton Park Collection, Record Series 31/13/5, University of Illinois Archives (hereafter APC); "Have Been Friends for 38 Years. Kauai's Allerton, 86, to Adopt 60-Year-Old Son," *Honolulu Star-Bulletin*, March 6, 1960, in Allerton Correspondence box, Juliet Rice Wichman Research Library, National Tropical Botanical Garden, Kalaheo, Hawai'i (hereafter NTBG).
2. "'Son' 30 Years Is Adopted by Allerton," *Chicago Daily Tribune*, March 5, 1960, 7.
3. For an insightful discussion of the absence of options of long-term male partners in this period of American history, see John Ibson, *Men without Maps: Some Gay Males of the Generation before Stonewall* (Chicago: University of Chicago Press, 2019), 16–17.
4. On open secrets and secrecy around relationships more generally, see Elizabeth Lapovsky Kennedy, "'But We Would Never Talk about It': The Structures of Lesbian Discretion in South Dakota, 1928–1933," in *Inventing Lesbian Cultures in America*, ed. Ellen Lewin (Boston: Beacon, 1996), 15–39; Colin R. Johnson, *Just Queer Folks: Gender and Sexuality in Rural America* (Philadelphia: Temple University Press, 2013), chap. 4; Rachel Hope Cleves, *Charity and Sylvia: A Same-Sex Marriage in Early America* (New York: Oxford University Press, 2014), xii–xiii, 203; Deborah Cohen, *Family Secrets: Shame and Privacy in Modern Britain* (New York: Oxford University Press, 2013).
5. On the community study, see George Chauncey, *Gay New York: Gender, Urban Culture, and the Making of the Gay Male World, 1890–1940* (New York: Basic Books, 1994); Elizabeth Lapovsky Kennedy and Madeline D. Davis, *Boots of Leather, Slippers of Gold: The History of a Lesbian Community* (New York: Routledge, 1993); Brett Beemyn, ed., *Creating a Place for Ourselves: Lesbian, Gay, and Bisexual Community Histories* (New York: Routledge, 1997); John Howard, *Men Like That: A Southern Queer History* (Chicago: University of Chicago Press, 1999); Marc Stein, *City of Sisterly and Brotherly Loves: Lesbian and Gay Philadelphia, 1945–1972* (Chicago:

University of Chicago Press, 2000); Nan Alamilla Boyd, *Wide-Open Town: A History of Queer San Francisco to 1965* (Berkeley: University of California Press, 2003). On the theme of movement and networking, see Martin Meeker, *Contacts Desired: Gay and Lesbian Communications and Community, 1940s–1970s* (Chicago: University of Chicago Press, 2006); Peter Boag, *Same-Sex Affairs: Constructing and Controlling Homosexuality in the Pacific Northwest* (Berkeley: University of California Press, 2003); John Howard, "Place and Movement in Gay American History: A Case from the Post–World War II South," in *Creating a Place for Ourselves*, ed. Beemyn, 211–25; Colin R. Johnson, "Casual Sex: Towards a 'Prehistory' of Gay Life in Bohemian America," *interventions* 10, no. 3 (2008): 303–20; Tim Retzloff, "Cars and Bars: Assembling Gay Men in Postwar Flint, Michigan," in *Creating a Place for Ourselves*, ed. Beemyn, 226–52; Nicholas L. Syrett, "A Busman's Holiday in the Not-So-Lonely Crowd: Business Culture, Epistolary Networks, and Itinerant Homosexuality in Mid-Twentieth-Century America," *Journal of the History of Sexuality* 21, no. 1 (January 2012): 121–40; Nicholas L. Syrett, "Mobility, Circulation, and Correspondence: White Queer Men in the Midcentury Midwest," *GLQ: A Journal of Lesbian and Gay Studies* 20, nos. 1–2 (2014): 75–94. On the transnational turn, see Robert Aldrich, *Colonialism and Homosexuality* (New York: Routledge, 2002); Julio Capó Jr., *Welcome to Fairyland: Queer Miami before 1940* (Chapel Hill: University of North Carolina Press, 2017); Emily K. Hobson, *Lavender and Red: Liberation and Solidarity in the Gay and Lesbian Left* (Berkeley: University of California Press, 2016); David Minto, "Perversion by Penumbras: Wolfenden, *Griswold*, and the Transatlantic Trajectory of Sexual Privacy," *American Historical Review* 123, no. 4 (October 2018): 1093–121.

6. By 1984 the Democratic Party Platform had at least acknowledged that gay men and lesbians were subject to "violent acts of bigotry, hatred and extremism," alongside women and racial and ethnic minorities, and that a "Democratic Administration will work vigorously to address, document, and end all such violence." See "1984 Democratic Party Platform," July 16, 1984 at https://www .presidency.ucsb.edu/documents/1984-democratic-party-platform. Of course, the Democrats lost the 1984 election.

7. For studies in activism, see, among many others, John D'Emilio, *Sexual Politics, Sexual Communities: The Making of a Homosexual Minority in the United States, 1940–1970* (Chicago: University of Chicago Press, 1983); Daniel Hurewitz, *Bohemian Los Angeles and the Making of Modern Politics* (Berkeley: University of California Press, 2008); Hobson, *Lavender and Red*; Martin Duberman, *Stonewall* (New York: Dutton, 1994); David Eisenbach, *Gay Power: An American Revolution* (New York: Da Capo, 2006); Lillian Faderman, *The Gay Revolution: The Story of the Struggle* (New York: Simon and Schuster, 2016); Stein, *City of Sisterly and Brotherly Loves*; Timothy Stewart-Winter, *Queer Clout: Chicago and the Rise of Gay Politics* (Philadelphia: University of Pennsylvania Press, 2015). On homonormativity, see Lisa Duggan, "The New Homonormativity: The Sexual Politics of Neoliberalism," in *Materializing Democracy: Toward a Revitalized Cultural Politics*, ed. Russ Castronovo and Dana D. Nelson (Durham, NC: Duke University Press, 2002), 175–94;

Michael Warner, *The Trouble with Normal: Sex, Politics, and the Ethics of Queer Life* (New York: Free Press, 1999).

8. For examples of those who saw it as a fiction, see Bruce Shenitz, "The Garden of Eden. Minus Eve," *Out*, September 2007, 88; Martha Burgin and Maureen Holtz, *Robert Allerton: The Private Man and the Public Gifts* (Champaign, IL: News-Gazette, 2009), 90.

9. Kennedy and Davis, *Boots of Leather, Slippers of Gold*. On class in the late nineteenth and early twentieth centuries, see Chauncey, *Gay New York*, chaps. 2 and 3, especially; Boag, *Same-Sex Affairs*, parts 1 and 2; Nayan Shah, *Stranger Intimacy: Contesting, Race, Sexuality and the Law in the North American West* (Berkeley: University of California Press, 2012); Margot Canaday, *The Straight State: Sexuality and Citizenship in Twentieth-Century America* (Princeton, NJ: Princeton University Press, 2009), 42–44; David D. Doyle, "'A Very Proper Bostonian': Rediscovering Ogden Codman and His Late-Nineteenth-Century Queer World," *Journal of the History of Sexuality* 13, no. 4 (October 2004): 446–76.

10. "Robert Henry Allerton," The Chicago LGBT Hall of Fame, http://chicagolgbthall offame.org/allerton-robert/.

CHAPTER ONE

1. Walter Scott Allerton, *A History of the Allerton Family in the United States, 1585–1885*, rev. ed. (Chicago: Samuel Waters Allerton, 1900), 13–14, 15; Nathaniel Philbrick, *Mayflower: A Story of Courage, Community, and War* (New York: Viking, 2006), 81.

2. Allerton, *A History of the Allerton Family*, 21–23, 27, 30; Eugene Aubrey Stratton, *Plymouth Colony: Its History and People, 1620–1691* (Salt Lake City: Ancestry Publishing, 1986), 44–46; Philbrick, *Mayflower*, 168–69.

3. Allerton, *A History of the Allerton Family*, 58, 85; Samuel W. Allerton to Kate R. and Robert H. Allerton, May 25, 1878, typescript in Robert Henry Allerton (hereafter RHA) Personal, Biographical folder, box 4, Allerton Park Collection, Record Series 31/13/5, University of Illinois Archives (hereafter APC).

4. Samuel Allerton to Kate and Robert Allerton; Allerton, *A History of the Allerton Family*, 83–84.

5. Samuel Allerton to Kate and Robert Allerton.

6. Ibid.

7. Allerton, *A History of the Allerton Family*, 86–87; Josiah Seymour Currey, *Chicago: Its History and Its Builders, a Century of Marvelous Growth* (Chicago: S. J. Clarke, 1912), 7; ads for the establishment of the First National Bank in *Chicago Daily Tribune*, July 13, July 17, July 21, July 24, July 30, 1863, and August 10, August 13, 1863, all on page 3.

8. "Union Stock Yard and Transit Company," *Chicago Daily Tribune*, January 13, 1865, 2 (italics in original).

9. Martha Burgin and Maureen Holtz, *Robert Allerton: The Private Man and the Public Gifts* (Champaign, IL: News-Gazette, 2009), 10.

10. Irene Priebe tribute to Allerton, 1, in RHA Personal, Biographical folder, box 4, APC; Burgin and Holtz, *Robert Allerton*, 10; 1880 Chicago Census, familysearch .org; "Folly," in Host, Betty folder, box 1, APC.

11. Albert Mudry, "The Role of Adam Politzer (1835–1920) in the History of Otology," Politzer Society, http://www.politzersociety.org/content.php?conid=683; Burgin and Holtz, *Robert Allerton*, 7.

12. Burgin and Holtz, *Robert Allerton*, 7; "Allerton Family," at Allerton Park and Retreat Center, allerton.illinois.edu/allerton-family/.

13. Brian Connolly, *Domestic Intimacies: Incest and the Liberal Subject in Nineteenth-Century America* (Philadelphia: University of Pennsylvania Press, 2014), 56–63, 81, 90–91.

14. Burgin and Holtz, *Robert Allerton*, 11; "Matrimonial: Papin-Allerton," *Chicago Daily Tribune*, November 12, 1885, 8; record for Francis Sidney Papin, at findagrave.com; marriage license of Kate Allerton Papin and Hugo Richards Johnstone, October 19, 1898, accessed via familysearch.org; "Mrs. Papin Wedded in New York," *Chicago Tribune*, October 22, 1898, 5.

15. "The Harvard School," http://www.illinoishsglorydays.com/id909.html; Arthur Stanwood Pier, *St. Paul's School, 1855–1934* (New York: Charles Scribner's Sons, 1934), chap. 1, 188, chap. 8, 213, 172–73; Priebe tribute to Allerton, 1, RHA Personal, Biographical folder, box 4, APC; Burgin and Holtz, *Robert Allerton*, 15–17.

16. Burgin and Holtz, *Robert Allerton*, 18; Roger L. Geiger, "Introduction," in *The American College in the Nineteenth Century*, ed. Roger L. Geiger (Nashville: Vanderbilt University Press, 2000), 1–36.

17. Bartlett quoted in Erne R. and Florence Frueh, "Frederic Clay Bartlett: Chicago Painter and Patron of the Arts," *Chicago History: The Magazine of the Chicago Historical Society* 7, no. 1 (Spring 1979): 16.

18. Samuel Allerton to Robert Allerton, January 1, 1886, transcription in Morgan, Jesse folder, box 1, APC.

19. Frederic Clay Bartlett, *Sortofa Kindofa Journal of My Own* (Chicago: Lakeside Press, 1965), 18, 19.

20. Ibid., 22, 24. See also Courtney Graham Donnell, "Frederic Clay and Helen Birch Bartlett: The Collectors," *Art Institute of Chicago Museum Studies* 12, no. 2 (1986): 86.

21. Bartlett, *Sortofa*, 4–5; Carroll Smith-Rosenberg, "The Female World of Love and Ritual: Relations between Women in Nineteenth-Century America," *Signs: A Journal of Woman in Culture and Society* 1, no. 1 (Autumn 1975): 1–25.

22. E. Anthony Rotundo, "Romantic Friendships: Male Intimacy and Middle-Class Youth in the Northern United States, 1800–1900," *Journal of Social History* 23, no. 1 (Autumn 1989): 1–25; Bartlett, *Sortofa*, 40.

23. See the examples in Rotundo, "Romantic Friendships"; Smith-Rosenberg, "Female World"; Karen V. Hansen, "'No Kisses Is Like Youres': An Erotic Friendship between Two African American Women during the Mid-Nineteenth Century," *Gender and History* 7, no. 2 (August 1995): 153–82; Jonathan Ned Katz, *Love Stories: Sex between Men before Homosexuality* (Chicago: University of Chicago Press,

2003), 24–25 and chap. 1. For a contrasting example of a same-sex couple of an earlier era that remained together in what many around them saw as a marriage, see Rachel Hope Cleves, *Charity and Sylvia: A Same-Sex Marriage in Early America* (New York: Oxford University Press, 2014).

24. Donnell, "Frederic Clay and Helen Birch Bartlett," 86.

CHAPTER TWO

1. "Richest Bachelor in Chicago," *Chicago Daily Tribune*, February 18, 1906, D1.
2. "Matrimonial Chances for Chicago Girls," *Chicago Daily Tribune*, April 14, 1907, F3.
3. David M. Halperin, *How to Be Gay* (Cambridge, MA: Belknap Press, 2012).
4. On various occupations and interests and their connections with homosexuality, see, for instance, Wayne Koestenbaum, *The Queen's Throat: Opera, Homosexuality, and the Mystery of Desire* (New York: Poseidon, 1993); D. A. Miller, *Place for Us: Essay on the Broadway Musical* (Cambridge, MA: Harvard University Press, 1998); John Clum, *Something for the Boys: Musical Theater and Gay Culture* (New York: Palgrave Macmillan, 2001); Michael Sherry, *Gay Artists in Modern America: An Imagined Conspiracy* (Chapel Hill: University of North Carolina Press, 2007); Phil Tiemeyer, *Plane Queer: Labor, Sexuality, and AIDS in the History of Male Flight Attendants* (Berkeley: University of California Press, 2013); Will Fellows, *A Passion to Preserve: Gay Men as Keepers of Culture* (Madison: University of Wisconsin Press, 2004).
5. Herbert Gans, *Popular Culture and High Culture: An Analysis and Evaluation of Taste* (New York: Basic Books, 1974), 10–11, 75–81.
6. Christopher Reed, *Art and Homosexuality: A History of Ideas* (New York: Oxford University Press, 2011), 1, 94, 105. On "artistic," see George Chauncey, *Gay New York: Gender, Urban Culture, and the Making of the Gay Male World, 1890–1940* (New York: Basic Books, 1994), 228–29; Reed, *Art and Homosexuality*, 1; on "aesthetic," see Nicholas L. Syrett, "The Boys of Beaver Meadow: A Homosexual Community at 1920s Dartmouth College," *American Studies* 48, no. 2 (Summer 2007): 9–18. On both, see David K. Johnson, *Buying Gay: How Physique Entrepreneurs Sparked a Movement* (New York: Columbia University Press, 2019), chap. 1. "Temperamental" is from a September 16, 1923, letter to the editor of the *Boston Herald*, quoted in Fellows, *A Passion to Preserve*, 20, which itself is quoting James M. Lindgren, *Preserving Historic New England: Preservation, Progressivism, and the Remaking of Memory* (New York: Oxford University Press, 1995), 131. On Oscar Wilde and aesthetics, see Sharon Marcus, "At Home with the Other Victorians," *South Atlantic Quarterly* 108, no. 1 (Winter 2009): 140–41; Reed, *Art and Homosexuality*, 94–95. See also Herbert Muschamp, "The Secret History of 2 Columbus Circle," *New York Times*, January 8, 2006; Halperin, *How to Be Gay*.
7. John Potvin, *Bachelors of a Different Sort: Queer Aesthetics, Material Culture, and the Modern Interior in Britain* (Manchester: Manchester University Press, 2014), 15, 24; Gail Bederman, *Manliness and Civilization: A Cultural History of Gender and Race in the United States, 1880–1917* (Chicago: University of Chicago Press, 1995); Clifford

Putney, *Muscular Christianity: Manhood and Sports in Protestant America, 1880–1920* (Cambridge, MA: Harvard University Press, 2003); E. Anthony Rotundo, *American Manhood: Transformations in Masculinity from the Revolution to the Modern Era* (New York: Basic Books, 1994), chap. 10.

8. Martha Burgin and Maureen Holtz, *Robert Allerton: The Private Man and the Public Gifts* (Champaign, IL: News-Gazette, 2009), 28.

9. "Robert Allerton," *Bulletin of the Pacific Tropical Botanical Garden* 3, no. 2 (April 1973): 21, in John Wyatt Gregg Allerton (hereafter JWGA) Personal folder, box 5, Allerton Park Collection, Record Series 31/13/5, University of Illinois Archives (hereafter APC); David Bowman, "The Allerton Chronology," 4, in Robert Henry Allerton (hereafter RHA) Personal, Biographical folder, box 4, APC; "Mrs. Papin Wedded in New York," *Chicago Tribune*, October 22, 1898, 5.

10. Frederic Clay Bartlett, *Sort of a Kind of a Journal of My Own* (Chicago: Lakeside Press, 1965), 22, 27, 40, 42; Allerton quoted in "The Allerton Legacy: Robert H. Allerton," 2–3, in RHA Personal, Biographical folder, box 4, APC.

11. "The Allerton Legacy: Robert H. Allerton," 2–3; Muriel Scheinman, *A Guide to Art at the University of Illinois* (Champaign: University of Illinois Press, 1995), 104; interview with John Gregg Allerton, transcript of Interview Tape 1, JWGA Personal folder, box 5, APC; Burgin and Holtz, *Robert Allerton*, 29; Michael Anesko, *Henry James and Queer Filiation: Hardened Bachelors in the Edwardian Era* (New York: Palgrave Macmillan, 2018), chap. 2., esp. 20.

12. "The Allerton Legacy: Robert H. Allerton," 2–3; statement on John Joseph Borie, RHA Personal, Biographical folder, box 4, APC; Anesko, *Henry James and Queer Filiation*, 18–19.

13. Borie statement; David L. Finnigan, *Inside Allerton: The Essential Guide to Robert Allerton Park* (Springfield, IL: G. S. Brenac, 2017), 7, 8–9, 10.

14. Finnigan, *Inside Allerton*, 51, 61.

15. Scheinman, *A Guide to Art at the University of Illinois*, 98; "The Allerton Legacy: Robert H. Allerton."

16. Tribute by Irene Priebe in RHA Personal, Biographical folder, box 4, APC.

17. Census listing from 1910 Piatt County Census, compiled by David Bowman, in RHA Personal, Biographical folder, box 4, APC; Cyril Cackett to David Bowman, July 3, 1994, same folder; Statement by Elmer Priebe, March 5, 1979, in Phalen, John folder, box 1, APC; Allerton Legacy statement in files at Juliet Rice Wichman Research Center, National Tropical Botanical Gardens Kalheo, Hawai'i (hereafter NTBG).

18. Ruth Schwartz Cohen, "The 'Industrial Revolution' in the Home: Household Technology and Social Change in the 20th Century," *Technology and Culture* 17, no. 1 (January 1976): 9–13; Susan Strasser, *Never Done: A History of American Housework* (New York: Henry Holt, 1982), 164.

19. Cackett to Bowman, July 3, 1994; Irene Priebe, "Robert Allerton—The Man," in RHA Personal, Biographical folder, box 4, APC; "Allerton Messages and Letters" transcription of postcards, same folder; John Gregg to Elmer Priebe, December 22, 1964, same folder.

20. "An Interview with Elmer Priebe," by J.M.H., in RHA Personal, Biographical folder, box 4, APC, 2, 4; "The Allerton Legacy: Robert H. Allerton."

21. Statement by Cyril Cackett, page 3, Cackett, Cyril folder, box 1, APC; Burgin and Holtz, *Robert Allerton*, 66. Book titles and inscriptions are in folders 1–4, Susan Enscore Inventory of Allerton Library, box 1, Allerton Family Collection, Record Series 31/13/20, University of Illinois Archives.

22. For "castle" and "palace," see "Narrow Escape," *Monticello Bulletin*, October 20, 1899, and "Robert Allerton's Castle," *Monticello Bulletin*, August 25, 1911, 1, both clippings in Main House folder, box 2, APC. "Lioness Brings Monticello Much Publicity," July 19, 1917, in RHA Personal, Biographical folder, box 4, APC; "Lion Is at Large with Armed Men Hunting Him," *Anaconda Standard*, July 15, 1917, 1; "Lure of the Mate," *Los Angeles Times*, July 17, 1917, I2; Priebe, "Robert Allerton— The Man," 10.

23. "Richest Bachelor in Chicago," D1; "At Allerton's Palatial Residence. Joseph Medill McCormick and Bride," June 11, 1903, in "The Farms," Pre-1946 folder, box 4, APC.

24. Nancy R____, "Week-End Party Given by Robert Allerton at His Country Place," *Chicago Daily Tribune*, October 1, 1927, 19.

25. "Oral Interview with Elmer Priebe," by Susan Gortner, March 1, 1983, 5–6, in Priebe, Elmer folder, box 2, APC; "Elmer Priebe," March 5, 1979, 9, in Phalen, John folder, box 1, APC; "Social Gossip," *Washington Post*, February 25, 1907, 7; Gregg quoted in Allerton Legacy Symposium, 1981, Allerton Legacy Symposium folder, box 7, APC; and second quotation from Allerton Legacy in NTBG files.

26. Fiona Brideoake, *The Ladies of Llangollen: Desire, Indeterminacy, and the Legacies of Criticism* (Lewisburg, PA: Bucknell University Press, 2017), xvi–xix.

27. Strawberry Hill House official website, accessed June 25, 2018 (http://www .strawberryhillhouse.org.uk/the-house/history/); Amanda Vickery, "Horace Walpole and Strawberry Hill," *Guardian*, February 19, 2010, https://www.the guardian.com/artanddesign/2010/feb/20/horace-walpole-strawberry-hill; Marion Harney, *Place-Making for the Imagination: Horace Walpole and Strawberry Hill* (Surrey, UK: Ashgate, 2013).

28. Dorothy Margaret Stuart, *Horace Walpole* (New York: Macmillan, 1927), 105; Harney, *Place-Making for the Imagination*, 83, xiv.

29. There are other examples of this phenomenon, which include E. F. Benson (who lived at Henry James's Lamb House in the 1920s with his brother) and Harold Acton (who restored his parents' Italian villa, La Pietra, after World War II), but both occupied their homes after the period that Allerton was building and designing his own. This is not to say that he might not have been aware of them or influenced by them after the fact, but they could not have served as inspiration in the way that Walpole or the Ladies of Llangollen might have. See Simon Goldhill, *A Very Queer Family Indeed: Sex, Religion, and the Bensons in Victorian Britain* (Chicago: University of Chicago Press, 2016); John Darnton, "Sir Harold Acton Is Dead; Prototypic Esthete of the 1920's," *New York Times*, March 1, 1994, 10.

30. "Cliff Dwellers in Chicago," *Chicago Daily Tribune*, November 7, 1907, 8; Helen

Lefkowitz Horowitz, *Culture and the City: Cultural Philanthropy in Chicago from the 1880s to 1917* (Lexington: University Press of Kentucky, 1976), 171.

31. Meyric R. Rogers, "The Robert Allerton Wing," *Bulletin of the Art Institute of Chicago* 34, no. 1 (January 1940): 4–6; "The Art Institute of Chicago Buildings, 1879–1988: A Chronology," *Art Institute of Chicago Museum Studies* 14, no. 1 (1988): 17, 20; John W. Smith, "The Nervous Profession: Daniel Catton Rich and the Art Institute of Chicago, 1927–1958," *Art Institute of Chicago Museum Studies* 19, no. 1 (1993): 61.

32. Kathleen D. McCarthy, *Noblesse Oblige: Charity and Cultural Philanthropy in Chicago, 1849–1929* (Chicago: University of Chicago Press, 1980), 84; Horowitz, *Culture and the City*, 51–52. On donations to the Honolulu Academy of Arts, see listings in Honolulu Academy of Arts folder, box 4, APC.

33. "Accessions and Loans," *Bulletin of the Art Institute of Chicago* 18, no. 4 (April 1924): 52; "Accessions and Loans," *Bulletin of the Art Institute of Chicago* 19, no. 9 (December 1925): 111; "Oriental Exhibitions," *Parnassus* 9, no. 1 (January 1937): 31; "Four Newly Acquired Examples of Japanese Art," *Art Institute of Chicago Quarterly* 52, no. 1 (February 1, 1958): 10–16.

34. Kay Bock, *Majestic Allerton* (Urbana: University of Illinois Foundation, 1998), 11, 24; [Par Danforth], *Robert Allerton Park* (Champaign: University of Illinois Press, 1951), 5, 7, 33. See also Kathryn Hulme, *The Robert Allerton Story, 1873–1964* (n.p.: n.p., 1979); Scheinman, *A Guide to Art at the University of Illinois.*

35. "Day's News in Society," *Chicago Daily Tribune*, March 16, 1925, 23; Nancy R_____, "Jane Morton Finds Hunter's Pink Auto Barred in Chicago," *Chicago Daily Tribune*, March 24, 1925, 27; "The Orientals, New Art Society, Organized," *Chicago Daily Tribune*, April 9, 1925, 21; "Leaders Arrange Persian Group for Pageant of the East," *Chicago Daily Tribune*, November 15, 1920, 23; "A Chinese Party," *Chicago Daily Tribune*, December 5, 1921, 20; Cousin Eve, "Cafferys Drip with Orchids as They Leave Rio," *Chicago Daily Tribune*, December 4, 1938, NWA2. On decoration, in particular, see Kristin L. Hoganson, "Cosmopolitan Domesticity: Importing the American Dream, 1865–1920," *American Historical Review* 107, no. 1 (February 2002): 55–83.

36. Amy Sueyoshi, *Queer Compulsions: Race, Nation, and Sexuality in the Affairs of Yone Noguchi* (Honolulu: University of Hawai'i Press, 2012), 48–49; Mari Yoshihara, *Embracing the East: White Women and American Orientalism* (New York: Oxford University Press, 2003). On queers and art collecting, see also Richard Meyer, "Mapplethorpe's Living Room: Photography and the Furnishing of Desire," *Art History* 24, no. 2 (April 2001): 292–311.

37. David Eng, *Racial Castration: Managing Masculinity in Asian America* (Durham, NC: Duke University Press, 2001); Paul C. P. Siu, *The Chinese Laundryman: A Study of Social Isolation*, ed. John Kuo Wei Tchen (New York: New York University Press, 1988); John Kuo Wei Tchen, *New York before Chinatown: Orientalism and the Shaping of American Culture, 1776–1882* (Baltimore: Johns Hopkins University Press, 2001).

38. Christopher Reed, *Bachelor Japanists: Japanese Aesthetics and Western Masculinities* (New York: Columbia University Press, 2017), 5, 35, 26.

39. Amy Sueyoshi, *Discriminating Sex: White Leisure and the Making of the American "Oriental"* (Champaign: University of Illinois Press, 2018), 157.

40. "An East Indian Print," *Bulletin of the Art Institute of Chicago* 20, no. 2 (February 1926): 22; "'Setting Table' Is an Art," *Chicago Daily Tribune*, December 3, 1920, 3; Potvin, *Bachelors of a Different Sort*, 27. Steiner quoted in Bridget Elliott and Janice Helland, "Introduction," in *Women Artists and the Decorative Arts, 1880–1935: The Gender of Ornament*, ed. Elliott and Helland (Aldershot, UK: Ashgate, 2002), 3; Elliott and Helland quotation on 2.

41. While one of those men, Russell Tyson, appears to have been married, the other, G. F. Porter, killed himself only two years later at the age of forty-five on the eve of his honeymoon, declaring to his wife that his suicide was the "inevitable result of a twisted life." See "G. F. Porter Suicide in Chicago Home," *New York Times*, February 24, 1927, 25. His obituary speculated that this was due to depression—clearly so—but the fact that he married only at forty-five and that he killed himself the night before the commencement of his honeymoon due to his "twisted life" does make one wonder if a struggle with same-sex desires might have had something to do with his decision.

42. Ghenete Zelleke, "David Adler: Benefactor and Trustee," in *David Adler, Architect: The Elements of Style*, ed. Martha Thorne (Chicago: Art Institute of Chicago, 2002), 57–58; "Accessions and Loans," *Bulletin of the Art Institute of Chicago* 19, no. 3 (March 1925): 39; "Gifts and Loans," *Bulletin of the Art Institute of Chicago* 23, no. 4 (April 1929): 44; "Accessions and Loans," *Bulletin of the Art Institute of Chicago* 19, no. 4 (April 1925): 51; "Accessions and Loans," *Bulletin of the Art Institute of Chicago* 19, no. 2 (February 1925): 26; Dan Klein and Margaret Bishop, *Decorative Art, 1880–1980* (Oxford: Phaidon/Christie's, 1986); Christa C. Mayer Thurman, *Textiles in the Art Institute of Chicago* (Chicago: Art Institute of Chicago, 1992), 6–8.

CHAPTER THREE

1. Peter Boag, *Same-Sex Affairs: Constructing and Controlling Homosexuality in the Pacific Northwest* (Berkeley: University of California Press, 2003); George Chauncey, *Gay New York: Gender, Urban Culture, and the Making of the Gay Male World, 1890–1940* (New York: Basic Books, 1994); Colin R. Johnson, *Just Queer Folks: Gender and Sexuality in Rural America* (Philadelphia: Temple University Press, 2013), chap. 3; Nicholas L. Syrett, "A Busman's Holiday in the Not-So-Lonely Crowd: Business Culture, Epistolary Networks, and Itinerant Homosexuality in Mid-Twentieth-Century America," *Journal of the History of Sexuality* 21, no. 1 (January 2012): 121–40.

2. St. Sukie de la Croix, *Chicago Whispers: A History of LGBT Chicago before Stonewall* (Madison: University of Wisconsin Press, 2012), 20–23; Jim Elledge, *The Boys of Fairy Town: Sodomites, Female Impersonators, Third-Sexers, Pansies, Queers, and Sex Morons in Chicago's First Century* (Chicago: Chicago Review Press, 2018), 2–3, 11, chap. 2, chap. 5, 52, 24. On the question of publicity surrounding same-sex desires in this era, see Lisa Duggan, *Sapphic Slashers: Sex, Violence, and American Modernity* (Durham, NC: Duke University Press, 2000).

3. De la Croix, *Chicago Whispers*, 20–23; Elledge, *The Boys of Fairy Town*, 59–61.

4. William Healy interview, 1960, quoted in Gregory Sprague, "On the 'Gay Side' of Town: The Nature and Structure of Male Homosexuality in Chicago, 1890–1935," 11–12, folder 12, box 5, subseries 5.1, Gregory Sprague Papers, Chicago History Museum.

5. Sprague, "On the 'Gay Side' of Town," 13–14; Lucinda Fleeson, "The Gay '30s," in *Out and Proud in Chicago: An Overview of the City's Gay Community*, ed. Tracy Baim (Chicago: Surrey Books, 2008), 44–45; Elledge, *The Boys of Fairy Town*, 20–22; "Cliff Dwellers in Chicago," *Chicago Daily Tribune*, November 7, 1907, 9.

6. De la Croix, *Chicago Whispers*, 35–39, chap. 7, 73; Sprague, "On the 'Gay Side' of Town," 18.

7. Chad Heap, *Slumming: Sexual and Racial Encounters in American Nightlife, 1885–1940* (Chicago: University of Chicago Press, 2009).

8. "Social Gossip," *Washington Post*, February 25, 1907, 7.

9. Allerton Legacy statement in Allerton Stuff box, Juliet Rice Wichman Library, National Tropical Botanical Gardens, Kalaheo, Hawai'i (hereafter NTBG); "Mrs. Ellen Rand, Noted Artist, Dies," *New York Times*, December 19, 1941, 25.

10. Michael Anesko, "Hardened Bachelors: Henry James and Queer Filiation in Edwardian London," *Henry James Review* 40, no. 1 (Winter 2019): 23; Robert Allerton to Ellen Emmet, May 11, 1901; Allerton to Emmet, September 26, 1911; Allerton to Emmet, July 31, 1901, copies of correspondence in possession of the author. My thanks to Maureen Holtz for sharing these letters with me.

11. Allerton to Emmet, July 15, 1901; Allerton to Emmet, August 26, 1901; von Glehn quoted in Anesko, "Hardened Bachelors," 27. See also Martha Burgin and Maureen Holtz, *Robert Allerton: The Private Man and the Public Gifts* (Champaign, IL: News-Gazette, 2009), 45.

12. Burgin and Holtz also note that while many of Emmet's relatives quite liked Robert Allerton, her mother seems to have been opposed to the union. See Burgin and Holtz, *Robert Allerton*, 49.

13. *New York Times*, May 7, 1911, 11; Georgia Soruika and Laura L. Klemt, "Robert Allerton: The Man and the Park," including oral history with John Gregg Allerton, 1970, 12–13, annotated copy in Allerton Stuff box (hereafter Soruika and Klemt), NTBG.

14. Birth records for Allerton and Vanderburgh Johnstone, 1900 and 1903, accessed at familysearch.org.

15. Chauncey, *Gay New York*, 196; John Borie business card in Train Tickets and Business Cards folder, box 1, Allerton Family Collection, Record Series 31/13/20, University of Illinois Archives; Anesko, "Hardened Bachelors," 23.

16. "Hotel Arrivals," *Miami Herald*, March 6, 1918, 7; Julio Capó Jr., *Welcome to Fairyland: Queer Miami before 1940* (Chapel Hill: University of North Carolina Press, 2017), chap. 3, 101–3, 13. On Deering and Villa Vizcaya, see also Althea McDowell Altemus, *Big Bosses: A Working Girl's Memoir of Jazz Age America*, ed. Robin F. Bachin (Chicago: University of Chicago Press, 2016), 9–38.

17. Oral Interview with Elmer Priebe conducted by Susan Gortner, March 1, 1983; Interview with Mr. Elmer Priebe, March 6, 1981, both in Priebe, Elmer folder, box

2, APC; Elmer Priebe statement, March 5, 1979, Phalen, John folder, box 1, APC; Karen Christel Krahulik, *Provincetown: From Pilgrim Landing to Gay Resort* (New York: New York University Press, 2005), 69–70, 72, 75.

18. "Big Crowd Sails Today," *New York Times*, January 24, 1912, 8. See "Liner Transatlantic Crossing Times, 1833–1952 (in days)," The Geography of Transport Systems, https://transportgeography.org/?page_id=2135; Anne de Courcy, *The Husband Hunters: American Heiresses Who Married into the British Aristocracy* (New York: St. Martin's Press, 2018).

19. Anesko, "Hardened Bachelors."

20. Ian Littlewood, *Sultry Climates: Travel and Sex since the Grand Tour* (London: John Murray, 2001), 3–5.

21. Burgin and Holtz, *Robert Allerton*, 32, 42, 57; "Charles Russell Hewlett," *Art and Progress*, February 1, 1914, 103; John Gregg Allerton Memoir, interview conducted by Nancy Becker, May 9, 1984, 10, available online at http://www.idaillinois.org/cdm/ref/collection/uis/id/883.

22. J. G. P. Delaney, *Glyn Philpot: His Life and Art* (Surrey, UK: Ashgate, 1999), 35–36.

23. Madame X, "English Artist Visiting Here May Paint Illinois Cornfields," *Chicago Daily Tribune*, September 21, 1913, E2.

24. Philpot quoted in Delaney, *Glyn Philpot*, 36–37.

25. Ibid., 37–38, 54; Gregg quoted in Soruika and Klemt, 15; Etta Arntzen to Valerie Langfield, September 2, 1997, in Quilter, Roger folder, box 2, APC; Burgin and Holtz, *Robert Allerton*, 82.

26. Delaney, *Glyn Philpot*, 38.

27. "Accessions and Loans," *Bulletin of the Art Institute of Chicago* 18, no. 5 (May 1924): 67; John Potvin, *Bachelors of a Different Sort: Queer Aesthetics, Material Culture and the Modern Interior in Britain* (Manchester: Manchester University Press, 2014), chap. 3. See also Matt Cook, *Queer Domesticities: Homosexuality and Home Life in Twentieth-Century London* (Hampshire, UK: Palgrave Macmillan, 2014), chap. 1; Michael Anesko, *Henry James and Queer Filiation: Hardened Bachelors in the Edwardian Era* (New York: Palgrave Macmillan, 2018).

28. Delaney, *Glyn Philpot*, 55; Valerie Langfield, *Roger Quilter, His Life and Music* (Suffolk, UK: Boydell Press, 2002), 34; Anesko, *Henry James and Queer Filiation*, 54, 68.

29. Robert Allerton to Roger Quilter, February 23, 1911, Add MS 70597, Roger Quilter Papers, British Library, sent via email by Valerie Langfield, July 20, 2007.

30. Langfield, *Roger Quilter*, 35.

31. "Big Crowd Sails Today," *New York Times*, January 24, 1912, 8; "Ocean Travellers," *New York Times*, April 19, 1913, 11; passenger records for *Mauretania*, coming from Liverpool to Ellis Island, April 18, 1913, accessed on familysearch.org; Robert Allerton to Roger Quilter, February 7, 1914, Add MS 70597, Roger Quilter Papers, British Library, sent via email by Valerie Langfield, July 20, 2007.

32. "Samuel Allerton, Pioneer Packer, Taken by Death," *Chicago Daily Tribune*, February 23, 1914, 1; Burgin and Holtz, *Robert Allerton*, 58, 90.

33. Will of Samuel Waters Allerton, SWA Will folder, box 4, APC; "Samuel W. Allerton Will Disposes of $4,000,000 Estate," *Chicago Daily Tribune*, April 23, 1914, 15; Burgin and Holtz, *Robert Allerton*, 59–60.

34. Passport application for Robert Allerton, November 23, 1915; passport application for Robert Allerton, January 11, 1919; passport application for Robert Allerton, January 3, 1921; passport application for Robert Allerton, December 19, 1922, all accessed on familysearch.org.

35. Chauncey, *Gay New York*; Boag, *Same-Sex Affairs*; Johnson, *Just Queer Folks*; Barry Reay, *New York Hustlers: Masculinity and Sex in Modern America* (Manchester, UK: Manchester University Press, 2010).

36. Robert Aldrich, *Colonialism and Homosexuality* (New York: Routledge, 2002), 8–9; Chauncey, *Gay New York*, 72.

37. Robert J. Morris, "Aikāne: Accounts of Same-Sex Relationships in the Journals of Captain Cook's Third Voyage (1776–80)," *Journal of Homosexuality* 19 (1990): 231–58; Lee Wallace, *Sexual Encounters: Pacific Texts, Modern Sexualities* (Ithaca, NY: Cornell University Press, 2003), chap. 1.

38. Aldrich, *Colonialism and Homosexuality*, 338.

39. Ibid., 8–9; Robert Aldrich, *The Seduction of the Mediterranean: Writing, Art, and Homosexual Fantasy* (London: Routledge, 1993), x.

40. Aldrich, *The Seduction of the Mediterranean*, 32.

41. Ibid., 124–33; Eugenio Zito, "'Amori et Dolori Sacrum': Canons, Differences, and Figures of Gender Identity in the Cultural Panorama of Travelers in Capri between the Nineteenth and the Twentieth Century," in *Homosexuality in Italian Literature, Society, and Culture, 1789–1919*, ed. Lorenzo Benadusi, Paolo L. Bernardini, Elisa Biano, and Paola Guazzo (Newcastle-upon-Tyne, UK: Cambridge Scholars, 2017), 129–54; Mario Bolognari, "Taormina and the Strange Case of Baron von Gloeden," in *Homosexuality in Italian Literature*, 155–83; Rachel Hope Cleves, *Unspeakable: A Life beyond Sexual Morality* (Chicago: University of Chicago Press, 2020).

42. Aldrich, *Colonialism and Homosexuality*, 157–59, 338 for the quotation.

43. Ibid., 337.

44. "Robert Allerton Gives a Million Dollars to the Pacific Tropical Botanical Garden," *Hawaiian Botanical Gardens Foundation Newsletter* 1, no. 4 (October 1964): 1, copy in Lawai-Kai, Post-Donation folder, box 4, APC; W. McC. McK., "The Drawing Collection," *Bulletin of the Art Institute of Chicago* 16, no. 6 (November 1922): 79; "Hawaiian Accessions and Loans," *Bulletin of the Art Institute of Chicago* 16, no. 4 (September 1922): 62; Littlewood, *Sultry Climates*, 171–72, 177.

45. Aldrich, *Colonialism and Homosexuality*, 127–35; Charles Warren Stoddard, *South-Sea Idyls* (Boston: James R. Osgood, 1873), 33, 39–40.

CHAPTER FOUR

1. "A Chinese Party," *Chicago Daily Tribune*, December 5, 1921, 20; "Cornell Glee Club Concert Proves Joy to Young and Old," *Chicago Daily Tribune*, December 28, 1921, 15.

2. Georgia Soruika and Laura Klemt, "Robert Allerton: The Man and the Park," n.d., typescript in Allerton Stuff box (hereafter Soruika and Klemt), Juliet Rice Wichman Botanical Garden Library, National Tropical Botanical Garden,

Kalaheo, Hawai'i (hereafter NTBG); John Gregg biographical statement, John Wyatt Gregg Allerton (hereafter JWGA) Biographical folder, box 5, Allerton Park Collection, Record Series 31/13/5, University of Illinois Archives (hereafter APC); John Gregg Allerton Memoir, transcription of interview with Nancy Becker, May 9, 1984, 1, http://www.idaillinois.org/cdm/ref/collection/uis/id /883.

3. See, for instance, Martha Burgin and Maureen Holtz, *Robert Allerton: The Private Man and the Public Gifts* (Champaign, IL: News-Gazette, 2009), 85.

4. John Gregg Allerton Memoir, 2.

5. On the question of men living together in boardinghouses, see John Ibson, *Men without Maps: Some Gay Males of the Generation before Stonewall* (Chicago: University of Chicago Press, 2019), 15; Howard Chudacoff, *The Age of the Bachelor: Creating an American Subculture* (Princeton, NJ: Princeton University Press, 1999). On men of wealth and status with wives and extensive same-sex relationships, albeit transient ones, see David D. Doyle Jr., "'A Very Proper Bostonian': Rediscovering Ogden Codman and His Late-Nineteenth-Century Queer World," *Journal of the History of Sexuality* 13, no. 4 (October 2004): 446–76.

6. John Gregg Allerton obituaries in JWGA Obituaries folder, box 5, APC; "John Wyatt Gregg Allerton," n.d., in Correspondence box, NTBG.

7. 1880 US Federal Census for Milwaukee; 1900 US Federal Census for Milwaukee; 1910 Federal Census for Milwaukee, 1920 Federal Census for Milwaukee (showing Katherine living with her husband, Frank Courtenay); Draft Registration Cards for Scranton Hugh Gregg, June 5, 1918, and John Wyatt Gregg, September 12, 1918, all available via familysearch.org. Kate Scranton Gregg's grave can be found here: https://www.findagrave.com/memorial/91036947/kate-gregg. Information on Gregg's parents' deaths is in biographies in JWGA Miscellaneous folder and JWGA Biographical folder, both in box 5, APC.

8. John Gregg Allerton Memoir, 2; John Gregg Allerton Oral History in Allerton Stuff box, 18, NTBG.

9. John Gregg Allerton Memoir, 3; *The 1924 Ilio*, 355, 472; *The 1925 Ilio*, 370; *The 1926 Ilio*, 382, 478; *The 1927 Ilio*, 78, 404.

10. *The 1924 Ilio*, 472; "Ku Klux Klan," October 15, 2012, University of Illinois Archives, https://archives.library.illinois.edu/blog/ku-klux-klan/; Stephen Kantrowitz and Floyd Rose, "Report to the Chancellor on the Ku Klux Klan at the University of Wisconsin-Madison," April 4, 2018, 10–11, https://news.wisc.edu/content /uploads/2018/04/Study-Group-final-for-print-April-18.pdf; Nicholas L. Syrett, *The Company He Keeps: A History of White College Fraternities* (Chapel Hill: University of North Carolina Press, 2009), 170.

11. "S. W. Allerton's Widow Victim of Long Illness," *Chicago Daily Tribune*, December 20, 1924, 12; "Mrs. Allerton's Will Disposes of $2,000,000," *Chicago Daily Tribune*, December 28, 1924, 17; Will of Agnes C. Allerton, Agnes C. Thompson Allerton Biographical folder (2 of 3), box 4, APC; "Allerton Family," *Americana* 15 (January–December 1921): 98.

12. John Gregg Allerton Oral History in Allerton Stuff box, 21, 16, NTBG.

13. William Wright, *Harvard's Secret Court: The Savage 1920 Purge of Campus*

Homosexuals (New York: St. Martin's Press, 2005); Nicholas L. Syrett, "The Boys of Beaver Meadow: A Homosexual Community at 1920s Dartmouth College," *American Studies* 48, no. 2 (Summer 2007): 9–18; Syrett, *The Company He Keeps*, 205–6.

14. Benjamin E. Wise, *William Alexander Percy: The Curious Life of a Mississippi Planter and Sexual Freethinker* (Chapel Hill: University of North Carolina Press, 2012), chap. 3; Justin Spring, *Secret Historian: The Life and Times of Samuel Steward, Professor, Tattoo Artist, and Sexual Renegade* (New York: Farrar, Straus and Giroux, 2010), 19.

15. Ina Russell, ed., *Jeb and Dash: A Diary of Gay Life, 1918–1945* (Boston: Faber and Faber, 1993), 21, 31; "The Real Jeb and Dash: The Quest for Carter & Isham," http://jebanddash.info/id2.html. "C.C. Dasham" is a pseudonym used by Bealer's niece when she published his edited diaries. Bealer and Hall are not pseudonyms.

16. Syrett, *The Company He Keeps*, 206–7, 223–24; Beth Bailey, *Sex in the Heartland* (Cambridge, MA: Harvard University Press, 1999), 53–4.

17. Soruika and Klemt, 18; on travel, see Nancy R____, "Frederic C. Bartlett and Robert Allerton Going on Art Quest," *Chicago Daily Tribune*, February 12, 1926, 27; "Ocean Travel," *New York Times*, March 2, 1926, 18. On the job with Adler, see documents in JWGA Miscellaneous folder, box 5, APC; David Bowman, "The Allerton Chronology," 4, in Robert Henry Allerton (hereafter RHA) Personal, Biographical folder, box 4, APC; JWGA Biography in Correspondence box, NTBG; Soruika and Klemt, 19. Schweikher quoted in interview with Betty Blum in series "Chicago Architects Speak," 28, transcription in JWGA Miscellaneous folder, box 5, APC.

18. On Gregg's living arrangements, see Bowman, "Allerton Chronology"; David Jeffrey Fletcher, "The Building of Allerton Park," *Illinois Magazine*, May 1979, 8–14; JWGA interviewed by Carl Caldwell in JWGA Personal folder, all in box 5, APC; John Gregg Allerton Memoir, 3; 1930 federal census accessed online via familysearch.org. On Gregg's architectural career, see Anthony Rubano to Steve Salny, March 18, 1996, Adler, David folder, box 1, APC.

19. "Society at the Opera," *Chicago Daily Tribune*, December 7, 1928, 39. On the uses of "gay," see Jonathan Ned Katz, *Love Stories: Sex between Men before Homosexuality* (Chicago: University of Chicago Press, 2001), 158; George Chauncey, *Gay New York: Gender, Urban Culture, and the Making of the Gay Male World, 1890–1940* (New York: Basic Books, 1994), 17.

20. Cousin Eve, "Ravinia Debut Attended by a Notable Throng," *Chicago Daily Tribune*, June 28, 1931, D1; "Opera in the Spotlight of Social Events," *Chicago Daily Tribune* December 17, 1933, E1. For more examples from the 1930s, see June Provines, "Front Views and Profiles," *Chicago Daily Tribune*, January 1, 1935, 31; "Robert Allerton on Way to Europe," *Chicago Daily Tribune*, January 17, 1937, F10; "Exchange Sale Held 2 Days at Harbor Point," *Chicago Daily Tribune*, August 28, 1938, E4; Ruth De Young, "Cruise to Call at Lonely Isles in South Atlantic," *Chicago Daily Tribune*, January 16, 1935, 17; De Young, "Travelers Will Bring Tales of Strange Lands," *Chicago Daily Tribune*, March 27, 1935, 12.

21. St. Sukie de la Croix, *Chicago Whispers: A History of LGBT Chicago before Stonewall* (Madison: University of Wisconsin Press, 2012), chaps. 3–8; Jim Elledge, *The Boys of Fairy Town: Sodomites, Female Impersonators, Third-Sexers, Pansies, Queers, and Sex Morons in Chicago's First Century* (Chicago: Chicago Review Press, 2018); Lillian Faderman, *Odd Girls and Twilight Lovers: A History of Lesbian Life in Twentieth-Century America* (New York: Columbia University Press, 1991), 24–25; Kevin P. Murphy, *Political Manhood: Red Bloods, Mollycoddles, and the Politics of Progressive Era Reform* (New York: Columbia University Press, 2008).

22. George Chauncey, "From Sexual Inversion to Homosexuality: Medicine and the Changing Conceptualization of Female Deviance," *Salmagundi* 58–59 (Fall–Winter 1983): 114–46; Chauncey, *Gay New York*; Peter Boag, *Same-Sex Affairs: Constructing and Controlling Homosexuality in the Pacific Northwest* (Berkeley: University of California Press, 2003); Nan Alamilla Boyd, *Wide-Open Town: A History of Queer San Francisco to 1965* (Berkeley: University of California Press, 2003); Lisa Duggan, "The Trials of Alice Mitchell: Sensationalism, Sexology, and the Lesbian Subject in Turn-of-the-Century America," *Signs* 18, no. 4 (Summer 1993): 791–814; Estelle Freedman, "'The Burning of Letters Continues': Elusive Identities and the Historical Construction of Sexuality," *Journal of Women's History* 9 (Winter 1998): 181–200; Katz, *Love Stories*; James Polchin, *Indecent Advances: A Hidden History of Crime and Prejudice before Stonewall* (Berkeley, CA: Counterpoint, 2019). On the Chicago connections, see De la Croix, *Chicago Whispers*, chap. 2, 82–84.

23. For same-sex sexuality facilitated by wealth, see Sharon Marcus, "At Home with the Other Victorians," *South Atlantic Quarterly* 108, no. 1 (Winter 2009): 119–45; Nigel Nicolson, *Portrait of a Marriage: Vita Sackville-West and Harold Nicolson* (New York: Atheneum, 1973); Judith Halberstam, *Female Masculinity* (Durham, NC: Duke University Press, 1998), chaps. 2 and 3; Diana Souhami, *The Trials of Radclyffe Hall* (New York: Doubleday, 1999); Helen Lefkowitz Horowitz, *The Power and Passion of M. Carey Thomas* (Champaign: University of Illinois Press, 1999); Faderman, *Odd Girls and Twilight Lovers*, 12, 30; Margot Canaday, *The Straight State: Sexuality and Citizenship in Twentieth-Century America* (Princeton, NJ: Princeton University Press, 2009), 22, 44–47. On Wilde, see Neil McKenna, *The Secret Life of Oscar Wilde: An Intimate Biography* (New York: Basic Books, 2005); Boag, *Same-Sex Affairs*, chap. 4.

24. "Richest Bachelor in Chicago," *Chicago Daily Tribune*, February 18, 1906, D1. See also "Matrimonial Chances for Chicago Girls," *Chicago Daily Tribune*, April 14, 1907, F3. On open secrets and silence, see Deborah Cohen, *Family Secrets: Shame and Privacy in Modern Britain* (New York: Oxford University Press, 2013), especially chap. 5 on "Bachelor Uncles."

25. Nancy Cott, "Passionlessness: An Interpretation of Victorian Sexual Ideology, 1790–1850," *Signs* 4 (1978): 219–36; Faderman, *Odd Girls and Twilight Lovers*, chap. 2; Katz, *Love Stories*, 52, 64–66.

26. Emily Skidmore, *True Sex: The Lives of Trans Men at the Turn of the Twentieth Century* (New York: New York University Press, 2017); Jen Manion, *Female Husbands: A Trans History* (New York: Cambridge University Press, 2020); Jesse Bayker,

"Before Transsexuality: Crossing Gender Borders in the United States, 1845–1920" (PhD diss., Rutgers University, 2019).

27. Horowitz, *Power and Passion*; Louise W. Knight, *Jane Addams: Spirit in Action* (New York: W. W. Norton, 2010); Lillian Faderman, *Surpassing the Love of Men: Romantic Friendship between Women from the Renaissance to the Present* (New York: Morrow, 1981), chaps. 4, 5. On the absence of male Boston marriages, see Ibson, *Men without Maps*, 16.

28. Rachel Hope Cleves, *Charity and Sylvia: A Same-Sex Marriage in Early America* (New York: Oxford University Press, 2014). There are limited examples of men living together in similar arrangements in the nineteenth century, however. See Susan Lee Johnson, *Roaring Camp: The Social World of the California Gold Rush* (New York: W. W. Norton, 2000), 335–37; Katz, *Love Stories*.

29. John Gregg Allerton Memoir, 3; JWGA Oral History in Allerton Stuff box, 21, NTBG.

30. Katz, *Love Stories*, 223, 170–72, 325. By contrast, aunt and niece Katherine Bradley and Edith Cooper—who lived in England between the mid-nineteenth century and the 1910s and wrote poetry under the pen name Michael Field—were lovers for more than forty years. Unlike the Allertons or Whitman, however, Bradley and Cooper were already related to one another and had no need to invent a filial status. See Emma Donoghue, *We Are Michael Field* (London: Bello, 2014).

31. Katz, *Love Stories*, chap. 16; David M. Halperin, "Is There a History of Sexuality?" in *The Lesbian and Gay Studies Reader*, ed. Henry Abelove, Michèle Aina Barale, and David M. Halperin (New York: Routledge, 1993), 416–31; John Addington Symonds, *A Problem in Greek Ethics, Being an Inquiry into the Phenomenon of Sexual Inversion, Addressed Especially to Medical Psychologists and Jurists* (1883; repr., London: privately printed, 1908), 8; Wise, *William Alexander Percy*, 44–51; Chauncey, *Gay New York*; Boag, *Same-Sex Affairs*; Doyle, "'A Very Proper Bostonian,'" 456, 467; Kate Fisher and Jana Funke, "The Age of Attraction: Age, Gender, and the History of Modern Male Homosexuality," *Gender and History* 31, no. 2 (July 2019): 266–83; Steven Maynard, "'Horrible Temptations': Sex, Men, and Working-Class Male Youth in Urban Ontario, 1890–1935," *Canadian Historical Review* 78, no. 2 (1997): 191–235; Nicholas L. Syrett, "Introduction" to "Sex across the Ages: Restoring Intergenerational Dynamics to Queer History," *Historical Reflections/Réflexions Historiques* 46, no. 1 (2020): 1–12. On the tendency of queer people to look backward to understand their relationships with one another, see Christopher Nealon, *Foundlings: Lesbian and Gay Historical Emotion before Stonewall* (Durham, NC: Duke University Press, 2001).

32. Katherine Parkin, "Adult Adoption and Intergenerational Same-Sex Relationships," *notches: (re)marks on the history of sexuality*, December 15, 2017, http://notchesblog.com/2017/12/15/adult-adoption-and-intergenerational-same-sex-relationships/. For women who likened their relationships to that between mother and daughter, see Julian Carter, "On Mother-Love: History, Queer Theory, and Non-Lesbian Identity," *Journal of the History of Sexuality* 14, nos. 1/2 (2005): 107–38.

33. Lee Virginia Chambers-Schiller, *Liberty, a Better Husband: Single Women in America: The Generations of 1780–1840* (New Haven, CT: Yale University Press, 1984), esp. chap. 6.

CHAPTER FIVE

1. "Robert Allerton Returns," *Chicago Daily Tribune*, June 28, 1931, D1; "Chicagoans Help Restore Ancient Chinese Palace," *Chicago Daily Tribune*, May 4, 1931, 20; Cousin Eve, "Opera in the Spotlight of Social Events," *Chicago Daily Tribune*, December 17, 1933, E1; Ruth De Young, "Cruise to Call at Lonely Isles in South Atlantic," *Chicago Daily Tribune*, January 16, 1935, 17.

2. John Wyatt Gregg quoted in "Robert Allerton," *Bulletin of the Pacific Tropical Botanical Garden 3, no. 2* (April 1973): 24, in John Wyatt Gregg Allerton (hereafter JWGA) Personal folder, box 5, Allerton Park Collection, Record Series 31/13/5, University of Illinois Archives (hereafter APC).

3. Bruce Shenitz, "The Garden of Eden. Minus Eve," *Out*, September 2007, 88, 90; Lucinda Fleeson, *Waking Up in Eden: In Pursuit of an Impassioned Life on an Imperiled Island* (Chapel Hill, NC: Algonquin Books, 2009), chap. 8.

4. For more on these points, see Nicholas L. Syrett, "'Lord of a Hawaiian Island': Robert and John Gregg Allerton, Queerness, and the Erasure of Colonization in Kaua'i," *Pacific Historical Review* 82, no. 3 (August 2013): 401.

5. For more on the separation of races on Kaua'i in the mid-twentieth century, as well as labor patterns, see Mike Ashman, *Kauai: As It Was in the 1940s and '50s* (Lîhu'e: Kaua'i Historical Society, 2004), 84–86.

6. *New York Times*, April 17, 1910, C3; on the Dillingham family, see George F. Nellist, ed., *The Story of Hawaii and Its Builders, with Which Is Incorporated Volume III, Men of Hawaii* (Honolulu: Honolulu Star-Bulletin, 1925), 97–99, 401–4.

7. Ralph S. Kuykendall, *The Hawaiian Kingdom, 1854–1874: Twenty Critical Years* (Honolulu: University of Hawai'i Press, 1953), 144; Nellist, *Story of Hawaii*, 171–73, 732–33; Edward Joesting, *Hawaii: An Uncommon History* (New York: W. W. Norton, 1972), 172; Joesting, *Kauai: The Separate Kingdom* (Honolulu: University of Hawai'i Press, 1984), 175, 177, 201.

8. Joesting, *Kauai*, 221; Nellist, *Story of Hawaii*, 620; Transcription of June 23 and August 16, 1978, interview of John Gregg Allerton with William Theobald (hereafter Theobald interview), 3, 15, 18–19, Allerton Stuff box, Juliet Rice Wichman Research Center, National Tropical Botanical Garden (hereafter NTBG); National Tropical Botanical Garden, "Allerton Garden History," https://ntbg.org /gardens/allerton/history.

9. Carol Wilcox, *Sugar Water: Hawaii's Plantation Ditches* (Honolulu: University of Hawai'i Press, 1996), 78; Joesting, *Kauai*, 221; Nellist, *Story of Hawaii*, 620.

10. Cousin Eve, "Society Welcomes New Year at Church Services and at Gay Parties," *Chicago Daily Tribune*, January 5, 1941, F1; "Robert Allerton," *Bulletin of the PTBG*, 24.

11. Theobald interview.

12. National Tropical Botanical Garden, "Allerton Garden Plant Collections," https://ntbg.org/gardens/allerton/collections; Theobald interview, 18, 6.

13. Theobald interview, 4, 15–16; Philip L. Rice to Larry Y. Nishikawa and Richard S. Mirikitani, December 9, 1938, Allerton Correspondence box, Allerton Stuff box, NTBG.

14. Robert Henry Allerton (hereafter RHA) to Helen Murphy (hereafter HM), March 20, 1940, 1940 folder, box 4, Allerton Family Collection, Record Series 31/13/20, University of Illinois Archives (hereafter AFC).

15. Theobald interview, 2–3; Ruth W. Patterson to Philip Rice, March 29, 1939, Allerton Correspondence box, NTBG.

16. JWGA to Philip Rice, September 4, 1939, in Allerton Correspondence box, NTBG.

17. RHA to HM, December 2, 1939, 1939 folder, box 4, AFC; RHA to HM, December 2, 1940, 1940 folder, box 4, AFC; RHA to HM, January 22, 1942, 1942 folder, box 4, AFC; JWGA to HM, December 23, 1938, 1937–1939 folder, box 5, AFC; JWGA to HM, January 31, 1942; August 4, 1942, 1940–1942 folder, box 5, AFC. For the situation on Kaua'i, see Ashman, Kauai, 84–86.

18. RHA to HM, March 15, 1943, 1943 folder, box 4, AFC. Wages are in RHA to HM, October 14, 1942, 1942 folder, box 4, AFC. Payroll Statement for June 1947, 1945–1948 folder, box 5, AFC. For average wages in 1943, see Susan B. Carter et al., eds., Historical Statistics of the United States, Earliest Times to the Present, Millennial Edition, 5 vols. (New York: Cambridge University Press, 2006), 2: 275, 277. For pay rates at the plantations on Kaua'i, see Ashman, Kauai as It Was, 149.

19. Greg Ward, The Rough Guide to Hawaii (New York: Rough Guides, 2011), 392; Suzanne Dworsky, "Two in the Tropics," Horticulture, March 1986, 59, copy in Lawai-Kai, Post-Donation folder, box 4, APC; Jon Letman, "A Tour of Hawaii's Rare Paradise," Christian Science Monitor, September 13, 2006, http://www.csmonitor.com /2006/0913/p13s01-lihc.html; Matthew Link, The Out Traveler Hawaii (Boston: Alyson, 2008), 140.

20. Robert J. Morris, "Aikāne: Accounts of Same-Sex Relationships in the Journals of Captain Cook's Third Voyage (1776–80)," Journal of Homosexuality 19 (1990): 231–58. See also Scott Lauria Morgensen, "Settler Homonationalism: Theorizing Settler Colonialism within Queer Modernities," GLQ: A Journal of Lesbian and Gay Studies 16 (2010): 105–31.

21. JWGA to HM, December 9, 1941, 1940–1942 folder, box 5, AFC; RHA to HM, late December or early January 1941/42, 1942 folder, box 4, AFC. On Gregg's assistant sheriff duties, see RHA to HM, late December or early January 1941/42, 1942 folder, box 4, AFC. On the Home Guard, see JWGA to HM, April 30, 1942; August 4, 1942, 1940–1942 folder, box 5, AFC. On the Red Cross, see RHA to HM, August 7, 1942; October 14, 1942, 1942 folder, box 4, AFC; JWGA to HM, August 12, 1942, 1940–1942 folder, box 5, AFC. On the Kaua'i Home Guard and Rice as sheriff, see Ashman, Kauai, 254–55, 248.

22. For more on the purchase, see Nicholas L. Syrett, "Queering Couplehood: Robert and John Gregg Allerton and Historical Perspectives on Kinship," Genders

(January 3, 2012): 55, https://www.colorado.edu/gendersarchive1998-2013/2012
/01/03/queering-couplehood-robert-john-allerton-and-historical-perspectives
-kinship. When Gregg talked about the purchase in correspondence, he tended
to explain it both as a matter of opportunity and to emphasize the beauty of
the location.

23. RHA to Herbert Gorsuch (hereafter HG), June 24, 1943, 1943 folder, box 4, AFC;
RHA to HG, June 1944; July 27, 1944; February 23, 1945, 1944–1945 folder, box
4, AFC.

24. Carlos Andrade, *Hā'ena: Through the Eyes of the Ancestors* (Honolulu: University
of Hawai'i Press, 2008), 82–84; Sally Engle Merry, *Colonizing Hawai'i: The Cultural Power of Law* (Princeton, NJ: Princeton University Press, 2000), 93–94. An
excellent summary of this process in regard to Hā'ena is available at http://
pacificworlds.com/haena/index.cfm.

25. Andrade, *Hā'ena*, 87–88, 99. William A. Kinney, of course, had been a partner in
the original McBryde Sugar Company, was the judge advocate who prosecuted
Queen Lili'uokalani in 1895, and attempted to rush through a treaty of annex-
ation with the United States two years later, before eventually switching his
allegiance to oppose the sugar dynasty.

26. Ibid., 104; Haw. Rev. Stat. § 668-1: Actions for Partition, passed in 1923, http://
codes.lp.findlaw.com/histatutes/4/36/668/668-1.

27. JWGA to HG, January 4, 1945; May 19, 1945, 1944–1945 folder, box 5, AFC; RHA
to HG, February 23, 1945; March 6, 1945, 1945 folder, box 4, AFC. On Brown, see
Nellist, *Story of Hawaii*, 305, 307.

28. "Three Appointed Commissioners for Haena Lands," newspaper clipping, n.d.,
in Allerton Correspondence box, NTBG; Andrade, *Hā'ena*, 109–15.

29. "Legal Notices," November 27, 1974, in Allerton Stuff box, NTBG; Charles Page
to William Theobald, April 1, 1988, Allerton Correspondence box, NTBG; memo
from David Bowman to Jerry Soesbe, April 17, 1995, JWGA Last Will and Testament folder, box 5, APC.

30. "Allerton Garden," http://ntbg.org/gardens/allerton.php; Andrew Doughty, *The
Ultimate Kauai Guidebook* (Lāhu'e, Hawai'i: Wizard Publications, 2009), 96. Another part of the hui, which was owned by Rice descendant Juliet Rice Wichman
after the partition, was donated to the National Tropical Botanical Garden by
her and her grandson, Chipper Wichman, now the director of the garden, over
the course of about thirty years. It is now the Limahuli Garden and is available
to visit for a fee.

31. JWGA to HG, July 30, 1945, 1944–1945 folder, box 5, AFC; JWGA to HG, February 7, 1950, 1949–1951 folder, box 5, AFC; Theobald interview, 4–6, 16. On Hawai'i
and extinction, see Tony Perry, "Is Hawaii the Extinction Capital of the World?"
Washington Post, April 25, 2016, https://www.washingtonpost.com/national
/health-science/is-hawaii-the-extinction-capital-of-the-world-exhibit-a-the
-alala-bird/2016/04/25/3f45c6ac-f210-11e5-89c3-a647fcce95e0_story.html.
On the National Tropical Botanical Garden's mission, see http://www.ntbg
.org/.

CHAPTER SIX

1. Robert Henry Allerton (hereafter RHA) to Philip Rice (hereafter PR), September 4, 1939, Allerton Correspondence box, Juliet Rice Wichman Research Library, National Tropical Botanical Garden (hereafter NTBG), Kalaheo, Hawai'i.

2. Rebecca Solnit, "More Equal than Others," *Financial Times*, May 24, 2013, https://www.ft.com/content/99659a2a-c349-11e2-9bcb-00144feab7de.

3. Matt Cook, *Queer Domesticities: Homosexuality and Home Life in Twentieth-Century London* (Hampshire, UK: Palgrave Macmillan, 2014), 3; Stephen Vider, "'Oh Hell, May, Why Don't You People Have a Cookbook?': Camp Humor and Gay Domesticity," *American Quarterly* 65, no. 4 (2013): 879; Vider, "Lesbian and Gay Marriage and Romantic Adjustment in the 1950s and 1960s United States," *Gender and History* 29, no. 3 (2017): 693–715; Sharon Marcus, "At Home with the Other Victorians," *South Atlantic Quarterly* 108, no. 1 (Winter 2009): 119–10; Marcus, *Between Women: Friendship, Desire, and Marriage in Victorian England* (Princeton, NJ: Princeton University Press, 2007); John Ibson, *Men without Maps: Some Gay Males in the Generation before Stonewall* (Chicago: University of Chicago Press, 2019), part 1.

4. Cook, *Queer Domesticities*, 3, chap. 1; Vider, "'Oh Hell, May'"; Marcus, "At Home," 137–38; John Potvin, *Bachelors of a Different Sort: Queer Aesthetics, Material Culture, and the Modern Interior in Britain* (Manchester: Manchester University Press, 2014), chap. 1; Ibson, *Men without Maps*, part 1.

5. "Best love": Helen Murphy (hereafter HM) to John Gregg (hereafter JWGA), July 18, 1934, 1934 folder, box 5, Allerton Family Collection, Record Series 31/13/20, University of Illinois Archives (hereafter AFC); JWGA to HM, May 16, 1935, 1935 folder, box 5, AFC; advice: HM to JWGA, March 12, 1937; and JWGA to HM, November 19, 1939; opera tickets: JWGA to HM, October 11, 1937; and HM to JWGA, November 14, 1938; lunch together: JWGA to HM, September 18, 1939, all in 1937–1939 folder, box 5, AFC; JWGA thanking HM: February 3, 1940, 1940–1942 folder, box 5, AFC; Republicans: HM to RHA, August 17, 1940; RHA to HM, October 8, 1940; HM to RHA, October 21, 1940; RHA to HM, November 1940, all in 1940 folder, box 4, AFC; visit to Lawai-Kai: PR to RHA and JWGA, June 8, 1939, Allerton Correspondence box, NTBG.

6. Responsibilities: RHA to HM, late December/early January 1941/1942; relatives gossip: HM to RHA, November 7, 1942, both in 1942 folder, box 4, AFC; Jen, the short, fat friend: HM to RHA, February 4, 1943, 1943 folder, box 4, AFC; ordering books: RHA to HM, June 1940; RHA to HM, May 1940; RHA to HM, July 29, 1940, all in 1940 folder, box 4, AFC; power of attorney: HM to RHA, December 19, 1941, 1941 folder, box 4, AFC.

7. Herbert Gorsuch (hereafter HG) to RHA, June 8, 1943; June 11, 1943; June 28, 1943; August 1, 1943; RHA to HG, August 16, 1943, all in 1943 folder, box 4, AFC; HG to RHA, June 2, 1944; October 9, 1944, 1944 folder, box 4, AFC; JWGA to HG, March 8, 1950, 1950 folder, box 5, AFC; Cook County, Illinois Death Records, March 2, 1950, accessible via familysearch.org.

8. Potvin, *Bachelors of a Different Sort*, 27; Cook, *Queer Domesticities*, 5.

9. Poem is in Allerton Legacy materials, Allerton Stuff box, NTBG; JWGA in Interview with Suzanne, WCIA's *PM Magazine*, JWGA Personal folder, box 5, Allerton Park Collection, Record Series 31/13/5, University of Illinois Archives (hereafter APC); 1981 interview with Elmer Priebe, Priebe, Elmer folder, box 2, APC.

10. David Jeffrey Fletcher, "The Building of Allerton Park," *Illinois Magazine*, May 1979, 8–14; Martha Burgin and Maureen Holtz, *Robert Allerton: The Private Man and the Public Gifts* (Champaign, IL: News-Gazette, 2009) 96–97; John Gregg Allerton interview with Carl Caldwell, UI Office of Public Affairs, JWGA Personal folder, box 5, APC.

11. Transcript of conversation with John Gregg and William L. Theobald, June 23, August 16, 1978, 8–10 (hereafter Theobald interview), JWGA Biographical folder, box 5, APC; JWGA to HM, December 16, 1938; December 23, 1938; January 16, 1939, 1937–1939 folder, box 5, AFC; JWGA to PR, October 9, 1939; JWGA to HM, December 10, 1939 (both on Lyman Watts), 1937–1939 folder, box 5, AFC; HM to RHA, sometime in December 1939; RHA to HM, December 14, 1939, both in 1939 folder, box 4, AFC.

12. RHA to HM, February 1941, 1941 folder, box 4, AFC; JWGA to HM, February 11, 1941; January 28, 1941; both in 1940–1942 folder, box 5, AFC.

13. JWGA to PR, September 18, 1939; Chicago Motor Club to Gregg, February 18, 1948, both in Allerton Correspondence box, NTBG; Hilary Hinds, "Together and Apart: Twin Beds, Domestic Hygiene, and Modern Marriage, 1890–1945," *Journal of Design History* 23, no. 3 (2010): 275–304.

14. RHA to HM, January 12, 1940, 1940 folder, box 4, AFC; JWGA to HM, January 8, 1941, 1940–1942 folder, box 5, AFC; Georgia O'Keeffe to RHA and JWGA, May 10, 1940, Allerton Stuff box, NTGB; JWGA to HG, March 18, 1947, 1945–1948 folder, box 5, AFC.

15. RHA to HM, February 4, 1940; March 2, 1940, 1940 folder, box 4, AFC.

16. RHA to HM, late December/early January 1941/42, 1942 folder, box 2, AFC; JWGA to HM, April 30, 1942, 1940–1942 folder, box 3, AFC; RHA to HM, Christmas letter 1941, 1941 folder, box 2, AFC; HM to JWGA, January 7, 1942, January 28, 1942, 1940–1942 folder, box 5, AFC; RHA to HM, February 25, 1942, 1942 folder, box 4, AFC.

17. *Robert Allerton Park* (Champaign: University of Illinois Press, 1951); Bowman chronology in RHA Personal, Biographical folder, box 4, APC; 1983 interview with Elmer Priebe, Priebe, Elmer folder, box 2, APC.

18. JWGA to HG, February 12, 1947, 1945–1948 folder, box 5, AFC; Eleanor Page, "Many Dinner Parties Precede Dance and Champagne Supper," *Chicago Daily Tribune*, January 11, 1947, 13; "Exhibition and Sale of the Robert Allerton Collection," *Chicago Daily Tribune*, October 20, 1946, 13; Edith Weigle, "Allerton Art Collection Is Offered Here," *Chicago Daily Tribune*, October 24, 1946, 29.

19. JWGA to HM, October 20, 1936, 1936 folder, box 5, AFC; HM to JWGA, September 12, 1939, 1937–1939 folder, box 5, AFC; HM to JWGA, July 29, 1940, 1940–1942 folder, box 5, AFC; JWGA to HM, September 18, 1939; HM to JWGA, December 11, 1939, both in 1937–1939 folder, box 5, AFC; HM to RHA, February 4, 1943, 1943 folder, box 4, AFC; RHA to HM, March 21, 1942, 1942 folder, box 4, AFC.

20. First quotation from Georgia Soruika and Laura Klemt, "Robert Allerton: The Man and the Park," n.d., typescript in Allerton Stuff box, NTBG; second quotation from "The Legacy Continues," panel #18, copy in JWGA Miscellaneous folder, box 5, APC.

21. HM to JWGA, May 13, 1936; September 8, 1936; April 17, 1936; and Treasury Department to HM, August 14, 1936, all in 1936 folder, box 5, AFC; JWGA to HM, March 3/2, 1940, 1940–1942 folder, box 5, AFC; JWGA to HM, Election Day, 1936, 1936 folder, box 5, AFC; JWGA to HM, May 31, 1940, 1940–1942 folder, box 5, AFC.

22. JWGA to HM, July 26, 1940, 1940–1942 folder, box 5, AFC.

23. RHA to HM, June 1, 1943, 1943 folder, box 4, AFC; RHA to HG, June 1944, 1944 folder, box 4, AFC; RHA to HG, February 23, 1945, 1945 folder, box 4, AFC; JWGA to HG, Easter morning, 1945; JWGA to Herbert and Ruby Gorsuch, May 19, 1945; JWGA to HG, July 5, 1945; and November 25, 1945, all in 1945–1948 folder, box 5, AFC.

24. RHA to HM, July 1941; HM to RHA, July 11, 1941; RHA to HM, July 1941, all in 1941 folder, box 4, AFC. They both revised wills in September 1944 as well.

25. Author's telephone conversation with Jane Gregg Schowalter, January 24, 2018. On trips to Milwaukee, see HG to JWGA, May 23, 1944, 1943–1944 folder, box 5, AFC; RHA to HG, April 1952; HG to JWGA, May 29, 1956, both in Allerton Correspondence box, NTBG; JWGA to Priebes, May 30, 1959, "Allerton Messages and Letters" in RHA Personal, Biographical folder, box 4, APC. On relatives, including cousin Allerton Miller, see JWGA to HG, June 22, 1945, 1945–1948 folder, box 5, AFC. On Allerton Johnstone: "Allerton Heir Leaps to Death at Coast Hotel," *Chicago Daily Tribune*, June 9, 1929, 1; Burgin and Holtz, *Robert Allerton*, 101–3. On Vanderburgh Johnstone: JWGA to HM, June 18, 1941, 1940–1942 folder, box 5, AFC; HG to RHA, November 16, 1956, Allerton Correspondence box, NTBG; memo from David Bowman to Jerry Soesbe, April 28, 1995, in RHA Obituaries, Will, Tributes folder, box 5, APC. On Gregg's family, especially his sister: RHA to HM, May 1940, 1940 folder, box 4, AFC; JWGA to HM, October 11, 1937; May 8, 1939, 1937–1939 folder, box 5, AFC; HM to JWGA, August 13, 1941, 1940–1942 folder, box 5, AFC.

26. RHA to HG, June 24, 1943, 1943 folder, box 4, AFC.

27. JWGA to HG, March 23, 1946; December 6, 1947, 1945–1948 folder, box 5, AFC; JWGA to HG, August 19, 1951, 1949–1951 folder, box 5, AFC; JWGA to HG, February 25, 1953, Allerton Correspondence box, NTBG.

28. JWGA to HM, May 25, 1938, 1937–1939 folder, box 5, AFC; postcard from JWGA to Katherine Gregg Courtenay, March 21, 1932, JWGA Miscellaneous folder, box 5, APC; "Robert Allerton Reaches China in Trip Around the World," *Decatur (IL) Morning Herald*, February 15, 1933, RHA Personal, Biographical folder, box 4, APC; Ruth De Young, "Cruise to Call at Lonely Isles in South Atlantic," *Chicago Daily Tribune*, January 16, 1935.

29. Vider, "'Oh Hell, May,'" 883; Allan Bérubé, *My Desire for History: Essays in Gay Community and Labor History* (Chapel Hill: University of North Carolina Press, 2011), 260–61, 265.

30. JWGA to HM, November 18, 1941, 1940–1942 folder, box 5, AFC.

31. "Robert Allerton Returns," *Chicago Daily Tribune*, June 28, 1931, D1; JWGA to HG, August 1, 1944, 1943–1944 folder, box 5, AFC; JWGA to HG, September 18, 1952, Allerton Correspondence box, NTBG; HG to JWGA, February 23, 1948, 1945–1948 folder, box 5, AFC; "Talk, Topics of Menfolk on Father's Day," *Chicago Daily Tribune*, June 18, 1944, F1; JWGA to HG, July 17, 1947, 1945–1948 folder, box 5, AFC; Justin Spring, *Secret Historian: The Life and Times of Samuel Steward, Professor, Tattoo Artist, and Sexual Renegade* (New York: Farrar, Straus and Giroux, 2010), 57

32. JWGA to HG, March 1946; April 8, 1948; HG to JWGA, April 13, 1948, all in 1945–1948 folder, box 5, AFC; JWGA to HG, April 26, 1949; HG to JWGA, May 17, 1949; JWGA to HG, May 17, 1949; February 7, 1950; May 11, 1951, all in 1949–1951 folder, box 5, AFC; JWGA to HG, September 18, 1952; May 29, 1956, Allerton Correspondence box, NTBG. On queer travelers in the Caribbean, see Julio Capó Jr., *Welcome to Fairyland: Queer Miami before 1940* (Chapel Hill: University of North Carolina Press, 2017), 118–23.

33. RHA to HM, April 20, 1942, 1940–1942 folder, box 5, AFC; Margot Canaday, *The Straight State: Sexuality and Citizenship in Twentieth-Century America* (Princeton, NJ: Princeton University Press, 2011), chap. 4.

34. JWGA to HM, October 22, 1942, 1940–1942 folder, box 5, AFC; JWGA to HG, April 19, 1945, 1945–1948 folder, box 5, AFC.

35. Betty Wilder, "Queen Emma's Kauai Cove Toured by Honolulu Party," *Honolulu Star-Bulletin*, December 15, 1956, in RHA Hawaii folder, box 4, APC; HG to RHA, December 28, 1956, Allerton Correspondence box, NTBG; "Great Tropic Garden," *Life*, March 17, 1958, 82–91; "Homosexuality in America," *Life*, June 16, 1964, 66–74.

CHAPTER SEVEN

1. Bartlett death: "F. C. Bartlett, Noted Chicago Artist, Dies," *Chicago Daily Tribune*, June 26, 1953, 14; Palmer death: https://www.findagrave.com/memorial /85826814/potter-palmer; Beatty death: https://www.findagrave.com /memorial/143948126/ethel-newcomb-beatty; Dillinghams: https://www .findagrave.com/memorial/106581823/louise-olga-dillingham#view-photo =76484493.

2. Allan Bérubé, *Coming Out under Fire: The History of Gay Men and Lesbians in World War Two* (New York: Plume, 1990), David K. Johnson, *The Lavender Scare: The Cold War Persecution of Gays and Lesbians in the Federal Government* (Chicago: University of Chicago Press, 2004); John D'Emilio and Estelle B. Freedman, *Intimate Matters: A History of Sexuality in America* (New York: Harper & Row, 1988), chap. 12; Margot Canaday, *The Straight State: Sexuality and Citizenship in Twentieth-Century America* (Princeton, NJ: Princeton University Press, 2009); Lillian Faderman, *Odd Girls and Twilight Lovers: A History of Lesbian Life in Twentieth-Century America* (New York: Columbia University Press, 1991), chaps. 5 and 6.

3. Alfred C. Kinsey, Wardell B. Pomeroy, and Clyde E. Martin, *Sexual Behavior in the Human Male* (Philadelphia: W. B. Saunders, 1948), chap. 21; Donald Webster Cory, *The Homosexual in America: A Subjective Approach* (New York: Greenberg, 1951);

David K. Johnson, *Buying Gay: How Physique Entrepreneurs Sparked a Movement* (New York: Columbia University Press, 2019); Martin Meeker, *Contacts Desired: Gay and Lesbian Communications and Community, 1940s–1970s* (Chicago: University of Chicago Press, 2006).

4. John D'Emilio, *Sexual Politics, Sexual Communities: The Making of a Homosexual Minority in the United States, 1940–1970* (Chicago: University of Chicago Press, 1983); Marcia Gallo, *Different Daughters: A History of the Daughters of Bilitis and the Lesbian Rights Movement* (New York: Carroll and Graf, 2006).

5. Howard Greer to John Gregg (hereafter JWGA) and Robert Allerton (hereafter RHA), April 25, 1954, Allerton Correspondence box, Juliet Rice Wichman Research Library, National Tropical Botanical Garden, Kalaheo, Hawai'i (hereafter NTBG); Howard Greer, *Designing Male* (New York: G. P. Putnam's Sons, 1949).

6. Walter Plunkett to RHA and JWGA, n.d., Allerton Correspondence box, NTBG.

7. Raymond to RHA, August 9, n.d., Allerton Correspondence box, NTBG; Meeker, *Contacts Desired*; Nicholas L. Syrett, "A Busman's Holiday in the Not-So-Lonely Crowd: Business Culture, Epistolary Networks, and Itinerant Homosexuality in Mid-Twentieth-Century-America," *Journal of the History of Sexuality* 21, no. 1 (January 2012): 121–40; Syrett, "Mobility, Circulation, and Correspondence: White Queer Men in the Midcentury Midwest," *GLQ: A Journal of Lesbian and Gay Studies* 20, nos. 1–2 (2014): 75–94.

8. Hugh to RHA and JWGA, September 16, 1956, Allerton Correspondence box, NTBG.

9. Ellen Herman, *Kinship by Design: A History of Adoption in the Modern United States* (Chicago: University of Chicago Press, 2008); Michael Grossberg, *Governing the Hearth: Law and Family in Nineteenth-Century America* (Chapel Hill: University of North Carolina Press, 1988), 268–80.

10. Grossberg, *Governing the Hearth*, 268–80; Thomas Adolph Pavano, "Gay and Lesbian Rights: Adults Adopting Adults," *Connecticut Probate Law Journal* 252 (1986–87): 260.

11. Jean-François Mignot, "Adoption in France and Italy: A Comparative History of Law and Practice (Nineteenth to Twenty-First Centuries)," *Population* 70, no. 4 (2015): 759–82; John D'Emilio, *Lost Prophet: The Life and Times of Bayard Rustin* (New York: Free Press, 2003), 483, 491; "Long before Same-Sex Marriage, 'Adopted Son' Could Mean 'Life Partner,'" National Public Radio, June 28, 2015, https://www.npr.org/2015/06/28/418187875/long-before-same-sex-marriage-adopted-son-could-mean-life-partner.

12. Justin Spring, *Secret Historian: The Life and Times of Samuel Steward, Professor, Tattoo Artist, and Sexual Renegade* (New York: Farrar, Straus and Giroux, 2010), 162–63.

13. "The Law: Adopting a Lover," *Time*, September 6, 1971, http://content.time.com/time/magazine/article/0,9171,943880,00.html; Chris Freeman and James J. Berg, "7 Things You Never Knew about Christopher Isherwood," *Huffington Post*, December 6, 2017; Christopher Isherwood, entry for June 8, 1977, *Liberation: Diaries*, vol. 3: *1970–1983*, ed. Katherine Bucknell (New York: HarperCollins, 2012), 543–44; Jaime Harker, *Middlebrow Queer: Christopher Isherwood in*

America (Minneapolis: University of Minnesota Press, 2013); quotations from Isherwood's diary and from Bachardy being interviewed are from *Chris and Don: A Love Story*, dir. Tina Mascara and Guido Santi (New York: Zeitgeist Films, 2008). For other examples of same-sex couples using adoption to secure inheritances, see Pam Belluck and Alison Leigh Cowan, "Partner Adopted by an Heiress Stakes Her Claim," *New York Times*, March 19, 2007, A1; "Gian Carlo Menotti," *Guardian*, February 3, 2007, https://www.theguardian.com/news/2007/feb/03/guardianobituaries.classicalmusic.

14. William K. Stevens, "The Illinois Inheritance Tax — Explanation and Suggested Improvements," *Northwestern University Law Review* 51, no. 6 (1956–57): 714–15, 695; "Illinois Adoption Laws Can Make a Son His Father's Elder," *Chicago Daily Tribune*, September 23, 1962, 25.

15. Pavano, "Gay and Lesbian Rights"; Peter N. Fowler, "Adult Adoption: A 'New' Legal Tool for Lesbians and Gay Men," *Golden Gate University Law Review* 14, no. 3 (1984): 667–708; Lawrence Friedman, *Dead Hands: A Social History of Wills, Trusts, and Inheritance Law* (Stanford, CA: Stanford Law Books, 2009), 56.

16. Friedman, *Dead Hands*, 99.

17. Fowler, "Adult Adoption," 686–87.

18. RHA to Elmer and Irene Priebe, n.d., "Allerton Messages and Letters," in RHA Personal, Biographical folder, box 4, Allerton Park Collection, Record Series 31/13/5, University of Illinois Archives (hereafter APC).

19. "'Son' 30 Years Is Adopted by Allerton," *Chicago Daily Tribune*, March 5, 1960, 7; "Allerton Adopts Gregg as His Son," *News-Gazette*, March 5, 1960, clipping in JWGA Adoption folder, box 5, APC.

20. Statement by First National Bank of Chicago, March 4, 1960; "Companion Adopted by R. Allerton," *Champaign-Urbana Courier*, March 5, 1960; "Robert Allerton Adopts Friend," March 5, 1960; "Robert Allerton, Piatt Park Donor, Adopts Companion of Many Years," March 4, 1960, newspaper clippings from unknown sources, all in JWGA Adoption folder, box 5, APC; "Have Been Friends for 38 Years. Kauai's Allerton, 86, to Adopt 60-Year-Old Son," *Honolulu Star-Bulletin*, March 6, 1960, in Allerton Correspondence box, NTBG; "'Son' 30 Years Is Adopted by Allerton."

21. "Trust Fund of $500,000 Presented to Art Institute," *Chicago Tribune*, June 28, 1963, 1; "Chicago Art Patron Gives $500,000 More," *New York Times*, July 1, 1963, 21.

22. "An Act to Charter by Act of Congress the Pacific Tropical Botanical Garden," Public Law 88-449, 88th Congress, S. 1991, August 19, 1964, https://ntbg.org/sites/default/files/generaluploads/ntbgcharterandamendments.pdf; National Tropical Botanical Garden, "Our Story," https://ntbg.org/about/story; *Champaign-Urbana Courier*, December 11, 1964, in RHA Hawaii folder, box 4, APC.

23. Martha Burgin and Maureen Holtz, *Robert Allerton: The Private Man and the Public Gifts* (Champaign, IL: News-Gazette, 2009), 118; *Chicago Sun-Times* clipping, December 23, 1964, Allerton Stuff box, NTBG; "Allerton Dies; Benefactor of Art Institute," *Chicago Daily Tribune*, December 23, 1964, A6; "Chicago Art Institute Donor Dead," *Chicago Daily Tribune*, December 23, 1964, D6.

24. Memorandum from David Bowman to Jerry Soesbe, April 28, 1995, RHA

Obituaries, Will, Tributes folder, box 5, APC; "R. H. Allerton Will Benefits Art Institute," *Chicago Daily Tribune*, December 30, 1964, A8.

25. John Gregg Allerton quoted in David Jeffery Fletcher, "The Building of Allerton Park," *Illinois Magazine*, May 1979, 11–12.

CONCLUSION

1. "Gregg Seeks New Name," *News-Gazette*, n.d. and "Adopted Son: Seeks Name of Allerton," news clipping from unknown source, January 15, 1965, both clippings in John Wyatt Gregg Allerton (hereafter JWGA) Adoption folder, box 5, Allerton Park Collection, Records Series 31/13/5, University of Illinois Archives (hereafter APC); JWGA quoted in Georgia Soruika and Laura Klemt, "Robert Allerton: The Man and the Park," n.d., p. 22, typescript in Allerton Stuff box, Juliet Rice Wichman Botanical Garden Library, National Tropical Botanical Garden, Kalaheo, Hawai'i (hereafter NTBG).

2. JWGA to Walter Keith, December 23, 1970, in JWGA Original Material; all subjects folder, box 5, APC; JWGA interview with Carl Caldwell, University of Illinois Office of Public Affairs (Raw Footage), transcript, n.d., p. 3, JWGA Personal folder, box 5, APC. See also John Gregg Allerton, "Interview with Suzanne," WCIA's *PM Magazine*, same folder.

3. "Legal Notices," November 27, 1974, Allerton Stuff box, NTBG; JWGA Obituaries folder, box 5, APC.

4. Will of John Wyatt Gregg Allerton, May 19, 1980, JWGA Last Will and Testament folder, box 5, APC.

5. See, for instance, Kathryn Hulme, *The Robert Allerton Story, 1873–1964* (n.p.: n.p., 1979), 10, available for sale at the NTBG gift shop; "Robert Allerton Park," tour guide script, in Tour Guide folder, box 2, APC.

6. Lucinda Fleeson, "The Gay '30s," in *Out and Proud in Chicago: An Overview of the City's Gay Community*, ed. Tracy Baim (Chicago: Surrey Books, 2008), 44; Marie J. Kuda, "Adopting New Ways," in *Out and Proud in Chicago*, 49; Bruce Shenitz, "The Garden of Eden. Minus Eve," *Out*, September 2007, 84-86, 88, 90.

7. Martha Burgin and Maureen Holtz, *Robert Allerton: The Private Man and the Public Gifts* (Champaign, IL: News-Gazette, 2009), 52–54, chap. 12; Lucinda Fleeson, *Waking Up in Eden: In Pursuit of an Impassioned Life on an Imperiled Island* (Chapel Hill, NC: Algonquin Books, 2009), 193–99; Shenitz, "The Garden of Eden," 88.

8. Rodger Steitmatter, *Outlaw Marriages: The Hidden Histories of Fifteen Extraordinary Same-Sex Couples* (Boston: Beacon, 2012); Rachel Hope Cleves, *Charity and Sylvia: A Same-Sex Marriage in Early America* (New York: Oxford University Press, 2014); Stephen Vider, "Lesbian and Gay Marriage and Romantic Adjustment in the 1950s and 1960s United States," *Gender and History* 29, no. 3 (2017): 693–715. See also Cleves, "'What, Another Female Husband?': The Prehistory of Same-Sex Marriage in America," *Journal of American History* 101, no. 4 (March 2015): 1055–81, though I disagree with Cleves about the degree to which it is appropriate to refer to many of the examples in her analysis as marriages if the law, which

regulates marriage, did not recognize them; if the participants themselves did not call them marriages; and if many of the participants (in the case of the female husbands) would not have thought of themselves as "same-sex" in the first place. See Jen Manion, *Female Husbands: A Trans History* (New York: Oxford University Press, 2020).

9. On homonormativity, see Lisa Duggan, "The New Homonormativity: The Sexual Politics of Neoliberalism," in *Materializing Democracy: Toward a Revitalized Cultural Politics*, ed. Russ Castronovo and Dana D. Nelson (Durham, NC: Duke University Press, 2002), 175–94; Michael Warner, *The Trouble with Normal: Sex, Politics, and the Ethics of Queer Life* (New York: Free Press, 1999). For the argument on strengthening the institution of marriage, see William Kuby, *Conjugal Misconduct: Defying Marriage Law in the Twentieth-Century United States* (New York: Cambridge University Press, 2018), epilogue; and on the connections between adulthood and marriage, see Nicholas L. Syrett, *American Child Bride: A History of Minors and Marriage in the United States* (Chapel Hill: University of North Carolina Press, 2016), conclusion.

10. There are, of course, exceptions to this rule, which include Nigel Nicolson, *Portrait of a Marriage: Vita Sackville-West and Harold Nicolson* (London: Weidenfeld and Nicolson, 1973); Anya Jabour, *Marriage in the Early Republic: Elizabeth and William Wirt and the Companionate Ideal* (Baltimore: Johns Hopkins University Press, 2002); Marilyn Yalom and Laura L. Carstensen, *Inside the American Couple: New Thinking, New Challenges* (Berkeley: University of California Press, 2002); Judith Stacey, *Unhitched: Love, Marriage, and Family Values from West Hollywood to Western China* (New York: New York University Press, 2011).

Index

Page numbers in italics refer to photos.